Swift as Priest and Satirist

Swift as Priest and Satirist

Edited by
Todd C. Parker

DELAWARE

Newark: University of Delaware Press

Associated University Presses
2010 Eastpark Boulevard
Cranbury, NJ 08512

The paper used in this publication meets the requirements of the American National Standard for Permanence of Paper for Printed Library Materials Z39.48-1984.

Library of Congress Cataloging-in-Publication Data

Swift as priest and satirist / edited by Todd C. Parker.
    p.   cm.
    Includes bibliographical references and index.
    ISBN 978-0-87413-044-7 (alk. paper)
    1. Swift, Jonathan, 1667–1745—Religion.   2. Authors, Irish—18th
century.   3. Satire—Religious aspects.   4. Religion and literature—Ireland.
I. Parker, Todd C., 1965–
PR3728.R4S95   2009
828'.509—dc22   2008028719

PRINTED IN THE UNITED STATES OF AMERICA

For Beverly, Earl, and Eric Parker,
With all my love.
Pax et bonum.

Contents

Acknowledgments

I WOULD LIKE TO THANK BOB MAHONY AND DON MELL FOR THEIR SUPPORT and encouragement as this project evolved. I am especially grateful to Don for his editorial expertise. I extend my sincere thanks and best wishes to the contributors to this volume, with each of whom it has been a pleasure to work. My thanks also to the brothers of the Society of St. Francis, American Province, for allowing me to continue editing *Swift as Priest and Satirist* even as I entered the novitiate and began formation in religious life.

Swift as Priest and Satirist

Introduction

Todd C. Parker

I

"Still it is a striking fact that Swift as a Christian divine has received comparatively little attention. His mystifying personal relationships, his political activities, his defense of Ireland—in these and other aspects he has been examined minutely, but no satisfactory detailed analysis of his religious views has yet appeared to provide a basis for a complete judgment."[1] When Louis Landa published these words in 1945, two hundred years after Jonathan Swift's death, he was one of the few scholars qualified to assess the accuracy of his own statement. Landa's landmark study, *Swift and the Church of Ireland* (1954), was the first to set Swift as priest in the intricate political and social environment of eighteenth-century Ireland. More recently, Christopher Fauske's *Jonathan Swift and the Church of Ireland 1710–1725* (2002) has shed new light on one of Swift's least conventionally "literary" periods and has given us a much clearer picture of Swift's relationship with his contemporary and sometimes antagonist, Archbishop William King. Fauske has juxtaposed Swift against King as a way to foreground the political nature of Swift's doctrinal positions. Fauske argues that, where "King based his critique [of Dissenters] upon an analysis of church doctrine, an analysis which then justified state-sanctioned protections for the Anglican church. Swift thought the church's social function justification enough for its privileges. Doctrine, for Swift, was of secondary importance to the church's social role; for King, the church's civic function was the consequence of its doctrine."[2] Swift's theology thus becomes less an affirmation of divine principle and more an expression of the realpolitik of the Church of Ireland. Fauske understands Swift as a career ecclesiastical politician, someone bent on preserving the Irish Establishment's heritage and what, by the beginning of the eighteenth century, was left of its prestige and power:

> Theology and political philosophy Swift left to others. His own inclinations and polemical skills led him to join the political debate not for

13

what he might accomplish but for what he could prevent. His efforts
were effectively a sustained rearguard action conducted against a back-
drop of ever-changing alliances and political expediency. Swift was engaged in an extended guerilla-like defense of an idealistic and
profoundly radical conservative concept. He took his allies where he
could, changed allegiances when need dictated and sought to engage
the enemy only when he had the twin advantages of surprise and momentum on his side. His main goal was to preserve what little power and
privilege he thought the Church of Ireland still enjoyed, and he believed
the struggle honourable and vital to society's well-being.[3]

Even if it isn't always entirely true that Swift left "theology and
political philosophy" to others, Fauske's remark aligns well with
much of the criticism on Swift as a religious figure. Few of Swift's
interpreters and critics take him seriously as a theologian. For Louis
Landa, he is rather a talented exponent of other people's arguments.[4] Likewise for Phillip Harth, Swift is a second-generation rationalist in the tradition of More, Stillingfleet, and Tillotson.[5] Harth
sees Swift as belonging to the tradition of "theologism," so that his
religious commentary, like that of the Anglican rationalist movement in general, "made no lasting contribution to the church in
whose defense it had been devised."[6] David Nokes, in what is probably the best essay to date on Swift's sermons, writes that they "are
homilies on social rather than spiritual topics. They seek to encourage dutiful behaviour and orthodox opinions by eschewing theological problems and recommending instead a simple, deferential and
conservative code of conduct to his parishioners."[7]

Nokes also writes that the young Swift, wavering between a career
in church or state, and increasingly unable to rely upon his patron,
Sir William Temple, "found his religious hero in the person of Archbishop Sancroft, the subject of his fourth ode. Sancroft was the
leader of the seven bishops condemned to the Tower by James II in
1688 for refusing to read his Declaration of Indulgence from their
pulpits. He subsequently confirmed his commitment to principles—or obstinacy—by refusing to acknowledge the authority of
William III either. Sancroft became a symbol of uncompromising
spiritual independence that sought no accommodation with the
temporal powers. He was, said Swift, 'a gentleman I admire at a degree more than I can express.'"[8] Sancroft wasn't, for Swift, a theological or spiritual model. What Nokes calls Sancroft's "spiritual
independence" signified the struggle of one institution for auton-
omy from another. What Swift seems to have admired about Sancroft was Sancroft's resistance to secular power, not because secular
power necessarily opposed the will or power of God, but because the

Church had to challenge the expansion of monarchical prerogatives to remain the Church. Whether or not the Church here is Christ's body or God's agency on Earth is irrelevant; it functions, vis-à-vis the king, as an institutional counterbalance. The civil functions of an established church are to police doctrine, to reinforce the structures of authority, and in its turn to be protected by that authority. What Swift admired in Sancroft was the archbishop's willingness to enforce the Church's contract.[9]

The late Michael DePorte commented of Swift that "in his satires, we often rub up against things that don't square with the orthodox assertions of the religious tracts and sermons."[10] DePorte concludes that, like the apostle Paul, Swift

> had not come early or easily to the Church. Like Paul, his writings had been misunderstood. And he, too, had tried to make up for his lateness by laboring "more abundantly than they all," fighting, as he had told Lady Worsley ten years before, "with Beast like St. Paul, not at Ephesus, but in Ireland" (*Correspondence* 4:79). This labor might well have seemed abundant to Swift because he appears to have performed it without Paul's experience of personal revelation, without Abraham's faith, which embraced impossibility and contradiction, and without clear expectation of that personal reward he assured his parishioners was the very basis of Christianity.[11]

DePorte's remark highlights one of the central concerns of criticism dealing with Swift in a religious context. Scholarship opening up Swift's work from ideological, economic, and historical perspectives teaches us much about the man and his century, but "religion" is something more than or in addition to the politics, sociology, or psychology of a foundational social institution. What we mean by "religious" isn't, for much of the world's population, only or simply a social phenomenon but must also include the possibility of transcendence; there is at the core of the religious experience "a clear overplus of meaning," to use Rudolph Otto's phrase, a sense of the holy as that which escapes "rationality," "meaning," and any other of the categories we use to approach it: "It will be our endeavor to suggest this unnamed Something to the reader as far as we may, so that he may himself feel it. There is no religion in which it does not live as the real innermost core, and without it no religion would be worthy of the name. It is pre-eminently a living force in the Semitic religions, and of these again in none has it such vigour as in that of the Bible. Here, too, it has a name of its own, viz. the Hebrew qādôsh, to which the Greek ἅγιος and the Latin *sanctus*, and, more accurately still, *sacer*, are the corresponding terms."[12] The Hebrew qā-

dôsh, or "holy," has at its root the meaning of "separate," "set apart." It is what is set apart, Otto's "Something," that we attempt to approach with terms like "transcendent," "divine," and "numinous," and the question is, did Jonathan Swift believe in it, experience it, and see himself in relation to it? Did he, like Abraham, believe in a *numen praesens* beyond himself even if he himself never touched nor was touched by it? This isn't the only question we should ask about Swift's religious writings and career, but neither should we forget entirely to ask it.

Swift famously wrote in "Thoughts on Religion" that "to say a man is bound to believe is neither true nor sense. You may force men, by interest or punishment, to say or swear they believe, and to act as if they believed: You can go no further." He also held that "the want of belief is a defect that ought to be concealed when it cannot be overcome."[13] Swift's "as if" creates a simulacrum of belief that may serve just as well as real faith, and in the wake of the Civil War, the Restoration, and 1688, it makes sense to read these statements as the conclusions of a man wary of social upheaval, but are they also the conclusions of a man who can't believe? This is, of course, a problem for Swift scholars who try to reconcile Swift's deeply hierarchical and mercantilist nature with his vocation as a priest in the Church of Ireland. Swift saw himself "in the capacity of a clergyman, to be one appointed by providence for defending a post assigned to me, and for gaining over as many enemies as I can. Although I think my cause is just, yet one great motion is my submitting to the pleasure of Providence, and to the laws of my country."[14] If this is Swift acknowledging God's existence, then it is at best a distant God, and one whose interests lie remarkably close to the state's. Insofar as "religion" may be divorced from personal faith, Swift was certainly religious. To the extent, though, that "religion" requires faith to be "religion," Swift's faith is unrecoverable to us except by the difficult process of interpreting his words and the record of his actions.

So, what do scholars do with Swift the priest? Do we consign him exclusively to the realm of politics and preferment? Do we attempt to raise from his textual record the ghost of a personal faith? Do we, with Fauske, see him primarily as a secular creature protecting social stability and operating of necessity in the guise of a priest? Do we see in his work the outlines of an agnostic or atheist entering the Church because a gentleman without wealth must have a polite profession? Are these even legitimate questions to ask in today's largely secular academic environment? No one answer, of course, encompasses the man or the complexity of his works. The purpose of this volume is to help open these questions to critical enquiry, to expand the critical horizons that Landa, Fauske, and DePorte have opened. While the contributors to this volume often reach very different conclusions, they each take seriously the linkage between Swift the priest and Swift the satirist.

It's this linkage between the priest and the satirist that makes Swift problematic and compelling. If his faith were obvious and key to his identity, then, surely, satire would serve faith. However good or bad the satires were, they would clearly operate within doctrinal and theological boundaries. Certainly Swift's friend, Alexander Pope, usually confined his satires to men, morals, and manners, and only rarely allowed his work to hint at a darker, less providential reality.[15] Pope's reputation has thus never suffered the same sustained attack or the same accusations of impiety that Swift's has endured. If, on the other hand, Swift's satiric genius necessarily brackets the question of his personal faith, can we nevertheless discern a kind of negative faith for Swift, one that emerges in contradistinction to his satiric attacks? Swift gives evidence of such a possibility in his prolix and sometimes awkward "Apology" to the *Tale*. Is "faith" thus built into Swift's texts, and can a true misanthrope also be a true priest? My own conclusion is that Swift, either as believer or as agnostic, is, finally, just as much a construct of the subjunctive mood as are the personae of his satires.

II

Early eighteenth-century Ireland was a nation radically split by its centuries-long conflict with England, and because of this conflict, split too by internal struggles. From Poynings' Law (1494) through the Declaratory Act of 1720, Ireland had been legally subject to a foreign power. Poynings' Law subjected the Irish to the English Crown; the Declaratory Act subjected the Irish people and the Irish parliament, nominally to the Crown, and actually to the English parliament.[16] These legal proscriptions made it relatively simple for succeeding English ministries to manipulate Ireland's political and economic foundations. Most notable were the Cattle Acts of 1666 and 1680, which restricted exportation of most Irish livestock, and the notorious Woolen Act of 1698–99, which banned absolutely any exportation of Irish woolens to any country other than England. This last act had the additional advantage of giving England a cheap and ready supply of wool for its own domestic market. Ireland thus found itself in the classic colonial situation: its raw materials ex-

ported at a loss, and little to nothing done to promote the even development of necessary social and economic infrastructures. The
Sacramental Test in England (1673), and Ireland (1704), required
anyone aspiring to political and social preferment to conform to the
sacraments of the Church of England; the act thus effectively
blocked Irish Catholics and dissenters, particularly Presbyterians,
alike from holding public office, and James II's Act of Toleration
(1689) only helped muddy the religious and political waters.[17]

When Swift was installed as Dean of St. Patrick's Cathedral on
June 13, 1713, this was the Ireland to which he returned—one split
unevenly three ways: among the Irish Establishment, the Catholic
majority, and the Scots-descended Presbyterians especially powerful
in the north, where Swift's first parish, Kilroot, was. Swift was a plu-
ralist, serving three parishes: unfortunately for Swift, "he had no
parish church in two of the three. The third parish did have a
church, without a company or a roof. Furthermore, in his three parishes he had almost no parishioners."[18] Pluralism was a necessary
evil of the time. Since so many powerful laymen had over time impropriated tithes and church lands under their control, clergy, especially lower clergy, often survived on subsistence-level preferments
and had to hold multiple parishes in order to make a living.[19] Non-
residence was often as much a sign of economic conditions as it was
of moral laxity, and the preference the Established Church should
have had was badly eroded by 1695 when Swift was ordained.[20]
Landa records that

> In County Antrim, where Swift's parishes lay, the dire condition of the
> Church in the middle of the seventeenth century is indicated by an In-
> quisition of 1657, which revealed that in the 65 parishes 30 churches
> were in ruins, 27 had no incumbents, 51 had no glebes, and the tithes
> of 32 were impropriate by laymen. And in 1693, a bare two years before
> Swift's incumbency, another report on Down and Connor emphasized
> its lamentable condition, among other things the clergy wrongfully dis-
> possessed of their glebe lands, incumbents restrained from claiming
> their legal rights for fear of offending their patrons or parishioners, non-
> residence widely prevalent, churches falling into disrepair and ruin.[21]

With glebe lands, the cultivable lands that should have belonged to
parish churches, providing revenues for laymen rather than for parish priests, and with local gentry expropriating the monies that
should have gone to parish upkeep and support of priests, it's small
wonder that lower clergy in the Church of Ireland often held several
parishes and were nonresident in any of them. The Church of Ireland was, nominally, the state church, but to think of church as coex-

tensive with state is to oversimplify Swift's situation. The Irish Establishment had legal precedence, and preserving that precedence was sometimes the best way also to preserve a peaceful status quo,[22] but the church that guaranteed that establishment was, at best, in a straitened condition, as Swift was well aware. When in 1704 Queen Anne remitted the First Fruits to the Church of England, the Irish clergy were quick to take notice:

> On her birthday Queen Anne had consented to remit the Crown's right to the "First Fruits and Twentieth Parts' of the Church of England, and had agreed to use the revenues for augmenting some poorer livings. The Convocation of the Church of Ireland quickly petitioned for a similar remission to be made in Ireland. The Queen made them a 'gracious answer' but no action followed. What was needed, Swift believed, was an envoy from the Church of Ireland to solicit the ministry in London to give effect to this remission. Moreover, if her Majesty would consent to give up not only the First Fruits, but also the Crown rents due on Church properties in Ireland, the value of the remission would be doubled for rather less than the cost of the grant made to the Church of England.[23]

Had the Queen, the head of the Church, really seen the Established Church in Ireland as coextensive with her state, she would have made the remission a priority, as would her ministers, but when Swift met with the Whig treasurer, the Earl of Godolphin, both men knew that the Church of Ireland's welfare was secondary to the ministry's political needs:

> In England Swift pleaded his cause with the Earl Godolphin, then First Lord of the Treasury, and with such other powerful Whigs as Somers, Pembroke, Wharton and Sunderland, all to no avail; and finally, when the Godolphin ministry fell, with Robert Harley and others among the Tories. So much has been said of Swift's inordinate ambition, of Swift the place-seeker, that we must look at this project from that vantage. He was not so naïve that he did not realize what might accrue to him from success, yet he could be selfless when his deepest convictions were affronted. Godolphin made clear that his government would consider favourably the pleas for remission of the First Fruits if the Irish churchmen supported the ministerial policy in Ireland, i.e., easing the plight of the nonconformists by removing the Test Act. Although we cannot in this day admire Swift's inflexible antagonism to dissent, we can understand it. Godolphin's bribe, as Swift conceived it, aroused his instincts for the safety of the Establishment.[24]

To deal with such degraded parishes would have been bad enough, but to compromise on the Test Act, the one piece of legislation central to preserving the Established Church and thus, in Swift's mind, the Protestant Establishment in Ireland, was too great a cost for the Church to pay, even if it meant improving the clergy's condition.

Swift also faced the obstacle of a thriving Presbyterian community. No group more aroused Swift's "inflexible antagonism to dissent" than this one. The Presbyterians, mostly descendents of Scots immigrants, were socially and economically powerful enough to nullify any legal advantage the Established Church had, and they outnumbered Establishment parishioners by a wide margin: "Anglican parishes often could not boast more than ten, sometimes not more than six, whereas 'the Presbyterian meetings [were] crowded with thousands'; so reported an Anglican dignitary three years before Swift arrived, adding that 'the county of Antrim especially . . . is the most populous of Scots of any in Ulster.' "[25] Militant Protestantism had diminished in both England and Ireland after Charles II was restored to the throne in 1660, and smaller groups, such as Quakers, Baptists, and Anabaptists played little role in Ireland's religious landscape. The Scots Presbyterians, on the other hand, settled northern Ireland in increasingly large numbers after 1600 and formed a much more cohesive, more disciplined community than any other of the dissenting sects: "For practical purposes, then, Irish Protestant Dissent meant Ulster Presbyterians, based on the Scottish immigrants who had been entering the province in irregular waves since the early seventeenth century."[26] Presbyterians naturally resented the tithe, and as their numbers grew, such unpopular taxes became more difficult to collect.[27] Not only would this have offended Swift's religious convictions; it also posed a threat to his and other priests' purses: "To the Anglican clergy of the eighteenth century it was axiomatic that the spiritual health of the Church depended on flourishing temporalities. Tithes, the divine tenth, were indeed divine."[28]

Presbyterians weren't the only denomination Swift had to deal with. Catholics, while politically the least powerful group in Ireland, were attaining numerical superiority by the time Swift became dean. Connolly reports that

> In the late seventeenth century the numerical weakness of the Protestants had to some extent been compensated by their strong positions in the towns. Although Catholics were far more numerous in the countryside, the Catholic bishop of Waterford and Lismore reported in 1672, 'in the cities the heretics are of equal number with the Catholics'. In Waterford itself, fifteen years later, Protestants still comprised up to half the population. Elsewhere the Protestant position was even stronger.

Drogheda, for example, was reported to be predominantly Protestant in 1670, while in Dundalk Catholics made up only a quarter of the population. By the early eighteenth century, this numerical superiority had in most cases eroded, as expanding urban centres drew in people from the surrounding countryside and earlier attempts to exclude Catholics from walled towns and other strategic centres were abandoned.[29]

As for Dublin, Swift's home after 1713, Connolly writes, "When a gentleman left his town house or an MP the parliament building on College Green, he stepped out onto the streets of what could still, if only just, be considered a Protestant city."[30] Urban centers were, especially, magnets for Catholic migration, as Catholics were the denomination mostly likely as a class to be poor;[31] they were most often the lowest level of tenant farmers whose livelihoods were precarious and dependent on both the weather and the whims of their absentee landlords; they were thus the economic class most often attracted to the employments cities offered. This isn't to say that all Catholics were poor or dispossessed. Their Protestant counterparts were often as just as distressed, and Landa quotes a 1718 letter from Bishop Evans to Archbishop Wake that makes clear the zero-sum game the poorest Catholics and Protestants engaged in: "I hear 1000 of Protestants go to American because their Landlords every where bear hard upon them & Papists succeed them in the Farms in severall parts of the Kingdom."[32] Catholics had also gained control of arable lands during the upheavals of 1641 and 1688, and in the ensuing political confusion, some lands ended up in Catholic hands that the Church of Ireland had previously controlled.[33]

Catholicism, more so than Anglicanism, exercised a spiritual power over its followers. Catholic priests were much more likely to come from local populations; priests thus shared both local traditions of piety and local economic depredations. Unlike the Church of Ireland, its association with an oppressive foreign regime didn't handicap Irish Catholicism: "As a persecuted church, it was not embarrassed by too close an identification with the state or the ruling class; the clergy attracted to a church without wealth or prestige were drawn from social backgrounds similar to those of their congregations. The same point was noted by some contemporaries. Berkeley, in 1735, queried 'whether it be not of great advantage to the church of Rome that she hath clergy suited to all ranks of men . . . whether her numerous poor clergy were not very useful in missions, and of much influence with the people.' "[34] Irish Catholicism had an internal consistency and loyalty that the Established Church lacked. Not only were Catholic priests like their parishioners, but be-

longing to a church under legal ban meant that promotion and preferment in the Catholic Church brought little improvement in
material circumstances. The same positions in the Church of Ireland would have given Irish Protestants sound, and sometimes
wealthy, livings, but native-born priests of the Church of Ireland
rarely reached the uppermost ranks of the church. As often as he
was at odds with the Protestant gentry, Swift sided with them in their
dissatisfaction with the English practice of appointing English clerics to Irish episcopacies: "Thus it became one of his persistent endeavours to build up a Church interest among the gentry of Ireland.
In practice this meant that he espoused the Irish (i.e. Anglo-Irish)
interest in the Church as opposed to the English interest—that is,
he wished preferment to be given more liberally to sons and relatives
of the Anglo-Irish gentry and less so the Englishmen."[35] Preferment,
such as it was worth, was at least one advantage the Catholic Church
had over the Established Church.

III

"Lions, bears, elephants, and some other animals, are strong or
valiant, and their species never degenerates in their native soil, except they happen to be enslaved or destroyed by human fraud: But
men degenerate every day, merely by the folly, the perverseness, the
avarice, the tyranny, the pride, the treachery, or inhumanity of their
own kind."[36]

What follows next is a practice reading, an attempt to suggest how
one can engage Swift's texts, specifically, his religious texts, in such
a way as to open the question of Swift's religious identity. Swift's dedication to the Church of Ireland certainly made him a theological
pragmatist whose arguments changed with the needs of his church.
And it is true that Swift's sermons are highly ancillary to his political
tracts and satires. But this does not mean that we cannot distinguish
the outlines of a "science of God" in Swift's religious writings. This
essay is not about what theology is, but about what Swift makes it out
to be as a structural element of his larger argument. Swift's belief in
God is axiomatic to his understanding of the properly constituted
state. As we find him in Swift's writings, God is thus a function of
state ideology; a governing rubric, as it were, under which the hierarchy of church and state regulates the transactions constituting cor-
porate and individual identity. Swift's God is, consequently, not a
personal God to whom one relates on an emotional or subjective
level. God exists instead somewhere between the unmoved and un-

emotional mover of deism and the unparsable God of fideism. Swift's theology is relational, but the relationship is between God and the state and not between the individual and the divine.

My reading will concentrate on two of Swift's sermons, "On the Poor Man's Contentment" and "On Brotherly Love." These sermons, probably composed in the teens or twenties,[37] reflect Swift's thinking on two fundamental and related issues: the value of the individual vis-à-vis the state, and the proper hierarchy within the state itself. Swift argues in "On Brotherly Love," for instance, that "The little Religion there is in the World hath been observed to reside chiefly among the middle and lower Sort of People, who are neither tempted to Pride and Luxury by great Riches, nor to desperate Courses by extreme Poverty."[38] This sentiment steers the sort of median way between wealth and poverty typical of Swift's discourses. It even allows Swift to castigate his poor parishioners for their greater sinfulness:

> [Y]ou of the meaner Sort are subject to fewer Temptations than the Rich; and therefore your Vices are more unpardonable. Labour subdueth your Appetites to be satisfied with common Things; the Business of your several Callings filleth up your whole Time; so that Idleness, which is the Bane and Destruction of Virtue, doth not lead you into the Neighbourhood of Sin: your Passions are cooler, by not being inflamed with Excess, and therefore the Gate and the Way that lead to Life are not so strait or so narrow to you, as those who live among all the Allurements to Wickedness. To serve God with the best of your Care and Understanding, and to be just and true in your Dealings, is the short Sum of your Duty and will be the more strictly required of you, because nothing lieth in the Way to divert you from it.[39]

This remarkable statement, from "On the Poor Man's Contentment," is, for most of us, Swift at his worst. Far from sympathizing with the poor, Swift actually raises the hurdle between them and heaven. I would, though, ask that we suspend temporarily any sense we may have of Swift's awfulness and instead ask ourselves what Swift says here about God's relationship to humans.

We might call the poor to whom Swift here refers "the providentially busy." These are the people whose struggle to get by "fills up their whole time" with appetite-subduing labor, and, presumably, passion-cooling weariness. They are thus preserved from the "Idleness" that characterizes the undeserving wealthy, who in their turn bear the brunt of God's disfavor by "living among all the Allurements to Wickedness." We know—because Swift tells us—that God is, if not directly responsible for doling out the material wealth of this life, at least willing to allow the undeserving to grab what they can to further their own damnation. Swift asks rhetorically, "If Men's Titles were to be tried before a true Court of Conscience, where false swearing, and a thousand vile Artifices, (that are well known, and can hardly be avoided in human Courts of Justice) would avail nothing; how many would be ejected with Infamy and Disgrace? how many grow considerable by Breach of Trust, by Bribery and Corruption? How many have sold their Religion, with the Rights and Liberties of themselves and others, for Power and Employments?"[40] Since no such "human Courts of Justice" can expose the true nature of human infamy, the court Swift hypothesizes here must be God's. This is the same court that will "strictly require" their duty of the sinful poor who miss the more capacious "Gate and Way that lead to Life" God has opened for them.

Indeed, Swift warns his audience not to misinterpret wealth as a sign of God's favor: "Now, if Riches and Greatness were such Blessings, that good Men without them could have their Share of Happiness in this Life; how cometh it to pass, that God should suffer them to be often dealt to the worst, and most profligate of Mankind? That they should be generally procured by the most abominable Means, and applied to the basest and most wicked Uses? This ought not to be conceived of a just, a merciful, a wise, and Almighty Being."[41] The question we must ask Swift then becomes "how poor is poor enough?" Swift's sermons presuppose an ideal materialism; just enough, that is, to avoid the hardships of abject poverty while at the same time escaping the immoral effect of wealth. Swift paraphrases the prayer of Agur, a figure from Proverbs, who asks that God "[G]ive me neither Poverty nor Riches; Feed me with Food convenient for me. Lest I be full and deny thee, and say, Who is the Lord? Or, lest I be poor, and steal, and take the Name of my God in vain."[42] Agur and his like would be Ireland's model citizens, neither wanting nor needing assistance, content with the balance they had achieved between human desire and God's providence.

The problem, though, is fixing the line that separates just enough from too little. When Swift theorizes the issue of poverty unironically, or at least as unironically as a satirist of his reputation can,[43] he insists that the greed of the "undeserving poor" hinders charity as effectively as the greed of the "undeserving wealthy." Those Swift calls the "foreign" poor, i.e., the poor who flock to Dublin from the surrounding countryside, compound the problem by diluting the effects of charity. Swift writes that "It is true, indeed, that sometimes honest, endeavouring Men are reduced to extreme Want, even to the Begging of Alms, by Losses, by Accidents, by Diseases, and old

Age, without any Fault of their own: But these are very few, in Comparison of the other; nor would their Support be any sensible Burthen to the Publick, if the Charity of well-disposed Persons were not intercepted by those common Strollers, who are most importunate, and who least deserve it."[44]

Nokes observes that Swift's "language is charged with moral opprobrium, and he sees poverty as the outward and visible sign of sinfulness. Hence compassion is ruled out of court as an accessory to the original vice that has brought the individual to penury."[45] I tend to agree with Nokes's interpretation, but I wonder what happens if we entertain seriously the proposition underlying Swift's argument. Nokes reacts to the "unpleasantly pharisaical" efficiency with which Swift divides Dublin's poor into the deserving few and the importunate many, but would an open purse to all be the moral alternative? In a way, Swift's sermons neatly encapsulate the central dilemma of mercantile capitalism. Who is responsible for the poor in the absence of a total welfare state, and who provides the resources (food, clothing, money, capital) to keep the unproductive poor alive? Even if we admit Nokes's contention that compassion is, for Swift, an accessory to vice, what response do we make to Swift's underlying question about the relationship between personal need and personal responsibility? But even more fundamental is the question of how much do the haves give, for whatever reason, to the have-nots? A nuanced answer does not permit us the simple response, "Swift is callous." That may be all too true, but his callousness has behind it the providential judgment of his God.

Swift offers to "vindicate" God's justice and mercy in dealing with the poor when he preaches that God "hath not dealt so hardly with his Creatures as some would imagine, when they see so many miserable Objects ready to perish for Want: For it would infallibly be found, upon strict Enquiry, that there is hardly one in twenty of those miserable Objects who do not owe their present Poverty to their own Faults; to their present Sloth and Negligence; to their indiscreet Marriage without the least Prospect of supporting a Family, to their foolish Expensiveness, to their Drunkenness, and other Vices, by which they have squandered their Gettings, and contracted Diseases in their old Age."[46] Is it ever ethical to blame the poor and suffering for their condition? Swift emphatically answers, "yes," especially if the alternative is to blame God. Swift's understanding of God calls for this theodicean justification, since the physical evil the poor suffer is a symbol of the moral evil they perpetrate and not the action of a "just" and "merciful" deity.

The problem here is, I think, with Swift's inherently hierarchical definition of the individual subject. The poor who suffer here do so, by Swift's account, as the result of their own imprudence: their free choice leads them where they do not wish to go. This is why Swift asks, "Is it any Way reasonable or just, that those who have denied themselves many lawful Satisfactions and Conveniences of Life, from a Principle of Conscience, as well as Prudence, should be charged with supporting Others, who have brought themselves to less than a Morsel of Bread by their Idleness, Extravagance, and Vice?"[47] What Swift calls "Conscience" comes from knowledge of God's will, not from any personal relationship with him. If these poor starve, it is their own fault, not God's, and most importantly, not Swift's. Swift characterizes their plight as the result of free choice in a physical world of consequences. What he does not theorize, of course, is the array of social, political, and cultural forces that collude against individual choice to render the individual needy. Swift's definition of individuality here implies that a person properly oriented toward God is also somehow competent to negotiate the transindividual circumstances defining a particular historical moment. Swift's position would probably be less objectionable to a modern liberal audience if he were to argue that unconditional aid to such people is a form of arrogance on the almsgiver's part; a means, that is, of infantilizing the poor that keeps them from bootstrapping their own way to self-sufficiency and social responsibility. But for Swift, aside from being a chronic annoyance, individual charity is pointless because it debases the giver without morally improving the receiver.

This notion appears to clash with Swift's concept of the individual in his sermon, "On Brotherly Love," in which Swift warns his parishioners that they may be unwitting agents in the struggle between political factions:

> Another cause of the great Want of Brotherly Love, is owing to the Weakness and Folly of too many among you, of the lower Sort, who are made the Tools and Instruments of your Betters, to work their Designs, wherein you have no Concern. Your Numbers make you of Use, and cunning Men take the Advantage, by putting Words into your Mouths, which you do not understand; then they fix good or ill Characters to those Words, as it best serves their Purposes: and Thus you are taught to love or hate, you know not what, nor why; you often suspect your best Friends and nearest Neighbours, even your Teacher himself, without any Reason, if your Leaders have once taught you to call him by a Name, which, they tell you, signifieth some very bad Thing.[48]

Here, the individual, always defined as of "the lower Sort," becomes the dupe of "cunning Men" who use him to ventriloquize their own party preferences. What Swift deplores in "On Brotherly Love" is this sort of instrumentalization of the working poor because it makes them as a class both misunderstand their own inherent best interests and challenge the authority of those who would instruct them in their social and religious duties—for Swift, there is no distance between the two. He deplores "that unhappy Disposition towards Politics among the Trading People, which hath been industriously instilled into them. In former Times, the middle and lower Sort of Mankind seldom gained or lost by the Factions of the Kingdom, and therefore were little concerned in them, further than as Matter of Talk and Amusement; but, now, the meanest Dealer will expect to turn the Penny by the Merits of his Party."[49] Swift warns, "where Party hath once made Entrance with all its Consequences of Hatred, Envy, Partiality, and Virulence, Religion cannot long keep its Hold in any State or Degree of Life whatsoever": "For, if the Great Men of the World have been censured in all Ages for mingling too little Religion with their Politicks, what a Havok of Principles must they needs make in unlearned and vulgar Heads? of which indeed the Effects are already too visible and melancholy all over the Kingdom."[50] If those at the top of society's natural hierarchy cannot resist the evils of party politics, what hope do the "unlearned and vulgar Heads" have?

The "Peace and mutual Love" Swift thus invokes as "the last Legacy of *Christ*"[51] turns out to be both a theological imperative and a form of ideological control. "In the early Times of the Gospel," Swift writes, "the Christians were very much distinguished from all other Bodies of men, by the great and constant Love they bore to each other; which, although it was done in Obedience to the frequent Injunctions of our Saviour and his Apostles, yet I confess, there seems to have been likewise a natural Reason, that very much promoted it. For the Christians then were few and scattered, living under Persecution, by the Heathens round about them, in whose Hands was all the civil and military Power; and there is nothing so apt to unite the Minds and Hearts of Men, or to beget Love and Tenderness, as a general Distress."[52] Brotherly love held the nascent Christian community together in the face of a mutual enemy. Theologically, this love originated in Christ, but in practical terms, it continued because of the "general Distress" bonding the faithful. Swift does not deny the theological origin of the virtue he promotes, but neither does he stress that virtue because of its salvific potential. Instead, he uses theology strategically, as he does throughout the sermons, as a means to bolster the social hierarchy. I don't doubt that Swift thought the hierarchical nature of his society was providentially ordained, but neither do I doubt that his motive for upholding that hierarchy had largely to do with the stability of his place in it.

Swift's definition of the individual is thus more coherent than it seems at first. The bootstrapping poor Swift dreams of are the same people who listen when teachers like Swift tell them how they should live their lives. Swift is deeply suspicious of the individual subject when that subject is "of the middle or lower Sort," but, at least when he speaks in the person of Dean of St. Patrick's, Swift endorses the hierarchical authority of the church-state apparatus. We know from his career, particularly his time in London, that Swift placed little worth in the words of the great. But what really matters to Swift is that the church speak authoritatively to the masses as a coherent counterweight to any individual, precisely because any individual has the potential to dissent, politically or theologically, from the church's doctrine. As Fauske argues, "Swift's belief that conduct was a sufficient guide to character . . . does gain a considerable measure of intellectual integrity when reviewed in the light of its author's conception of Christian doctrine as being at least as much of a social code of ethics as a matter of faith."[53] But whether or not Swift's defense of the church springs from his political or religious beliefs, the effect of Swift's sermons is to place God squarely on the side of those who submit to the duly ordained agents of institutional authority. Michael DePorte writes, "As a public spokesman for the church, Swift's views are straightforward. He sought to secure its position from attack, to discredit the motives of those who took part in such attacks, and to demonstrate that Christianity itself, particularly the doctrine of eternal rewards and punishments, is the only sure foundation of moral life."[54] Swift's argument is political, but what undergirds it is a providential theology that demands obedience to the ordained order first, and individual faith or understanding only second. In a way, Swift's position makes sense, since as the public face of the church, Swift's function is to promote action, not to foster faith where it does not already exist.

Swift's sermons make it clear that he identifies much more closely with the figure of God than he does with the compassionate Christ. Or, if we wish to invoke Christ, it is Christ the King, Christ the majestic Pantocrator, rather than the humble and very human person from Nazareth. Swift is, I contend, powerfully attracted to the idea of a remote God represented in this world not by his salvific son, but by that God's law, a law that saves—if it saves at all—not through charity but through structure. In America, Swift's God would feel comfortably at home, since it is his kind of morality that underwrites the means testing of our social welfare system and fails to count the increasing number of "discouraged workers," those who have given up the search for work, in our national unemployment figures. It is his kind of morality that preserves the proprieties of bureaucracy in the face of increasing need. Swift knew, of course, about the needs of the poor; the range of his works, from his sermons to "A Modest Proposal" to the Drapier's letters to his various proposals for giving badges to beggars, show his outrage toward rich and poor alike for colluding with the system that produced both. But a God removed from the individual, a God who is himself all sufficient, and not the image of the generous householder or his messianic mediator, proves the ultimate model for the Dean's theology.

IV

The aim of the following essays is to reevaluate Swift's tenure as a priest in the Church of Ireland vis-à-vis his identity as one of the Enlightenment's premier satirists. To that end, the contributors have adopted a variety of approaches, some examining the historical contexts of Swift's works, others reading Swift from particular literary-critical and theoretical perspectives, and while we don't always agree in our methods or conclusions, each of the contributors has produced a powerful and original reading.

Robert Mahony's essay, "Certainty and Irony in Swift: Faith and the Indeterminate," identifies the conventions that signify "faith" in Swift's texts and notes a shift in those conventions that leaves Swift vulnerable to charges of agnosticism and infidelity. Mahony finds that during Swift's day, the proof of faith shifted away from belief in the credal and doctrinal positions of the Church and toward a more subjective and personal engagement with the question of belief. By privileging sentiment over fidelity to doctrine, Mahony argues, we moderns have failed to give Swift his due because we no longer recognize his kind of fidelity. Swift's "faith" is a function of belief in scripture that both creates and guarantees the certainty one seeks in vain in extrascriptural texts and thus in the world beyond scripture. Using Swift's sermons in particular, Mahony shows how Swift accepts as given a degree of truth in scripture that he cannot, and in fact does not, accept anywhere else. By thus elevating the truthfulness of scripture, Swift creates a two-tiered hermeneutic system consistent both with his understanding of scripture and with his use of satire.

My own essay, " 'The Idlest Trifling Stuff That Ever Was Writ,' or Why Swift Hated His Sermons," argues that Swift's sermons by their very nature undermine the stable boundaries between sacred and satiric texts that Swift very much wished to reinforce, especially as his fame as a satirist grew and clashed with his desire for ecclesiastical preferment. Because Swift couldn't control the way readers would receive his texts, and particularly because his public persona as priest and dean had to coexist with his persona as a major satirist, he could never effectively police the boundary between satiric and nonsatiric texts. Swift's sermons thus become the occasion for a crisis of interpretation precisely because "satire" isn't a genre, but a mode of interpretation; once Swift is identified as a satirist, he loses the power to determine which of his texts are satire, and which aren't.

Brian A. Connery's " 'Wild Work in the World': The Church, the Public Sphere, and Swift's Abstract of Collins's *Discourse*" begins with the late seventeenth- and early eighteenth-century attacks on ecclesiastical authority that opened the discussion of religion and reason to the general public. Collin's *Discourse* offered itself as a way to unseat mystery and revelation as the Church's privileged means of maintaining social authority, and Swift's satiric abstract of Collins's text is his most direction rejection of Enlightenment liberalism and of deists' and freethinkers' arguments for free speech and the open public forum. Connery stresses that, for Swift, the value of the Church of England lay primarily in its stability as a social institution and only secondarily as a repository of Christian doctrine. To counter what he saw as the damage of the debate over reason versus mystery, Swift adopted a satiric strategy designed to silence both the Church's critics and its defenders. Connery argues that, ironically, Swift's reaction to Collins itself fed the debate over the reasonableness of Christianity and thus helped to accelerate the very processes Swift wished to suppress.

Christopher Fox's essay, "Swift and the Rabble Reformation: *A Tale of a Tub* and the State of the Church in the 1690s," is one of the best short histories of Scots Presbyterian influence on Swift since Louis Landa. Fox shows the consequence of Scots Presbyterianism on the origin and development of Swift's *Tale;* more importantly, Fox articulates the relationship between the Scots migration to Ireland in the 1680s and the state of crisis in the Church of Ireland when Swift first went to Kilroot to take up his cure. Kilroot was directly across the bay from southwest Scotland, where the rabblings began in 1688, and Fox points out that by a conservative estimate, more than 40,000 Scots Presbyterians fleeing famine would settle in northeastern Ireland during the first half of the eighteenth century. The constant influx of people hostile to the Established Church

would have deeply concerned Swift, especially since these same people had successfully disestablished the Church in Scotland during
King William's reign. Fox argues persuasively that the character of
Jack in the *Tale* embodies Swift's fear, not just of Presbyterianism in
general, but in particular those who lived in Kilroot and who were
related by ties of blood and sympathy to the Scots agitators who had
torn Establishment clergy from their homes and publicly humiliated
them as representatives of a hated episcopacy. For Fox, Jack embodies a nagging anxiety in Swift's character that the Scots and their
detestable church will eventually control Ireland as well as Scotland.

Anne B. Gardiner's "*A Tale of a Tub* and the Great Debate over
Substance, with Regard to Sacrament, Church, and Nature," argues
that Swift's *Tale* is an important theological intervention in the early
eighteenth-century controversy surrounding the nature of Christ's
body in the Eucharist. Swift, according to Gardiner, rejects Descartes' and Calvin's reduction of "substance" to matter and extension. She shows how Swift artfully expands his satire to include what
seemed to him to be dubious arguments replacing Christ's real presence in the Church and in its central sacrament with conciliar
edicts, papal decretals, and narrowly literal readings of the Bible. To
equate substance and extension, as Descartes and Calvin did, is, for
Swift, to impoverish and to dehumanize the fully human. Instead,
Swift supports an earlier, pre-Cartesian way of thinking, in which the
internal, "real" nature of a thing can't be known materially. Gardiner's perspective is especially useful because she places Swift in the
context of the fractious eighteenth-century debate over the nature
of Christ's divinity and how best to understand spiritual realities in
a largely material age. Gardiner thus shows us a Swift rarely seen in
modern criticism.

James Ward's punning title, "Pastures and Masters: Swift the Pastor and the Politics of Pastoral," foregrounds the material conditions of Swift's tenure as an Anglican priest holding both authority
over and responsibility for the land that produced his income and
for the local population that made (or should have made) up his
congregation. As a satirist, Ward contends, Swift used the language
of the pastoral tradition to insert himself into the political struggle
of the Church of Ireland to maintain its social, and particularly its
economic, position. Swift's use of the "pastor" was part of a wider
cultural phenomenon whereby elements of the pastoral genre were
used to dramatize issues of ownership, patronage, and expropriation that were germane to the postcolonial society of eighteenth-
century Ireland. As a political enactment of these issues, Ward discusses the tithe agistment controversy of the early-mid 1730s, which

was part of the continuing struggle between the Church and the gentry to assert rights of stewardship over the land and its people. Swift thus used the language of pastoral in an attempt to portray the Church of Ireland as a victim of the ideological struggles of the 1730s, and thus as a way to give voice to his own rancorous relationship to his "flock." Swift's pastoral language becomes, in effect, a form of payback for the ungrateful sheep he, as pastor, must pasture.

Daniel Lupton rejects as unproductive the history of allegorical readings of *Gulliver's Travels* in favor of an approach that takes seriously Swift's oft-repeated claim of faith in the Christian revelation. In "Swift's Idea of Christian Community," Lupton holds that his method of reading agrees with Swift's sense of his own identity and helps to reconcile Swift the priest with Swift the satirist. Lupton argues that Swift's Christianity was, by conscious choice, void of the complicated theology Swift thought inappropriate for the average Establishment churchgoer. Instead, Swift's sermons suggest that the true Christian engages society actively with an aim of reforming vice and promoting virtue; abstruse theologizing simply obstructs this process, so when Swift embodies Christian principles—particularly those of brotherly love and compassion—in *Gulliver's Travels,* he does so by showing the consequences of their conspicuous absence. Calling the Houyhnhnms "constitutionally immune to revealed wisdom," Lupton makes the point that the Houyhnhnms can neither accept nor benefit from such Christian concepts a sin or grace. Nor, for that matter, can Gulliver. Lupton provocatively argues that Christian readers should recognize both the limitations of Houyhnhnm society and Gulliver's sinfulness in refusing to sacrifice his comfort or pride for the sake of the reviled Yahoos.

Probably the greatest strength of Louise Barnett's essay, "Swift and Religion: Notes Toward a Psychoanalytic Interpretation," is that Barnett discusses Swift's religious views vis-à-vis Freudian psychoanalysis without trivializing or stereotyping either man. Barnett clearly situates Swift in a Freudian dynamic of paternal loss, and thus of paternal idealization, but she does so without either simplistically reducing God to a lost father figure or reducing Swift's life to a deterministic psychoanalytic pattern. Using William James as the fulcrum between Swift and Freud, Barnett shows how Swift searches for a father, as for example in Archbishop William King, without naively substituting such father surrogates for God or imagining that the reality of God, psychic or otherwise, in itself compensates for the miseries of existence or the reality of death. Swift's own despair, in other words, never blinds Swift to the necessity of God as a sociopolitical reality, nor does it cause Swift to seek refuge in the easy security of deism or atheism.

For John Shanahan, the shock value of Swift's satire in *Gulliver's Travels*' third book is the disparity between the promise of some utopian future and the savage reality of the present imposed by those who value what might be over what actually is. "'in the mean time': Jonathan Swift, Francis Bacon, and Georgic Struggle" argues that this tension between present and future fuels Swift's indignation and his moral activism. Shanahan uses the model of Virgil's *Georgics* as a lens through which to view Swift, first because Swift's situation in the post–civil war era paralleled that of Virgil after the civil wars that ended the Roman republic. Second, and more important, the *Georgics* concern themselves with the here and now of agriculture and husbandry, something infinitely attractive to those who had lived through the apocalyptic and eschatological traumas of the seventeenth century. For Shanahan, Swift's Anglicanism was ultimately "georgic" in its approach to the world, i.e., "practical and prudential," in that Swift resisted theological abstractions that either ignored political and social realities or, worse, shoehorned them into an irrelevant model of human conduct more appropriate to end-time fears—fears of a future that comes so late as to be irrelevant to the material conditions of the living. It is in this spirit that Swift condemns the tendency of systematizing thinkers to worship their own arguments in the place of the divine, thus idolizing human intellection at the expense of divine *sophia*. Such theories, themselves by necessity short-sighted and incomplete, pose as general and eternal truths and thus obscure the hard work of knowing reality as it really is. For all his distrust of Bacon, Swift sympathized with Bacon's disdain of inductive science, which preferred the easy and convenient truth of the moment to the hard-won work of real experience. It was, as Swift saw, simpler all around to substitute convenient human schemes for the frustrating perplexities of the real creation.

NOTES

1. "Swift, the Mysteries, and Deism," reprinted in *Essays in Eighteenth-Century English Literature* (Princeton: Princeton University Press, 1980), 90.

2. *Jonathan Swift and the Church of Ireland 1710–1724*, (Dublin: Academic Press, 2002), 39–40.

3. Ibid., 5.

4. See Landa's introduction to the sermons in *The Prose Works of Jonathan Swift,*

Vol. IX, *Irish Tracts and Sermons 1720–1723,* ed. Herbert Davis and Louis Landa (Oxford: Basil Blackwell, 1968), 196.

5. See *Swift and Anglican Rationalism* (Chicago: University of Chicago Press, 1961), 46–51.

6. Ibid., 51.

7. "Swift and the Beggars," *Essays in Criticism* 26 (1976): 219.

8. *Jonathan Swift: A Hypocrite Reversed* (Oxford: Oxford University Press, 1985), 24.

9. S. J. Connolly sees James II's Act of 1689 as a major blow to the Established Church's prerogative: "The Toleration Act of 1689 had not only recognized the rights of Dissenters to worship in their own manner. It had also permitted large numbers to abandon religious practice altogether, and had fatally weakened the coercive discipline exercised through the ecclesiastical courts" (*Religion, Law, and Power: The Making of Protestant Ireland 1660–1760* [Oxford: Clarendon Press, 1992], 172).

10. "Public Certainty, Private Doubt: Swift In and Out of the Pulpit," paper presented at the Symposium on Jonathan Swift and Christianity, St. Patrick's Cathedral, Dublin, October 19 2002; 1: www.unh.edu/english/swift/2002.deporte.htm.

11. Ibid., 8.

12. Rudolph Otto, *The Idea of the Holy* (Oxford: Oxford University Press, 1958), 5–6, 11.

13. Davis and Landa, *Irish Tracts and Sermons,* 261.

14. Ibid., 261.

15. Think, for instance, of the bleak vision with which the 1743 *Dunciad* ends. Having absented itself, the divine no longer guides humanity or its affairs.

16. See Fauske, *Swift and the Church of Ireland 1710–1724,* 82–89, for further details.

17. G. J. Schochet remarks, "The Toleration Act at least left Protestant Dissenters somewhat better off than it had found them. . . . It had the further consequence, with the failure of comprehension, of forcing into their number the Presbyterians, who had to surrender their hope of reuniting with the Church of England" ("The Act of Toleration and the Failure of Comprehension: Persecution, Nonconformity and Religious Indifference," quoted in Fauske, 31).

18. Louis Landa, "Jonathan Swift: Not the Gravest of Divines," reprinted in *Essays in Eighteenth-Century English Literature,* 68.

19. Swift knew the pinch of impropriated tithes: "Swift himself . . . possessed only a portion of the tithes of his parishes, the remainder being in lay possession; and it will also be recalled that he purchased the impropriate tithes of Effernock to improve the income of the vicars of Laracor" (Louis Landa, *Swift and the Church of Ireland* [Oxford: Clarendon Press, 1954], 166).

20. The Church of Ireland wasn't the only church to endure absenteeism. Connolly reports that the Roman Catholic Church also suffered: "One complaint, throughout the early and mid-eighteenth century, was the number of bishops who failed to reside in their diocese, preferring to live either elsewhere in Ireland or, in some cases, in one of the more pleasant corners of Catholic Europe. A report in 1739 listed no less than six habitual absentees, three of whom were said not to have lived in their diocese for ten years or more" (*Religion, Law, and Power,* 153–54).

21. Landa, *Swift and the Church of Ireland,* 11.

22. The 1689 Toleration Act has been read as one promoting religious freedom, but its intention was to liberate Catholics from the restrictions of the Act of Uniformity without unduly undermining Ireland's Protestant Establishment: "In reality,

however, the purpose of the Act [of 1689] was not to light a beacon of religious liberty, but rather to get around a practical problem: how to nullify the provisions of the Act of Uniformity, which gave the Church of Ireland its privileged status, and made non-attendance at its services punishable by law, without embarrassing the king by too direct an attack on the Anglican establishment" (*Religion, Law, and Power*, 157).

23. Nokes, *A Hypocrite Reversed*, 70–71.

24. Landa, "Not the Gravest of Divines," 72–73.

25. Ibid., 68.

26. Connolly, *Religion, Law, and Power*, 161.

27. In Archbishop King's opinion, Presbyterians "are a people embodied under their lay elders, presbyteries and synods and come to their sacraments in crowds of three or four thousand from 20 or 40 miles about, and they make laws for themselves and allow not that the civil magistrate has any right to control them and will be just so far the king's subjects as their law elders and presbyteries will allow them." Quoted in Connelly, *Religion, Law, and Power*, 168.

28. Landa, "Not the Gravest of Divines," 68–69.

29. Connelly, *Religion, Law, and Power*, 145–147.

30. Ibid., 147.

31. We should remember what the Proposer has to say on this point: "FOR, *First*, as I have already observed, it would greatly lessen the *Number of Papists*, with whom we are yearly overrun; being the principal Breeders of the Nation, as well as our most dangerous Enemies; and who stay at home on Purpose, with a Design to *deliver the Kingdom to the Pretender*; hoping to take their Advantage by the Absence *of so many good Protestants*, who have chosen rather to leave their Country, than stay at home, and pay Tithes against their Conscience, to an idolatrous *Episcopal Curate*." See "A Modest Proposal" (Davis and Landa, *The Prose Works of Jonathan Swift*, Vol. XII, *Irish Tracts and Sermons*), 114–15.

32. Landa, *Swift and the Church of Ireland*, 156.

33. Ibid., 160–161.

34. Connelly, *Religion, Law, and Power*, 152.

35. Landa, *Swift and the Church of Ireland*, 169.

36. "Further Thoughts on Religion," Davis & Landa, *Irish Tracts and Sermons*, 264.

37. See Landa's introduction, *Irish Tracts and Sermons*, 133.

38. Davis and Landa, *Irish Tracts and Sermons*, 174.

39. Ibid., 196.

40. "On the Poor Man's Contentment," *Irish Tracts and Sermons*, 194

41. *Irish Tracts and Sermons*, 195.

42. Ibid.

43. For more on the relationship between Swift's sermons and his satires, see my essay, "'The Idlest Trifling Stuff That Ever Was Writ,' or, Why Swift Hated His Sermons," below.

44. *Irish Tracts and Sermons*, 191.

45. "Swift and the Beggars," 223.

46. "Causes of the Wretched Condition of Ireland," *Irish Tracts and Sermons*, 206.

47. Ibid.

48. Ibid., 173.

49. Ibid.

50. Ibid., 174–75.

51. Ibid., 171.

52. Ibid.

53. Fauske, *Swift and the Church of Ireland 1710–1724*, 43.

54. "Swift, God, and Power," *Walking Naboth's Vineyard: New Studies in Swift,* ed. Christopher Fox and Brenda Tooley (Notre Dame: University of Notre Dame Press, 1995), 81.

Certainty and Irony in Swift:
Faith and the Indeterminate

Robert Mahony

JONATHAN SWIFT'S CHRISTIAN FAITH—OR MORE COMMONLY HIS LACK OF it—used to excite considerable interest. In his own lifetime he was often regarded as an unbeliever, not because he denied any elements of Christian doctrine over his long career as a priest of the Church of Ireland, but rather for his seeming misanthropy: it was cause for wonder how a man with the loathing for humankind that *Gulliver's Travels* apparently exhibits, especially in Part 4, could possibly believe in a redeeming God. Such a sentimentalized Christianity was one indication of the advance of humanitarianism in eighteenth-century British culture, which made greater strides still in the nineteenth century. In the twentieth century, humanitarianism had outpaced religion entirely, and by contrast to the critical mass of comment on Swift's personal psychology, his political views or his relationships with women, no more than a handful of scholars paid attention to his faith. The fact that Swift was an active clergyman meant that his most assiduous biographer, Irvin Ehrenpreis, took his religion seriously; the fact that a few of his sermons survive has meant that their outstanding twentieth-century editor, Louis A. Landa, not only compared different texts but examined their ecclesiastical as well as their political contexts. Landa's essay of 1944, produced while he was preparing his edition of the sermons (as vol. 9 of the "Prose Writings," *Irish Tracts 1720–1723 and Sermons*), remains a foundational commentary.[1] But Landa here and in his even more important study of *Swift and the Church of Ireland* wisely refrained from pronouncing or even speculating upon the *authenticity* of Swift's Christianity.[2] Swift could be presented as a Churchman, a strong defender of the prerogatives of the Church of Ireland and its position in the state as the established church, and as homilist accomplished in the plain style ascendant in the Church by the beginning of the eighteenth century, without probing into his personal faith. Of Landa's contemporaries, Samuel Holt Monk

thoroughly overset the common perception of Swift as misanthrope
by demonstrating his steadfastness to Christian doctrine.[3] Despite
their efforts and those of succeeding scholars to fill in the picture of
Swift's Christianity,[4] however, most of his readers probably find it
easier to see the Dean of St. Patrick's as a misanthrope or otherwise
an unbeliever than as a convinced and committed Christian. For
Swift the believer is more difficult by far to fathom than Swift the
ecclesiastical dignitary or politician or, indeed, moralist. His expressions of faith in sermon and pamphlet embrace the conventional,
whereas his procedure throughout a long writing career often ridicules convention; when speaking about the Divine he adopts a cool-
ness of tone that, while it could be taken as assured, more often
marks out distance in an area where tonal intensity has been taken
as pointing to commitment.

Indeed, what is said to constitute Christian authenticity has altered significantly over the last three hundred years; instead of belief
as the test—the acceptance of Scripture as the Divine Word and the
creeds as valuable conciliar formulations of scripturally-based
truths—we have since the eighteenth century continued to validate
sentiment as a mark of the true Christian, a mark that tends to exclude Swift. Nobody would argue that he was touched deeply by the
insistence of belief that so distinguishes the faith of evangelical
Christians, by the humane urgencies we associate with Christian
charity, nor even by the serenity that often accompanies the faith of
the more intellectual. Because he was a clergyman, we may consider
that Swift should be easier to associate with such intensities than he
is, and disparage him accordingly. This is unfair, of course. Alexander Pope's Catholicism was at least as steadfast and undemonstrative
as Swift's Anglicanism, but as a layman belonging to a minority faith
legally restricted if not consistently persecuted, Pope seems more devout—despite his having left little record of the good works that
Catholicism privileges. To jump one generation later, Samuel Johnson's "emotional life is recorded in his private prayers,"[5] and Johnson wasn't even a clergyman. And the fact that Swift had so little
regard for his sermons, which limited the scope of the inventiveness
he valued, compromises for us their assertions of the intelligibility
and value of Christianity as a claim to personal belief. In those sermons Swift's invocatory and exegetical formulae tend to the commonplace, but that is true of most Anglican clergymen in the
eighteenth century (they had the *Book of Common Prayer* as a tem-
plate, an intoxicating influence upon devotional expression).
Doubts persist about Swift's Christian sincerity because it still seems
suspicious that one so comfortable with satire should profess Chris-

tian belief. Apart from abetting religious sentimentalism, such an approach misapprehends the nature of Swift's satiric practice as misanthropic and thus preclusive or hostile to (a sentimentalized) Christianity. Swift's satire is less misanthropic, commonly, than mocking (in both senses of that term) of generally assumed certainties. His underlying ironies discover human reality as fluid, undetermined, lacking the certainties we tend to cloak it with; accordingly, whatever of reality that the literal sense of a given passage can reflect for Swift is undetermined; indeed, his ironies often reveal or even embody indeterminacy, in the face of our preference to see certainty instead. Part 4 of *Gulliver's Travels* is only misanthropic if we glamorize as aspiration—to describe human pride, ambition, intolerance, and lust politely—what Swift sees more clearly as sin. Rather than an argument for his lack of belief, Part 4 becomes an argument against our human tendency to veil injustice. Actual Christian faith, however, tested not by emotional intensity but by acceptance of God's word in scripture, rests upon literal certainty, which Swift professes. He trusts scripture not only as an imperative guide to action or behavior, but also, in its descriptions of the divine character with no relation to any human behavior, as determining belief in God. For God is at pains to demonstrate that His being is beyond human understanding—for instance in the divine name "I am who am"—and must be accepted on faith. Swift makes no play about resisting the power of doubt because he is not tempted to doubt. Faith is not a mystical challenge, but an antidote to evil if one welcomes its obligations and fulfills its responsibilities. Swift does that: he is not only a dutiful but a devoted minister (what other than devotion explains why in his church he "bowed to the Holy Table like a Papist"?)[6] and a prayerful employer (neither as clergyman nor employer was he obliged to conduct prayer services for his household of servants; they were conducted discreetly—lest the leader of household prayers seem a Pharisee—and it is a far greater leap to consider that they derive simply from a sense of duty than that they are owing to belief).

SERMONS AND CERTAINTY

In Viscount Bolingbroke's portion of a letter he and Alexander Pope wrote to Swift, apparently in March of 1732, he recalls a sentence from a letter the Dean had written to him: "the passage I mean, is that where you say that you told Dr. * the Grand Points of Christianity ought to be taken as infallible Revelations. &c."[7] The

doctor cryptically starred is Swift's friend and fellow clergyman Patrick Delany; the passage Bolingbroke recollects is from a letter from
Swift to him that has not been recovered, so it is not certain whether
Swift was recounting in that letter a conversation with Delany or another letter that hasn't been recovered. Hence the statement to Delany is rendered to us at a third remove, and Bolingbroke may have
misremembered Swift's actual phrasing as well, since "infallible" is
a term Swift usually uses archly (or perhaps Bolingbroke was himself
using the term mockingly). But the sentiment is accurate, as Landa
maintained by citing it to conclude his 1944 essay, for it is certainly
the case that Swift never questions the truth of Christianity. "On the
Trinity," one of the few sermons of Swift to survive and that to which
Landa reckoned the statement to Delany as having special relevance, is worth noting also as Swift's only work that he says "probably
I should not have chosen" to write at all. He was, however, "invited
to it by the Occasion of this Season, appointed on Purpose to celebrate the Mysteries of the Trinity, and the Descent of the Holy
Ghost,"[8] more an institutional than a scriptural invitation, since the
Church determines Trinity and Whit (Pentecost) Sundays. It was an
invitation that enabled him, nonetheless, to use his reluctance as an
affirmation of faith, which often "invites" action from which we
would prefer to refrain; in this sense his reluctance to write about
the doctrine of the Trinity, overcome by that invitation, resembles
in miniature the difficulty of believing the doctrine, overcome by a
sterner, scriptural injunction: "God commandeth us, by our Dependence upon his Truth and his holy Word, to believe a fact that we
do not understand."[9] The complementary syntax of God's Truth
and God's Word presents the faithful as trusting or relying upon
God *and* believing his Scripture, for faith is not restricted absolutely
to Scripture, but extends to the interpretive authority of the Church.
Thus not only does Swift perceive the ecclesiastically mandated occasion of Trinity Sunday as sufficiently weighty to overcome any personal hesitation about dealing with a matter of theology rather than
morals (an area in which his other sermons manifest his greater
comfort), but he also glances beyond the scriptural foundations of
Christian faith to consider the credal formulae determined by the
early councils of the Church, even though he reckons the theological issues underlying these as rather too arcane for the ordinary believer. But they are encompassed within Christian tradition, and the
trust of the believer, founded upon scripture, extends to the
Church, which supports the believer in that active trust, as guardian
of faith and the interpretive authority for scripture and the credal
Mysteries of the Incarnation and the Trinity.

In fact, Swift's reluctance about the Trinity as his subject is not only a matter of his own homiletic preference for moral over theological discussion, but also invokes a long and respectable Christian tradition of hesitancy toward examining the Mysteries, because they are by definition beyond human reasoning. Writing in the fourteenth century, Thomas à Kempis cautions almost at the very beginning of *The Imitation of Christ*, "What is a Man the better, for entring into the Sublime Mysteries of the Trinity, and being able to dispute nicely upon that adorable Union; if in the mean while he want that Meekness and Humility, without which he must needs lie under the Displeasure of the Trinity?"[10] Thomas advocates humility rather than an exercise of reason that might approach arrogance, what Catholics know as an "occasion of sin." The Lutheran reformer Philip Melanchthon also discredited theological abstraction, though as a waste of effort that can obscure the significance of faith: "We do better to adore the mysteries of Deity than to investigate them . . . there is no reason why we should labor so much on those exalted topics such as God, the Unity and Trinity of God, the Mystery of Creation and Incarnation. What, I ask you, did the Scholastics accomplish during the many ages when they were examining only these points . . . always trifling about universals, formalities, connotations and various other foolish words? Their stupidity could be left unnoticed if those stupid discussions had not in the meantime covered up for us the gospel and the benefits of Christ.[11]

And in Swift's own time, his fellow clergyman Matthew Hole recommended that "we shall better celebrate the Holy Trinity by a profound Silence and Adoration, than by disputing about it, or prying too curiously into the Manner of it."[12] Accepting the Trinity is an act of faith, mandated by Scripture; probing it is to question Scripture and so threaten that faith. The standard formula for believing in the Christian Mysteries, then, is to assert their overarching rationality: they are, as Swift puts it, "above our Reason without being contrary to it."[13] Swift adheres to the tradition of unquestioning faith, even to cautioning those of his cloth whose probing, he fears, may have raised scruples among the otherwise faithful.[14]

Swift's resort to the standard formula is the more important for the strong stance he takes against "those who are Enemies to all Revealed Religion," the freethinkers he often attacked.[15] Since Swift as churchman is more often taken as religiously dutiful than faithful, it is tempting to interpret his argument with freethinkers in this sermon as fundamentally a political defense of the Church. They are the nemesis of the Church, which is at once his employer and a bulwark of the traditional sociopolitical order. But he actually takes issue with the essential hostility of freethinkers to religious faith, their doctrine, as it were, that Christianity is an excellent moral system, but an excrescence as organized into a religion. Faith in what can't be understood by human reason is delusive, they would hold, to say nothing of the trappings of religion—the clergy, the hierarchy, the temporal power and wealth of the Church. By dismissing or opposing Christian religion, however, the freethinkers exhibit the flaw Swift finds with classical philosophy as the source of a moral code. For what he termed the "Excellency of Christianity," its superiority to the "Heathen Wisdom" of the "Gentile Sages," derives from its projecting eternal rewards and punishments for good and bad behavior—Heaven and Hell.[16] The ancients had no eschatology to validate moral doctrine that was similar in its consistency to the Christian, an eschatology depending for its credibility entirely upon religious faith. The matter of faith is at the core of Swift's Trinity sermon: it is a doctrine that can only be taken on faith, its credibility resisting that test of human logic to which freethinkers would subject divine actions and attributes. Accepting it on faith denotes submission to the forthright statement of the Scriptures, for, as the text for Swift's sermon attests, the doctrine of the Trinity is "positively affirmed in Scripture."[17] The basis of that faith is God's "Truth and his holy Word," the theological fundamentals Swift termed "the Scripture system"[18] and thought formulated best in the moderate Protestant version of traditional Christianity represented by the Church of England and its sister Church of Ireland. Anglican moderation is manifest in Swift's brief excursus on faith; based upon Scripture, it exhibits itself and flowers in works:

> Our Saviour is perpetually preaching Faith to his Disciples, or reproaching them with the Want of it; and Saint *Paul* produceth numerous Examples of the Wonders done by Faith. And all this is highly Reasonable; for Faith is an entire Dependence upon the Truth, the Power, the Justice and the Mercy of God; which Dependence will certainly incline us to obey him in all Things. So that the great Excellency of Faith, consisteth in the Consequence it hath upon our Actions: As, if we depend upon the Truth and Wisdom of a Man, we shall certainly be more disposed to follow his Advice. Therefore, let no man think that he can lead as good a moral life without Faith, as with it; for this Reason, Because he who hath no Faith, cannot, by the Strength of his own Reason or Endeavours, so easily resist Temptation, as the other who depends God's assistance in the overcoming his Frailties, and is sure to be rewarded for ever in Heaven for his Victory over them. *Faith*, says the Apostle, *is the Evidence of Things not seen. . . .*[19]

The eloquence of this passage is its plainness, its refusal to drift into headstrong rhetoric. It is utterly Anglican in moving from nonspecific scriptural description ("Our Saviour is perpetually preaching Faith . . . and Saint *Paul* produceth numerous Examples") through a discursive invocation of human reason, the attributes of God, and domestic example ("As, if we depend upon the Truth and Wisdom of a Man . . ."), to the point to be driven home, the superiority of Christian faith as the imperative for a moral life, and finally to a specific reference to Scripture ("*Faith,* says the Apostle . . .") There is much here of the formulaic, but the formula imparts a sense of certainty. "A 'mighty Weight' was laid upon faith, and the mere revelation of spiritual mysteries through the scriptures was sufficient for their acceptance,"[20] notes J. A. Downie of Swift's practice here. He was entirely orthodox in that respect, as Matthew Hole, the very prominent contemporary commentator on the liturgy and catechism of the Church of England, maintains that in the face of the Trinity as a concept our "reason be at a loss, and our weak Understandings cannot comprehend this ineffable Mystery, yet have we a firm foundation for our Faith in it; being built upon the Basis of Divine Revelation, and the Discoveries that God hath been pleas'd to make to us of himself."[21] What the Scriptures reveal is to be believed on faith, that is, because, as Bolingbroke's recollection of Swift's phrasing has it, "The grand points of Christianity ought to be taken as infallible revelations." Such infallibility inevitably recalls that claimed for the papacy, which *A Tale of a Tub* ridicules as Peter, the eldest brother, searches through the will left by his father to his brothers and himself to find approval for his extraordinary alterations to the coats their father bequeathed them—the coats that the father's will specifically stated should never be altered—and always finds the desired alterations allowed.

The certainty Swift claims for faith, and claims of it as well, contrasts with the indeterminacy of the world beyond scripture, and the very expansion of the import of the literal sense that Swift ridicules in the allegorical sections of the *Tale,* he actually cultivates to underscore that contrast in the world at large. This indeterminacy Swift's irony often mocks, in the sense both of imitating and subverting it: he often deploys irony to broaden the range of his literal sense, "mining" rather than simply undermining it; even as the literal expands, moreover, it points to itself, often with some black humor.

IRONY AND THE INDETERMINATE LITERAL

Irony is Swift's métier, as *A Modest Proposal* confirms in a concentrated essence: for a reader to take it literally would prompt immediate scorn. Of course, readers and scholars are anything but united about how to understand the *Proposal,* if not literally. Interpretations abound, to the point that multivalence in the import of the work seems intended, as though Swift actually *meant* his irony to facilitate a spectrum of meanings. And such an inference emerges all the more when we venture beyond the *Proposal,* where irony diverges less demonstratively from the literal meaning of a passage.

Notice, for instance, how Swift celebrates himself as ironist in *Verses on the Death of Dr. Swift:*

> ARBUTHNOT is no more my Friend,
> Who dares to Irony pretend;
> Which I was born to introduce,
> Refin'd it first, and shew'd its Use.

> (lines 56–59)

John Arbuthnot, who had been Queen Anne's physician, was a very close friend of Swift's, intimately associated with him and Pope in the Scriblerus Club and its most lasting joint production, the *Memoirs of Martinus Scriblerus;* he was author of the satirical *History of John Bull* and an easygoing, jovial man by all accounts, a friend Swift valued, and not least for knowing how greatly Arbuthnot valued him. Two decades earlier, having fallen ill shortly after his arrival in Dublin following the accession of George I, Swift lamented that he was

> Remov'd from kind Arbuthnot's aid,
> Who knows his art, but not his Trade,
> Preferring his regard for me
> Before his credit, or his Fee.

> ("In Sickness," 9–12)

Their friendship had not abated in the interval; thus Swift's reference to Arbuthnot in the *Verses on the Death* does not mean what he says literally, that he is no longer friends with Arbuthnot, and readers discount that statement accordingly. We would tend to hesitate, however, to discount his assertions about introducing irony and taking the lead in refining it, because we *know* that Swift considered himself a great ironist. We may suspect that we ought not to take him at face value either about Arbuthnot or irony but cannot determine so easily what respective value we should give the Arbuthnot and irony clauses. "Arbuthnot is no more my friend" should probably be read as overstatement, factually unreliable because intended jocularly, whereas "Which I was born to introduce, etc" is to be read as overstatement that is more reliable because merely hyperbolic; the jocularity of the earlier, obviously unreliable, clause signals to us that the later clause, about irony, is an exaggeration. It is not on that account self-deprecating, however, if self-deprecation means reversing the import of the literal sense, which would have Swift thus mocking his own pretensions to irony. The passage as a whole appears to mean that Swift, though Arbuthnot's friend, regards himself as an ironist not only superior to him but as supreme; in other words, Swift says what he *doesn't* mean so obviously that he must mean something else; but that much of that something else is actually quite close to what he says in the first place.

Most readers are introduced to irony, of course, as something that means either the opposite of what it says literally, or means at some noticeable variance from that literal sense. As we grow more familiar with irony we may come to understand it less restrictively than just as contradicting or undermining what the literal sense conveys, but a vestige of the initial instruction lingers in our discomfort with a definition of irony that includes opening or broadening the literal as well as subverting it. In the immediate context of this passage in the *Verses*, Swift has been citing features of his friends' achievements that remind him of his own inadequacies or are otherwise mildly irritating; Pope fixes more meaning in one couplet than Swift can in six, and so forth. Arbuthnot fits here as another friend, but neither he nor anyone else had ever made any pretense that his achievement as an ironist was actually in the same league with Swift's. And the larger context of the poem is its breathtaking narcissism. This is no mock-eulogy, though sometimes, as in this passage, it can almost appear that way. It is a genuine eulogy, though to be sure it is composed by the deceased-to-be himself, so we can't help but think of it in somewhat mocking terms, as, perhaps, the obituary he would have liked somebody else to write, though he couldn't trust anyone else to praise him so unreservedly. Considering these contexts, we interpret the passage more intuitively than logically. Unfastened from the literal in the sense of the strict import of the words on the page, that is, we seek some kind of terra firma, but we will be disappointed. If we recall Wayne Booth's categories of stable and unstable irony, this passage would at first appear to instance the stable, since it obviously doesn't mean what it says on the page; except that in a palpable way it *does* mean some version of what it says.[22] Swift does not really want to abandon his friendship with Arbuthnot, but regardless of any feint at self-deprecation, he very much regards himself as a master ironist. The meaning is discernible; indeed it is rather close to the literal sense itself, strictly interpreted, but that meaning isn't *determined* either by attending simply to the literal sense or by a simple process of subverting it.

Of course, irony is often like that. The sort of irony we see most frequently is what Booth considers "stable"—as when one says, on a rainy day following many rainy days, "We really need that rain," since it is obvious that we don't. Less commonly, irony untethers us from the literal sense with no comparably certain alternative mooring. Our moorings seem more difficult to find with Swift than with most writers before the twentieth century, for Swift characteristically reveals the haphazardness of our interpretive conventions (of which the Arbuthnot passage above is a very mild example) or calls clashing, even contradictory interpretations into play, in uneasy balance. It is as though he distrusts or finds the unequivocal unsatisfying, by comparison with an ironic practice that veers commonly toward Booth's category of the unstable. Such ironic practice rarely reverses the literal sense of his words; frequently it adheres to that literal sense, or perhaps more exactly mines it, cultivating the very range of meaning, the spectrum of import, which the literal can allow to a sentence or a passage, a range that colloquial conventions or idioms tend to narrow. The literal offers him room to play, enabling him to make his work intelligible to ordinary people, a matter of considerable importance to Swift, who recommends to a young clergyman "the Method observed by the famous Lord *Falkland*" of observing whether what was written could be understood by servants,[23] even while he was suspicious of strictness of interpretation as a drawback inhering in the "literal" as well. *A Tale of a Tub* satirizes the Church of Rome for (among other defects) its straying from strict scriptural literalness, but that satire is pressed home in an allegory—a device that poses a consistent alternative to the literal sense—as though Swift recognizes that the more unequivocally colloquial literalness is driven, the less forceful it becomes.

In the "Digression upon Madness" from *A Tale of a Tub*, for instance, Swift uses a completely unremarkable conventional idiom, and we as readers have long been certain of his meaning, or so we would like to think: "Last Week I saw a Woman *flay'd*, and you will hardly believe, how much it altered her Person for the worse."[24] We *know* this is ironic, and would tend conventionally to describe the irony as "understatement." But where in fact *is* the understatement? The literal sense is horrible to ponder, on its own; what distracts us from pondering it is the colloquial "you will hardly believe," which is, however, not understatement at all, but a statement of fact. The very phrase, in its very conventionality, because it is so often used merely as a notional intensifier, tempts us think that it functions the same way here, though in actual fact it is utterly literal in its import: the sight of a woman flayed is so appalling, so grotesque, that we want to turn away, we want (or will) *not* to believe it. The idiomatic veneer of "you will hardly believe," which appears to be designed to distract the reader from the sheer depth of the gruesome in the passage, is so overwhelmed by the horror of that literal gruesomeness as to become literally accurate. What seems at first a rhetorical throwaway inappropriate to the horror recounted, has the effect instead of registering, even enhancing, that horror. It is our practice of discounting idioms that makes this one seem like understatement, an effect buttressed by the dry "how much it altered her Person for the Worse." But that legalistic or philosophical use of "person" for "body" isn't understating: the words are in fact quite literally accurate. Swift is hiding the extensiveness of his meaning in plain sight here; it isn't the subversion of the literal sense, but the insistence upon it, which makes this sentence ironic. At first reading, the irony appears directed at the Tale-teller, the "speaker" who so often bears Swift's burdens, who here is discussing the common human preference for the superficial over the probing; we take him as certainly unbalanced in his mind, to mute the horror of the scene with so matter-of-fact a tone of voice. Or, to put it differently, to relate an action so horrifying with a dryness that seems intended to obscure or distract from the horror, to cover it from our view. And as soon as we put the case this way, we can see that the reader is targeted by Swift's irony as much as the Tale-teller, through the ironic manipulation of what is expected of the literal. We are *supposed* to think that the speaker is crazy, and as such somebody to dismiss from serious consideration, somebody who is "other" rather than like us. But since our own aversion to contemplating what lies beneath the surfaces of life makes what underlies threaten to undermine, just as the speaker notices at length in the "Digression upon Madness," our turning away from the underlying befits a species of madness to which we are susceptible—indeed, the species typified by those who seek felicity in being well deceived by appearances. The sentence, thus, means simultaneously what it says (the sight of a woman flayed is too horrible to believe) and what it says about us (we prefer language to disguise rather than to reveal); there is no single meaning determined.

Such breadth of import in the literal sense can be occluded in the *Tale* because stock rhetoric and idioms are rife in colloquial practice, whether spoken or written. Our tendency is to discount the literalness of such phrases, to dismiss them as vacant fillers, meant originally to intensify meaning but by now so stale from overuse as to inhibit that function, while hardly projecting or even contributing to meaning in their own right. The *Tale* abounds with examples of conventional usage that thereby impart an ironic dimension to the literal sense. The "Digression in Praise of Digressions" offers an illustrative rhapsody of phrases describing the method preferred among the Moderns to become learned "without the Fatigue of *Reading* or of *Thinking*," by getting

> a thorough Insight into the Index, by which the whole Book is governed and turned, like *Fishes* by the *Tail.* For, to enter the Palace of Learning at the *great Gate,* requires an Expence of Time and Forms; therefore Men of much Haste and little Ceremony, are content to get in by the *Back-Door.* For, the Arts are all in a *flying* March, and therefore more easily subdued by attacking them in the *Rear.* Thus Physicians discover the State of the whole Body, by consulting only what comes from *Behind.* Thus Men catch Knowledge by throwing their *Wit* upon the *Posteriors* of a Book, as Boys do Sparrows with flinging *Salt* upon their *Tails.* Thus Human Life is best understood by the wise man's Rule of *Regarding the End.* Thus are the Sciences found like *Hercules*'s Oxen, by *tracing them Backwards.* Thus are *old Sciences* unravelled like *old Stockings,* by beginning at the *Foot.*[25]

Even for the notoriously prolix Tale-teller, this is profusely manic; the insistency of the catalog of similes amuses and impresses the reader with the teller's insecure grip on reality. Veering away from the normal, Swift seems to imply, eccentricity can become madness in almost no time at all. Considered closely, though, the catalog is less starkly determinative; indeed, it seems to be questioning determinacy. There is a conventional way to acquire learning, by "*Reading*" and "*Thinking*"; the Moderns can't be bothered with the time and effort the long-established method entails, but they like the appurtenances of learning, so they resort immediately to that very respectable shortcut for recognizing facts and those who understand them, indeed a sign that a work is learned, the index—placed at the end of a book and quite literally an assortment of points. That sort of regarding or pointing from the end can be paralleled to a number of time-honored, very human habits—the taxonomy of methods given for gaining some knowledge from aftereffects. The irony doesn't arise from subverting the literal sense of the passage, in the whole or at any one stage, but from the very inventiveness of the teller's list, the unexpected congruities of his similes; it doesn't seem quite right that there ought to be so many ways to find knowledge from results. We are surprised, thus, that there are, and amused at their general applicability to the intellectually unrespectable shortcut being proposed to gain learning. The indeterminacy becomes diverting as well as destabilizing.

The "Digression concerning Madness" offers quite a few ironies of indeterminacy. One appears very early in the text, the story of Henri IV of France:

A certain Great Prince raised a mighty Army, filled his Coffers with infinite Treasures, provided an invincible Fleet, and all this without giving the least Part of his Design to his greatest Ministers or his nearest Favourites. Immediately the whole World was alarmed; the neighbouring Crowns, in trembling Expectation, towards what Point the Storm would burst; the small Politicians, every where forming profound Conjectures. Some believed he had laid a Scheme for Universal Monarchy: Others, after much insight, determined the Matter to be a Project for pulling down the *Pope,* and setting up the *Reformed* Religion, which had once been his own. Some, again, of a deeper Sagacity, sent him into *Asia* to subdue the *Turk,* and recover *Palestine.* In the midst of all these Projects and Preparations; a certain *State-Surgeon,* gathering the Nature of the Disease by these Symptoms, attempted the Cure, at one Blow performed the Operation, broke the Bag, and out flew the *Vapour;* nor did any thing want to render it a compleat Remedy, only, that the Prince unfortunately happened to Die in the Performance. Now, is the Reader exceeding curious to learn from whence this *Vapour* took its Rise, which had so long set the Nations at a Gaze? What secret Wheel, what hidden Spring could put into Motion so wonderful an Engine? It was afterwards discovered that the Movement of this whole Machine had been directed by an absent *Female,* whose Eyes had raised a Protuberancy, and before Emission, she was removed into an Enemy's Country. What should an unhappy Prince do in such ticklish Circumstances as these? He tried in vain the Poet's neverfailing Receipt of *Corpora quæque;* For
    Idque petit corpus mens unde est saucia amore;
    Unde feritur, eo tendit, gestitq: coire. LUCR.
Having to no purpose used all peaceable Endeavours, the collected Part of the *Semen,* raised and enflamed, became adust, converted to Choler, turned head upon the spinal Duct, and ascended to the Brain. The very same Principle that influences a *Bully* to break the Windows of a Whore, who has jilted him, naturally stirs up a Great Prince to raise mighty Armies, and dream of nothing but Sieges, Battles, and Victories.
    ————*Teterrima belli*
  Causa- [26]

The satire here obviously inhabits the distinction made between the motivations ascribed to Henri's bellicosity by various contemporary observers, and what the Tale-teller finds to be impelling him. And we don't know whether to take the latter at face value (Henri was simply motivated by lust, nothing grander), since the Tale-teller is not a reliable narrator. The instability that results enhances/produces the satire, of course. Henri IV had extended toleration to

Protestants within the French state with the Edict of Nantes, which
Louis XIV in 1685 revoked, and the effects of that revocation were
evident enough in Ireland, Swift's homeland, where a number of
Huguenot families immigrated. Henri was, then, an historical figure
of whom an Irish Protestant clergyman like Swift might be expected
to approve. Swift never says he disapproves of Henri, of course, nor
even does the Tale-teller; what is averred rather is that lust was the
engine of his martial scrappiness, a rangy, rapacious lust at that (*cunnus* having for Horace a slangy, even more extramural connotation
than "lust" has in English), which Horace deeply disapproves of as
a cause for war. What this means is that Henri, whatever his politics
as a ruler, was ruled by his appetites, not something we should admire. Indeed, so far from admiring any such motivation, we are
loath to ascribe royal behavior to it, preferring to cite geopolitical or
religio-political reasons. So what Swift is saying is that kings put on
their trousers—or more to the point, take them off—one leg at a
time, just like the rest of us would. The satire ridicules us even more
than the king, since we have expectations of kings that one like
Henri wouldn't have had of himself. Of course, if Henri had professed such motives as the desire to shake off the papal yoke, or liberate Palestine from the Turks, he would have been a hypocrite. But
Henri in this passage ascribes no such grand motive to his actions;
the charge of hypocrisy attaches more accurately to those observing
the court, who reckon as a matter of course that activities of state
have a grander imperative than lust. Those observers' tendency to
look for more appropriately regal springs of action is ironized, first
by the mention of those regal springs, secondly by the grandilo-
quent rhetoric for describing the effects of lust. But the irony becomes very evident when the Tale-teller descends to vulgarity with
words like Bully and Whore—at which point we see that Henri, too,
has become the butt of irony. The confusion—first making us think
the observers were satirized, then letting us see that Henri is—makes
for ironic indeterminacy. Radically this has to do with the clash between the way kings behave and the way we would have them behave; we are unwise to think a king would suppress human urges any
better than an ordinary man, perhaps, but a king who does not control himself loses his reputation. If history and human nature form
our study, it is only prudent to expect hypocrisy in the great, foolish
to respect it, yet surprise and deference are more common reac-
tions. That ironic indeterminacy Swift underscores by omitting the
word *cunnus* from his latter quotation for the fifth (1710) and later
editions of the *Tale*. The quotation is unattributed, but is taken from
Horace, *Sermones* 1.3.107: *Nam fuit ante Helenam cunnus teterrima belli /*

causa (since, before Helen, lust was the cause of most terrible wars). It was hardly an obscure passage; David Hume in 1742 cites it as an expression of Horace, in tracing the origin of good and evil, but reproves Horace, along with Sallust, Ovid, Lucretius, and Juvenal, for a "licentiousness and immodesty" of style, which he then illustrates by quoting each one.[27] Swift in revising the work for the fifth edition dropped the word *cunnus,* which Hume retains, which makes him a bit coyer than Hume. The quotation from Horace punctuates the whole passage, and the quotation needn't have been attributed, because it was a well-enough known classical tag; the Tale-teller's display of erudition is also a self-conscious concern to give an authority even for matters that are easily enough demonstrated without citing a classical author. The initial *cunnus* superadded a verbal lubricity that Swift evidently decided was unnecessarily overt, and by omitting it he underscores the effect of indeterminacy, so vital in the clash between anticipation and actuality in Henri IV's motives for affrighting the world.

The breadth of that spectrum of meaning that the literal sense of colloquial discourse offers to Swift provides one reason he presents so much of his writing *as* discourse: "A Letter to" this one or that, for instance. In normal colloquial practice much of this range goes uninvoked, whether ignored or occluded, allowing him a considerable capacity in the literal to exploit for the purposes of irony; thus the balances and even clashes of meanings on the literal "level" enable irony as much as undermining or inverting those "surface" meanings. Notice, for instance, the account of Gulliver's invitation to attend the King of Luggnagg, in the *Travels,* part 3; to "*lick the Dust before his Footstool*" is "the Court Style, and I found it to be more than Matter of Form," for he was intended to do just that as, crawling upon his belly, he approached the royal person.[28] Because Gulliver was a stranger, there wasn't much dust; but literal adherence to this "Court Style" is expected of the king's own subjects, who might find that the floor was strewn with dust on purpose, or even with poison, if they had an enemy at court or if the king wished to put them to death, for literal obedience was enforced by making spitting or wiping one's mouth in the royal presence a capital crime. Of course, if the attending subject's enemy at court plotted to poison him, there could be consequences for that enemy, or for a court page entrusted with the strewing; but these were merely a "Matter of Form" if in fact the attending subject was intended by the king to die in this way, without blame attaching directly to the king. Or if the victim's death, though perhaps not intended at the time, was not so displeasing to the king upon reflection: "I myself heard him [the king] give Directions, that one of his Pages should be whipt, whose Turn it was to give Notice about washing the Floor after an Execution, but maliciously had omitted it; by which Neglect a young Lord of great Hopes coming to an Audience, was unfortunately poisoned, although the King *at that Time* had no Design against his Life. But this good Prince was so gracious, as to forgive the Page his Whipping, upon Promise that he would do so no more, *without special Orders* [italics mine]."[29] Because the Luggnaggians were used to offering this form of respect to their king, that is, a means was readily at hand to execute whomever the king wanted removed, or decided after the fact that he didn't mind being removed: responsibility would only attach to the king if so he wished. It was, to use a modern term of art, "deniable," a capacity signaled to the reader by the phrases italicized above; it may be that Gulliver is meant to be understood as repeating such phrasing, unaware of this signal they convey to the rest of us, for this is a king whom Gulliver commends above the "monarchs of *Europe.*"[30] If that is the case, then these phrases inform a situational irony at Gulliver's expense, since he doesn't realize the degree to which the king is responsible for fatalities that can seem accidental. But this would mean that Gulliver is tipping us off to his becoming an ironic target. That can happen; when he is making a great display of his English patriotism in conversation with the king of Brobdingnag and the master Houyhnhnm, he falls into this self-ironizing trap. In those cases, however, he is being shown up as a jingoistic fraud by comparison with an enlightened foreign ruler, and that is not the case in this instance. It is at least as likely here that Gulliver knows the significance of such phrasal enablers of royal deniability, and is deliberately tipping us off, for the tip-offs are entirely aboveboard, overt rather than subversive; there is no understatement. He is talking about the dangers, after all, lurking in (or better, littering) a literal adherence to a customary show of obeisance. The truth stares us in the face, concealed in plain sight. The irony consists in the acceptability—on our part as readers, not only on Gulliver's—of this sort of royal activity, the denial of responsibility for behavior that could include certain kinds of killing. We would rather not believe that kings do that sort of thing, while knowing that of course they do; we prefer trusting that their intentions are benign to being reminded that kings can betray such trust. That the phrases that tip us off aren't hidden implies that such behavior becomes kings, after all; and that we accept as much ourselves. Though without wishing to confront it directly, indeed because we prefer to avoid confrontation, we become complicit in royal misbehavior.

It is fitting indeed that one with Swift's respect for hierarchical society should show such concern about the moral practice of kings; royal misbehavior constitutes one index, in Swift's writing career, of the gap between what is and what ought to be, or, to use the metaphor of the *Tale,* what fits. That gap is the dwelling place of irony, and it is mistaken, when examining Swift's works, to see it as stable; what the irony imports is ultimately indeterminate, nor is the method of its portending constant—even in the rare case where Swift uses a nearly identical verbal formula. In chapter 5, Part 4 of the *Travels,* Gulliver is describing to his Houyhnhnm master "the whole State of *Europe,*" indicating when certain martial activities are legitimate by civilized standards: "If a Prince send Forces into a nation, where the People are poor and ignorant, he may lawfully put half of them to death, and make Slaves of the rest, in order to civilize and reduce them from their barbarous Way of Living."[31] There is no question here that Swift is opposed to such policy, nor indeed that he has Ireland in mind, in connection with which he often uses such terms as "poor and ignorant" and "Slaves" found in this passage, though the application is hardly exclusive. Gulliver is as much the ironist as Swift himself, since he is no longer the apologist for European practice that he was in part 2, when his account of Europe drew the King of Brobdingnag to respond famously, "I cannot but conclude the Bulk of your Natives, to be the most pernicious Race of little odious Vermin that Nature ever suffered to crawl upon the Surface of the Earth."[32] The ironic treatment of colonialist policy in part 4 implicates rulers, of course, but also the public for tolerating the policy apparatus that makes such actions "lawful"—or more than tolerating, profiting by it as many ordinary people did from colonialism. It is a far more determined irony than Swift used in his earlier years, indicating some shift in view. In his little-known "Fragment of the History from William Rufus" continuing the equally unremembered "Abstract of the History of England," just before the point at which this unfinished work ceases, Swift recounts the rationale of Henry II for invading Ireland in 1169, "reducing the savage people of *Ireland* from their brutish way of living, and subjecting them to the crown of England."[33] The formula is used in the "Abstract" with more than a little irony; Swift has in the pages just before it detailed the venality and faithlessness of Henry II, and his capacity to manipulate the papal court in his favor when the pope was Adrian IV, the Englishman Nicholas Brekespear. Rome had helped him to evade a provision in his father's will to leave his

younger brother Geoffrey in peaceful possession of the dukedom of
Anjou; and he was applying to Rome as well for leave to invade Ireland. But following this account of Henry's faults, Swift provides a
lengthy description of the barbarity of the native Irish, and the reasons for it (their factionalism and their remoteness), which suggests
that even while he considered Henry II a rogue, he also thought that
the Irish needed to be colonized and properly Christianized. To an
extent, this tolerance toward Henry reflects Swift's general tendency
in the "Abstract" to treat kings "kindly, extenuating their shortcomings, enhancing their physical appearance, and making the most of
their virtues."[34] But there is a strong sense here that civilizing Ireland was so important to Swift as a mission that it mitigated the bad
motives of a scoundrel king, and certainly those of a grasping
pope—by Swift's account, Adrian IV was primarily interested in col-
lecting the annats, or annual dues, owed to Rome by the Irish
church, which he reckoned Henry would be sure to remit. It was an
important mission, indeed, even though he implies his awareness
that after five and a half centuries of English colonization, Ireland
was still far from civilized: taking up in 1719 the manuscript fragment that he had left unfinished in 1703 and had all but forgotten,
and planning to dedicate it to the Count de Gyllenborg, Swedish
ambassador in London in Queen Anne's time, Swift notes that since
her death he has spent his life "in a most obscure disagreeable country, and among a most profligate and abandoned people."[35] This
sentiment comports with a good many others from the early 1720s,
disparaging life in Ireland; the colonial project that Henry II had
launched was a failure, and Swift knew it but wasn't yet willing to
acknowledge it as such. He could not at all have made that acknowl-
edgment when writing *A Tale of a Tub*, where the tolerance for kingly
faults of character, in the case of Henri IV of France, becomes an
ironic vehicle for observing the common human aversion to ascrib-
ing low motives to kings. But by the time Swift was writing part 4 of
the *Travels*, he could have Gulliver's Houyhnhnm master respond to
Gulliver's description of colonialist practice with the damning ver-
dict upon Europeans that "instead of Reason, we were only possessed of some Quality fitted to increase our natural vices."[36] And
the difference was, of course, the experience Swift had had, by the
time he came to complete the *Travels*, with the affairs of Ireland. For
Ireland defeated the colonial project, inasmuch as that project was
meant to civilize the country; what was left of it was the naked exercise of power by one group over the rest—which as Swift's own experience of Ireland and colonization deepened, seemed indeed to be
the whole point of the project. It was not Henry II's ostensibly Chris-

tian civilizing purpose for invading Ireland and "reducing" its natives, but his venal motive that had come over the centuries to dominate the project for colonizing them. For much of his writing career, Swift was able to cultivate the ironies potential in broadening the import of the literal sense of a passage or verbal formula; irony, after all, made the experience of the human expulsion from Eden, our distance from God, less amenable to our powers of self-delusion. Scripture alone conveys truth. But in Ireland, the perversions of truth that colonialism inflicts are so penetrating, so intimate, as to flatten irony to simple subversion of the literal, normalizing, in effect, the topsy-turvy.

NOTES

1. Landa, "Swift, the Mysteries, and Deism," in *Studies in English, Department of English, The University of Texas 1944* (Austin: University of Texas Press, 1945), 239–56, reprinted in Landa, *Essays in Eighteenth-Century English Literature* (Princeton: Princeton University Press, 1980), 89–106.

2. Landa, *Swift and the Church of Ireland*, Oxford: Clarendon Press, 1954.

3. Monk, "The Pride of Lemuel Gulliver," *The Sewanee Review* 63 (Winter 1955), 48–71, reprinted in James L. Clifford, *Eighteenth-Century English Literature* (New York: Oxford University Press, 1959), 112–29.

4. Among the best commentaries in recent years are those of Camille R. LaBossière, "'Upon Sleeping in Church': Swift's Sermons and the Ethics of Wit," *Canadian Journal of Irish Studies* 19, no. 1 (July 1993): 1–11; and Todd C. Parker, "'The Idlest Trifling Stuff That Ever Was Writ': or Why Swift Hated His Sermons" (in this volume).

5. Donald Davie, "Introduction," *The Late Augustans* (London: Heinemann, 1958), xxiii.

6. Laetitia Pilkington, *Memoirs of Mrs. Laetitia Pilkington* (London: Griffiths and Woodfall, 1748), 1:52–53.

7. Pope and Bolingbroke to Swift, [March 1732] *Correspondence of Jonathan Swift, D.D.*, vol. 3, ed. David Woolley (Frankfurt am Main: Peter Lang, 2003), 3:458.

8. Swift, "On the Trinity," *Irish Tracts 1720–1723 and Sermons* (*Prose Works of Jonathan Swift*, vol 9 [Oxford: Blackwell, 1948]), 168.

9. Ibid.

10. [Thomas À Kempis, *Imitation of Christ*, as] *The Christian's Pattern. Or a Treatise of the Imitation of Jesus Christ*. trans. George Stanhope, 4th edition (London: M. Roberts for D. Brown, 1704), 2. Stanhope's translation, first published in 1698, was the version most often reprinted during Swift's lifetime.

11. Philip Melancthon, *Loci Communes Theologici*, 1521, trans. L. J. Satre, rev. by W. Pauck, in *Melanchthon and Bucer*, Library of Christian Classics 19, ed. Wilhelm Pauck. (Philadelphia: Westminster Press, 1969), 21.

12. Matthew Hole, *Practical Discourses on the Liturgy of the Church of England*, ed. J. A. Giles (London: William Pickering, 1837), 3:6 [originally published in 1716].

13. Swift, "On the Trinity," 164.

14. Ibid., 160.

15. Ibid., 159.

16. Swift, "A Sermon [upon the Excellency of Christianity]," *Irish Tracts and Sermons*, 242, 241 et seq. "A Letter to a Young Gentleman lately entered into Holy Orders," *Irish Tracts and Sermons*, 73–74.

17. "On the Trinity," 162. Swift seems to have been aware that the text he chose for this sermon, 1 John 5:7 ("For there are three that bear record in heaven, the Father, the Word and the Holy Ghost, and these three are one") had a disputed history. The passage was discarded as inauthentic by Erasmus in his Greek edition of the New Testament in 1516, and only reinstated because of various pressures brought to bear upon Erasmus; Luther and Zwingli both rejected the passage, and Tyndale placed his English translation of it in brackets, but it was gradually accepted as genuine on both sides of the Reformation during the later sixteenth century. This textual history is probably that to which Swift refers in the "Argument against Abolishing Christianity" when inveighing against "Free-Thinkers" who take Christianity "as a Sort of Edifice, wherein all the Parts have such a mutual Dependance upon each other, that if you happen to pull out a single Nail, the whole Fabrick must fall to the Ground. This was happily expressed by him, who had heard of a Text brought for the Proof of the Trinity, which in an ancient Manuscript was diferently read; he thereupon immediately took the Hint, and by a sudden Deduction of a long *Sorites,* most logically concluded; Why, if it be as you say, I may safely whore and drink on, and defy the Parson" (*Prose Writings*, vol. 2, *Bickerstaff Papers and Pamphlets on the Church* [Oxford: Blackwell, 1939]), 38. Known in Scripture scholarship as the "Johannine Comma," the passage began to fall out of favor again in the nineteenth century and is regarded as spurious by Catholic and many Protestant commentators, though its authenticity is strenuously defended by the more evangelically inclined Protestant scholars. Among the treatments of the controversy most apprehensible to those only slightly versed in Scripture controversies are Raymond E. Brown, "Appendix IV: The Johannine Comma," in Brown, ed. and trans., *The Anchor Bible: The Epistles of John* (Garden City, NY: Doubleday, 1982), 775–87, and Joseph M. Levine, "Erasmus and the Problem of the Johannine Comma," *Journal of the History of Ideas* 58, no. 4 (Winter 1997): 573–96. That the authenticity of the passage from Scripture that Swift takes as his text for a sermon insisting that God commands our belief in the Trinity is (or by Swift's day, had been) a matter of scholarly dispute, and that Swift was likely to have been aware of this, would give his sermon, for many modern readers, an ironic cast. We can perceive that Swift's attitude toward scriptural integrity is hardly absolute, as the passage quoted above from the "Argument against Abolishing Christianity" indicates; but neither is he implying the Catholic consideration that more important than the entire accuracy of the text of Scripture is the sense or interpretation of it established over time. The middle ground is hard to discern, though; Swift may well have been content to treat the accuracy of Scripture opportunistically, as indeed many generations of Christians have done.

18. Swift, "Further Thoughts on Religion," *Irish Tracts and Sermons*, 264.

19. Swift, "On the Trinity," 164.

20. J. A. Downie, *Jonathan Swift: Political Writer* (London: Routledge, 1984), 101.

21. Hole, *A Practical Exposition of the Church-Catechism: In several Discourses On All the Parts of it.* In Two Volumes [continuous pagination]. The Second Edition. (London: Printed by J. D. for T. Varnum et al., 1715) [1:]340.

22. Booth, *A Rhetoric of Irony,* Chicago: University of Chicago Press, 1974, passim.

23. Swift, "A Letter to a Young Gentleman," 65.

24. Swift, *A Tale of a Tub*, vol. 1, *Prose Works of Jonathan Swift* (Oxford: Blackwell, 1957), 109.

25. Ibid., 91.

26. Ibid., 103–4.

27. Hume, "Of the Rise and Progress of the Arts and Sciences," 1742

28. Swift, *Gulliver's Travels*, vol. 11, *Prose Works*, 204.

29. Ibid., 204–5.

30. Ibid., 205.

31. Ibid., 246.

32. Ibid., 132.

33. Swift, "A Fragment of the History from William Rufus," *Miscellaneous and Autobiographical Pieces, Fragments and Marginalia*, vol. 5, *Prose Works*, 76.

34. Irvin Ehrenpreis, "Swift's History of England," *JEGP* 51 (1952): 181.

35. Swift, "A Fragment of the History," 11.

36. Swift, *Gulliver's Travels*, 248.

"The Idlest Trifling Stuff That Ever Was Writ," or, Why Swift Hated His Sermons

Todd C. Parker

THE JONATHAN SWIFT I CONJURE UP FOR MY STUDENTS IS USUALLY THE one who enjoins us to "Abi Viator / Et imitare, si poteris, / Strenuum pro virili / Libertatis Vindicatorem."[1] Swift's "saeva Indignatio," or "savage indignation," has long been one powerful rubric under which his major satires, particularly "A Modest Proposal," have been read. As David Nokes observes: "*A Modest Proposal* is often produced as a *locus classicus* of [Swift's] mature ironic style. In it he challenges us to register our own humanity by supplying those human qualities which his rhetorical and logical formulae deliberately leave out of account."[2] It is against just this sort of humane inscription, though, that Nokes warns us when it comes to interpreting Swift's sermons: "Yet in accepting this challenge we must beware of allowing our liberal principles to prejudice our understanding of what Swift must have meant, supplying lacunae where none was left, and laying virtues to Swift's charge of which he was not guilty" (219). Indeed, Nokes's observation that the sermons "are not of a kind to warm the hearts of humanitarians," puts it mildly, to say the least (219). Here, for instance, is a brief excerpt from Swift's sermon, "On the Poor Man's Contentment": Lastly, As it appeareth from what hath been said, that you of the lower Rank have, in Reality, a greater Share of Happiness, your Work of Salvation is easier, by your being liable to fewer Temptations; and as your Reward in Heaven is much more certain, than it is to the Rich, if you seriously perform your Duty, for Yours is the Kingdom of Heaven; so your Neglect of it will be less excusable, will meet with fewer Allowances from God, and will be punished with double Stripes."[3] Even granting the rigid structures of class and race relations in early eighteenth-century Ireland, this Swift exerts few charms. Swift aims his indignation here at the poor for aspiring to sin above their station, and yet this too is presumably the Swift whose heart was lacerated by social injustice. As a substantive figure of eighteenth-century literature, Swift suffers more from the quotidian hypocrisies of life; not, I contend, because he was more of a hypocrite than his contemporaries, but because he left us a paper trail of his vagaries. More importantly, our own assumption that the author of "A Modest Proposal" should not in all seriousness chastise the poor for the moral quality of their poverty is a function of the coherence we invest in "Swift" as author and moralist. The reverend dean has received comparatively little critical attention as compared to his tub-flinging, linen-draping, and cannibalistic others, in part, I believe, because the modern critic shies away from the harsh dogmatism of Swift's sermons and the mundanity of their prose. I will argue, though, that Swift's identity as the great satirist of the modern age is incomplete without an understanding of his sermons and the effect they have on Swift's authorial persona.

Swift himself was famously ambivalent toward both his reputation as a preacher and his sermons. When John Winder, Swift's successor at Kilroot, wrote to Swift about the sermons Swift had left behind there, Swift replied: "Those sermons . . . will utterly disgrace you, unless you have so much credit that whatever comes from you will pass. They were what I was firmly resolved to burn, and especially some of them, the idlest trifling stuff that ever was writ. . . . They will be a perfect lampoon on me whenever you look upon them, and remember they are mine" (*Irish Tracts and Sermons*, 97). Given the strict Anglican orthodoxy of those sermons that survive, we should ask what constitutes the idle and trifling character from which Swift is so eager to dissociate himself. Swift's sermon, "On the Trinity," for instance, reasons that comprehending the mystery of the Trinity is much less important than accepting it as received teaching of the Church: "God commandeth us, by our Dependence upon his Truth and his holy Word, to believe a Fact that we do not understand. And, this is no more than what we do every Day in the Works of Nature, upon the Credit of Men of Learning. Without Faith we can do no Works acceptable to God; for if they proceed from any other Principle, they will not advance our Salvation; and this Faith, as I have explained it, we may acquire without giving up our Senses, or contradicting our Reason" (*Irish Tracts and Sermons*, 168). Since it is through the Church that God speaks to his servants, it is to the Church that we must turn to clarify the relation between reason and faith. Just as we accept the reasonable, if incomprehensible, workings of nature "upon the Credit of men of Learning," so we should accept the divinely incomprehensible, the "Fact that we do not understand," by submitting to the Church and its ordained representatives. By making "reason" an act of obedience and not of understanding, Swift reinforces the authority of the Church, which becomes the guarantor of those "facts" upon which we bring our "reason" to bear. That we can "know" facts we cannot understand is typical of the Anglican rationalism of Swift's day, and Swift's sentiments would not have seemed out of place in either Irish or English pulpits of the time. As Louis Landa explains in his introduction to the sermons, "*On the Trinity,* which is Swift's most elaborate statement on Christian doctrine, exhibits clearly the orthodoxy and conventionality of his religious views. The Earl of Orrery praised this sermon as 'one of the best in its kind,' but a contemporary who had read or listened to some conventional Trinity Sunday sermons would have found little in Swift's sermon, either in ideas or phraseology, that had not been utilized often by his fellow-clergymen in their many defenses of the Trinity and the other mysteries of Christianity" (*Irish Tracts and Sermons,* 107).

Indeed, Swift's Trinitarian theology is consistent with the rationalist projects of such figures as Henry More, Edward Stillingfleet, John Tillotson, and other prominent divines.[4] Swift's orthodoxy was hardly "trifling": as a vigorous defender of the Church and its privileged position vis-à-vis the state, Swift remains constant from his early days as a parish priest in Kilroot to his discouraged last years in Dublin. Michael DePorte argues that Swift's identification of Christianity with the Church of England was so profound that "opposition to the church in both England and Ireland had made him give up 'all hopes of Church or Christianity.'"[5] Writing to Charles Ford, Swift notes, "A certain author (I forgot his name,) hath writ a book (I wish I could see it) that the Christian Religion will not last above 300 and odd years. He means, there will always be Christians, as there are Jews; but it will be no longer a Nationall Religion" (79).

Since his doctrine and rhetoric conform to the conventions of the time, why are the sermons so offensive to Swift? These texts were a necessary part of a parish priest's life and insured his ongoing presence in the public discourse of his community; they were, after all, one important way Swift exercised what limited authority he possessed as a priest of the Church of Ireland. Moreover, as Swift's clerical authority came increasingly under attack after *A Tale of a Tub* was published in 1704, the sermons could have stood as public proof of his orthodoxy. Why, then, did Swift abhor his sermons and wish them destroyed? Why do Swift's sermons remain among the least regarded texts in his canon?

What if, I would like to propose, it is not the content of his sermons that Swift belittles as trifling, but rather their position and context within the totality of his writings? The sermon puts a public face on Swift's piety, certainly, but it also imposes a generic orthodoxy, in that texts marked as sermons invoke a different concept of authority and audience—at least ideally—from the kind of response one elicits with a satiric text. And herein lies Swift's dilemma. The authority behind the author of *A Tale of a Tub*, one who can hypothesize "A Panegyrical Essay upon the Number THREE," must somehow reconcile with the authority of an Anglican dean. Swift the satirist and Swift the divine work in such parodic proximity to each other that the difference between parody and orthodoxy often erodes; the alignment of the terms "satirist/priest" too easily reinforces that of "satire/sermon," so that texts that should read least like religious commentary or theology may be mistaken for their parodic others. To write as a satirist, that is, requires Swift to reject the sermons, not because he disagrees with their doctrine, but because they surrender themselves so easily to what Swift, as a churchman and dean, must view as perverse interpretation. Ironically, Swift can safeguard his identity as a priest only by abjecting the sermons and thus separating them from the body of his satire.

If we look at the introduction to Swift's *Tale*, for example, we find the narrator excluding "the *Bench* and the *Bar*" from his "List of Oratorial Machines" less because they are inappropriate to the list than because "it were sufficient, that the Admission of them would overthrow a Number which I was resolved to establish, whatever Argument it might cost me; in imitation of that prudent Method observed by many other Philosophers and great Clerks, whose chief Art in Division has been, to grow fond of some proper mystical Number, which their Imaginations have rendered Sacred, to a Degree, that they force common Reason to find room for it in every part of Nature; reducing, including, and adjusting every *Genus* and *Species* within that Compass, by coupling some against their Wills, and banishing others at any Rate."[6] Here, form takes precedence over content; worse, an arbitrary form dictates content; worst of all, the author acknowledges both the arbitrariness of the form and its adequacy to his purpose in the same rhetorical gesture. Irvin Ehrenpreis argues that "the satire is directed against the polemical writers who produced a great controversy over the doctrine of the Trinity during the years around the turn of the eighteenth century. It is not directed against the doctrine."[7] But the problem with Ehrenpreis's contention is that satire as a mode of expression cannot be so easily stabilized. Ehrenpreis is not alone in seeing the possibility of determinate meaning in the *Tale*. Peter E. Morgan, for example, writes that "happiness, according to the illustrious philosopher responsible for the *Digression concerning* Madness in *A Tale of a Tub*, is *a perpet-*

ual Possession of being well Deceived. How fad[ing] and insipid, he
continues, do all Objects accost us that are not convey'd in the Vehicle of *Delusion.* Of course, these are the rambling speculations of a
madman: Swift is making the narrative persona out to be a fool, so
we need not credit what he has to say, and ought not take it at face
value.[8]

Morgan's "of course" depends for its obviousness on the assumptions (1) that Swift as author controls the *Tale*'s narrative voice and
(2) that the reader indeed recognizes "the rambling speculations
of a madman" as such. It is, for Morgan, simple common sense to
see the narrator as a fool, because otherwise the narrator's comments become dangerously suggestive—of what, we may not be
sure, but we do know that readers who approach the narrator unaware of his madness do so at their own risk. These seem to me
problematic assumptions, first, because Morgan's reading simply
projects the question of authorial intention onto the persona—
which displaces, not resolves, the issue of intentionality—and, second, because once contained as speculations "we need not credit,"
Swift's digression loses its radical character as a species of social critique. There is, moreover, something uncanny in the way that such
positivist statements on authorial intent mirror the *Tale*'s own posi-
tivism: "'tis easie to Assign the proper Employment of a *True Antient
Genuine Critik;* which is, to travel thro' this vast World of Writings:
to pursue and hunt those Monstrous Faults bred within them: to
drag out the lurking Errors like *Cacus* from his Den; to multiply
them like *Hydra*'s Heads; and rake them together like *Augea*'s Dung.
Or else to drive away a sort of *Dangerous Fowl,* who have a perverse
Inclination to plunder the best Branches of the *Tree of Knowledge,*
like those *Stimphalian* Birds that eat up the Fruit" (*Tale,* 312). Morgan's comment that we "ought not take" the narrator "at face
value" cannot, I submit, be made qualitatively different from the
narrator's own dicta about critics. Both Morgan and the narrator
make the same kind of categorical statements about their subjects;
both find it "easie to Assign" the correct value to the authorial
function; neither contextualizes his own statement as susceptible to
ironic subversion; both thus neutralize the possibility of an improper or contestable reading. In other words, the more insane the
narrator's position, the easier it is to claim a satiric meaning for his
text, and—consequently—the easier it is to define his "real" intention. It makes less difference that we know what this intention is
than that we know that some other intention underwrites it; under
this interpretive model, the determinate meaning of a text is always
other than the available meaning. That is why Swift's satires, scan-

dalous as they are, yield so easily to the neutralizing certainties of commonsense criticism.

As a member of the clergy, Swift had firsthand experience with satire's corrosive effect on the appearance of propriety:

> According to tradition, Swift was greeted on the day of his installation as dean of St. Patrick's by an anonymous verse tacked to the front door of the cathedral:
>
>> Look down, St. Patrick, look down we pray
>> On thine own church and steeple;
>> Convert the Dean on this great day;
>> Or else, God help the People.
>
> (quoted in DePorte, 73)

Swift faced charges of apostasy, lunacy, and atheism throughout his career and after his death, so it is hardly surprising that he takes issues with those who see the "mystical number" of oratorial machines in the *Tale* as an attack on the Trinity.[9] In a passage critics such as Ehrenpreis and Morgan would mark as satiric (and thus hermeneutically containable), the *Tale*'s narrator obsesses with strictly formal criteria: "Now among all the rest, the profound Number THREE is that which hath most employ'd my sublimest Speculations, nor ever without wonderful Delight. There is now in the Press, (and will be publish'd next Term) a Panegyrical Essay of mine upon this Number, wherein I have by most convincing Proofs, not only reduced the *Senses* and the *Elements* under its Banner, but brought over several Deserters from its two great Rivals SEVEN and NINE" (*Tale*, 292). But the formal criteria that privilege THREE over SEVEN and NINE result not from some internal logical necessity of the number itself, but rather from the author's own idiosyncratic intention. The dean's argument against Socinians and anti-Trinitarians exploits the same strategy: "But there is another Difficulty of great Importance among those who quarrel with the Doctrine of the Trinity, as well as with several other Articles of Christianity; which is, that our Religion abounds in Mysteries, and these they are so bold to revile as Cant, Imposture, and Priest-craft. It is impossible for us to determine for what Reasons God thought fit to communicate some Things to us in Part, and leave some Part a Mystery. But so it is in Fact, and so the Holy Scripture tells us in several Places" ("On the Trinity," 162). For Swift's opponents, the Trinity has no internal logic or necessity. As "Cant, Imposture, and Priest-craft," it is an empty, external construct imposed upon the gullible as if it were the wholly internal and self-authorizing plenitude of "mystery." There is no answer to this charge, except to refute it through the competing authority of "Fact." The Trinity thus becomes a function of readerly intention in much the same way as satire operates as "a sort of Glass, wherein Beholders do generally discover every body's face but their Own."[10] Either one accepts the Trinity through faith in the authority of scripture, or one rejects it as an external imposition of form over content: either way, it is the interpretive act that brings the Trinity, like satire, into being as such. Swift's defense of the Trinity is made even more difficult by the question surrounding the scriptural source for the term "Trinity" itself: "Thus it happened with the great Doctrine of the Trinity; which Word is indeed not in Scripture, but was a Term of Art invented in the earlier Times to express the Doctrine by a single Word, for the Sake of Brevity and Convenience. The Doctrine then, as delivered in Holy Scripture, although not exactly in the same Words, is very short, and amounts to only this, That the Father, the Son, and the Holy Ghost, are each of them God, and yet that there is but One God" ("On the Trinity," 159–60). Crucially, how different is the "Trinity" as "a Term of Art invented in the earlier Times" from the "Art" of those "other Philosophers and great Clerks" who force doctrine and scripture to their own ends in the *Tale* (294)? Can the "Trinity" in any way be read as "a great Mystery, being a Type, a Sign, an Emblem, a Shadow, a Symbol, bearing Analogy to the spacious Commonwealth of Writers, and to those Methods by which they must exalt themselves to a certain Eminency above the inferiour World" (*Tale*, 296)? In commenting on this passage, Greenberg and Piper write "In this and the next few paragraphs the professed author gives his reader an example of the deductions, or, as he will call them, the exantlations, of deep meanings which, he insists, are persistently present within his work. If one follows the author's example in studying his whole system of oratorial machines, he may exantlate the drop of sense from *that* and find it to be simply, this is an amusing book. By comparing this small measure of meaning with the elaborate discourse in which it was hidden, the reader may test the validity of this discourse and judge the mind, the sensibility, that would compose and publish it" (*Tale*, 466 n. 33). To follow the author's example as Greenberg and Piper suggest, however, the reader must already have decided that the "deep meaning" of the *Tale* in some manner involves Swift's nonidentity with the *Tale*'s "professed author." The doctrine of the Trinity is an approximation "not exactly in the same words" of a meaning from scripture that cannot be localized in any particular verse. The "term of Art" that signifies the Trinity is, then, a signified without local signifiers, and its adequacy to the doctrine it symbolizes depends, perhaps disturbingly, on the skill of those readers "of an earlier Time to express, the Doctrine by a single word for the Sake of Brevity and Convenience." In other words, Trinitarian dogma is founded on a kind of exegetical shorthand that translates God's intent from the missing text of His word.

Again, Swift negotiates here between authorial intent and readerly competence. For Swift, the Trinity is "real," even if it can only be inferred from scripture. It is "really" there in a way that the mystery of the "Oratorial Receptacles" cannot be, even though the "Trinity," like Swift's receptacles, depends at some point or another on exegetical expertise. The "Trinity" is not, after all, a word in scripture, and its legitimacy depends on the reader's ability to piece various references together in just such a fashion as to produce the correct meaning. Fostering this sort of readerly competence is no easy task, as Swift admits when he describes the Athanasian Creed's limited catechetical value: "This Creed is now read at certain times in our Churches, which, although it is useful for Edification to those who understand it; yet, since it containth some nice and philosophical Points which few People can comprehend, the Bulk of Mankind is obliged to believe no more than the Scripture-Doctrine, as I have delivered it. Because that Creed was intended only as an Answer to the *Arrians* in their own way, who were very subtle Disputers" ("On the Trinity," 160). If the Athanasian Creed exists principally to defend the Trinity from "very subtle Disputers," but is itself too subtle to be useful to the laity, then the Creed subverts its own purpose; if, that is, the "meaner sort" Swift addresses in his sermons cannot tell the difference between the subtlety of heresy and that of right doctrine, all that is left to them is the form of obedience. Scripture in itself is impeccable, but that is not the issue. At some point, Scripture must be construed if it is to give up the fullness of its meaning, and it is in the moment of reading that competence may fail, perhaps without even giving a readable sign of its failure.

Twice in "On the Trinity," Swift cites the authority of precedent as a guarantee for the reading process: once when he refers his auditors to the "Credit of Men of Learning" to "believe a fact that we do not understand," and once when he invokes those unnamed scriptural exegetes who "invented in the earlier Times" a term competent to describe the Triune God. For Swift the priest, epistemological certainty results from prior authority. But did these earlier authorities know that their "Term of Art" would play such a foundational role in Christian theology, and even if they did, can we be certain that the precedent they set in reading Scripture is one that Swift's parishioners cannot claim for themselves? Swift as dean argues that one only has liberty of conscience in religious matters if one has "thoroughly examined by Scripture, and the Practice of the ancient Church, whether those points are blamable or no. . . ."[11] The "ancient Church" authorizes Swift's certainty, but what in its turn authorizes the ancient church? In the *Tale,* the father's will enacts its own self-referential interpretation: "*You will find in my will* (here it is) *full Instructions in every particular concerning the Wearing and Management of your Coats; wherein you must be very exact, to avoid the Penalties I have appointed for every Transgression or Neglect, upon which your future Fortunes will entirely depend. I have also commanded in my Will, that you should live together in one House like Brethren and Friends, for then you will be sure to thrive, and not otherwise*" (*Tale,* 302). The father's deictic gesture ("here it is") closes the referential circle and ensures that this moment in history cannot be counterfeited or reproduced; as a moment of origin, the father's final commandment marks itself as unique. As Swift reads his own text, any deviation from the father's will is thus an intentional act on the sons' part, no matter how hard they work to justify their disobedience or to disguise it as legitimate exegesis. But we already know that the concept of the Trinity cannot be traced to one specific moment, only to "the earlier Times." History in the sermons is, consequently, inaugural and vague, foundational and untraceable. History authorizes Swift's exegesis, but no one moment is in itself authoritative. "History" as such thus becomes the principal trope of instability, yet another feature Swift's satires and his sermons share. Because Swift cannot legitimize the privilege he accords history, his only recourse is to deploy that privilege as if it were an inherent characteristic of his signifier: the "Term of Art invented in the earlier Times" must be made to authorize itself in a way that terms and doctrine resulting from "the Liberty of Conscience which the Fanaticks are now openly in the Face of the World endeavouring at with their utmost Application" cannot (*Irish Tracts and Sermons,* 151). The degree to which the authority of history fails is, therefore, the degree to which Swift's texts may be misappropriated by his audience.

Swift's identity as satirist is thus open to the contesting interpretations of his audience, and even his own attempts to stabilize his intention—and to clear his reputation—fall short. Swift argues, for example, that those who see the *Tale* as impious or atheistic do so only by violently misconstruing his intentions:

There are three or four other Passages which prejudiced or ignorant Readers have drawn by great Force to hint at ill Meanings; as if they glanced at some Tenets of Religion, in answer to all which, the Author solemnly protests he is entirely Innocent, and never had it once in his Thoughts that any thing he said would in the least be capable of such Interpretations, which he will engage to deduce full as fairly from the most innocent Book in the World. And it will be obvious to every Reader, that this was not any part of his Scheme or Design, the Abuses he notes being such as all Church of England Men agree in, nor was it proper for his Subject to meddle with other Points, than such as have been perpetually controverted since the Reformation. ("An Apology For the, &c," *Tale*, 267)

These are odd readers: on the one hand forcing prejudiced and ignorant misconstructions of Swift's design; on the other hand able to read the author's obvious meaning without error. As with "On the Trinity," what is reasonable for Swift is what accords with the power of authority, particularly the author's authority to determine his own meaning.

This same desire to fix meaning informs Swift's sermons on conditions in Ireland. If we return to the question of social justice, we find Swift describing the role of parish charity-schools for the deserving Irish poor: "In these Schools, Children are, or ought to be trained up to read and write, and cast Accompts; and these Children should, if possible, be of honest Parents, gone to Decay through Age, Sickness, or other unavoidable Calamity, by the Hand of God; not the Brood of wicked Strolers; for it is by no means reasonable, that the Charity of well-inclined People should be applied to encourage the Lewdness of those profligate, abandoned Women, who croud our Streets with their borrowed or spurious Issue."[12]

These eighteenth-century welfare mothers presumably correspond to the "deservedly poor" wretches Swift chastises in "On the Poor Man's Contentment." These unworthies suffer as a consequence of their own "Laziness or drunkenness, or worse Vices" and "are not to be understood to be of the Number" of those to whom society must extend its limited resources in good Christian conscience (*Irish Tracts and Sermons*, 191). Nokes describes this attitude as "unpleasantly pharisaical" and Swift's example as "a distasteful inversion of the parable of the lost sheep" (223), but I wonder if Swift's "distasteful" proposals are in reality any more or less ethical than the satirical suggestions of "A Modest Proposal." Nokes sees this as a point of convergence for Swift and his satiric persona: "For the crucial similarity between Swift's tone and that of the proposer is that both see the problem from the viewpoints of the hard-pressed alms-giver called upon to support an idle population. There is never any consideration of the situation from the view of the beggars themselves" (231). But the peculiarity of this argument is that while Swift and the proposer become increasingly similar rhetorically and politically, they remain, at least for Nokes, stubbornly individual in terms of morality. Swift's sermons are "distasteful" and "pharisaical" because they originate with Swift himself and not with some dim-witted cleric or public benefactor in one of Swift's satires. Nokes, along I suspect with many of the rest of us, deplores the sentiments of the sermons because Swift's notion of charity is so punitive; worse yet, the Dean has no difficulty defining and policing the category of the "deserving poor" despite those social and political complexities that would render the designation impossibly open in practical terms. Swift clearly desires that his policies belong to, and be shared by, what Claude Rawson calls "the world of practical action": "Nor were the badges a solitary fancy of Swift's own. At the time of the *Proposal,* they were already notionally in place, partly in execution of an earlier recommendation by Swift. The idea was to identify the parish from which the beggars came, which was the institution legally responsible for supporting them when they could not support themselves. Beggars were unproductive, by definition, and since, in Swift's view, most of them were able-bodied and capable of employment, they fell into the category which mercantilist thinking . . . described as 'undeserving.' "[13]

We can date the thinking behind Swift's 1737 "Proposal for Giving Badges to Beggars" at least as far back as 1726.[14] Licensing beggars with mandatory and visible badges distinguishes "those who have proper title to our charity" from those "sturdy Vagrants" who divert limited charitable resources.[15] Swift is most concerned to distinguish Dublin's "Original Poor," those who owe their poverty to circumstances beyond their control, from the "undeserving vicious Race of human Kind" who make up "the Bulk of those who are reduced to Beggary, even in this beggarly Country": "For, as a great Part of our Public Miseries is originally owing to our own Faults (but, what those Faults are I am grown by Experience too wary to mention) so I am confident, that among the meaner People, nineteen in twenty of those who are reduced to a starving Condition, did not become so by what Lawyers call the Work of GOD, either upon their Bodies or Goods; but merely from their own Idleness, attended by all Manner of Vices, Particularly Drunkenness, Thievery, and Cheating" ("Badges to Beggars," 135). Here, Swift reserves his savage indignation for the majority of Dublin's poor people. Having warned people publicly about their own imprudence and excess to no purpose (the "faults" Swift "is grown by Experience too wary to mention"), he now turns his attention to the fate these individuals deserve. "Nineteen in twenty" are by their own choice, after all, an unproductive, parasitic annoyance to urban life who should be driven from the city. Swift has no compassion for these folk even in their old age: "As for the Aged and Infirm, it would be sufficient to give them nothing, and then they must starve or follow their Brethren" ("Badges to Beggars," 138).

This Swift hardly accords with the (albeit ironic) champion of the people the author of "A Modest Proposal" has become in liberal academic criticism. Even as he argues for a more rigorous understanding of Swift's rhetorical ploys, Nokes still desires an authoritative voice that rules and subordinates those other, more radical voices we find in Swift's texts.[16] But hearing Swift's true voice through the babble of his personae is, in reality, an attempt to stabilize the body of texts we read as "Swift" in accordance with our own desires. As compared to "A Modest Proposal" or the *Tale,* are Swift's sermons any more monologic, any more serious, or any more controllable by authorial intention than his more conventionally "satiric" works? Louise K. Barnett warns that reading Swift "requires that we relinquish the security of genre itself, its authority to confer and name coherence . . . What is difficult to tolerate when we approach a work through genre is plurality, a degree of latitude that obliterates generic boundaries entirely rather than merely emphasizing their existence by over-stepping them."[17]

It is also appropriate to recall Foucault's observation that "if we wish to know the writer in our day, it will be through the singularity of his absence and his link to death, which has transformed him into a victim of his own writing."[18] What Swift resists in his sermons is satire's rapacious applicability, the difficulty of claiming that a text is *not* satire. As "a victim of his own writing," Swift cannot prove what the sermons are not, any more than he can prove what his satires are. I would argue that positing the impossibility of generic stability is, in effect, the same thing as acknowledging a text's openness to satiric subversion, even co-optation by the unruly or incompetent reader. Nokes's reading, good as it is, depends upon our ability to control Swift's identity as author as well as the reliability of generic distinctions between "sermon" and "satire." What makes the modest proposer's anthropophagic musings "satire" is the genre-based conviction that Swift's prose is multilayered, polyvalent, even duplicitous. But what enables Noke's—and probably our own—ire is the understanding that the Swift of the sermons is univocal, that he successfully intends an un-ironic text, and that his readers will know the lack of irony when they don't see it. That is, the message of "A Modest Proposal" or of the *Tale* is awful; Swift cannot mean it; the message of the sermons is awful; Swift must mean it. Ultimately, neither Swift nor his intentions are proof against satire, since satire is no positive quality that can be isolated or quarantined. The author of Swift's sermons is one constituted at the expense of its own integrity, both in a moral and a rhetorical sense, because the same notions of authority and genre inform satire and its other. Perhaps, then, a more accurate genre for Swift's sermons might be "the literary abject," because to forestall the misreading of his sermons as satire or his satires as atheism is to suppress one body of texts in favor of the other.[19] If Swift forgets, loses, or burns the sermons, they can no longer "be a perfect lampoon" on him, but only because the only way to contain satire is to obliterate its medium. To read unironically means to abject the subject, to halt the play of signifiers, and, finally, to bury the body that was once so savagely indignant.

NOTES

1. "Go, traveler, and imitate if you can one who with all his might championed liberty." Translated in Victoria Glendinning's *Jonathan Swift: A Portrait* (New York: Henry Holt and Company, 1998), 275.

2. David Nokes, "Swift and the Beggars," *Essays in Criticism* 26 (1976): 219.

3. "On the Poor Man's Contentment," in *The Prose Works of Jonathan Swift*, Vol. 9, *Irish Tracts 1720–1723 and Sermons*, ed. Herbert Davis and Louis Landa (Oxford: Basil Blackwell, 1968), 196. This is Swift's constant theme in this sermon. See the introduction, n37 for a similar passage.

4. See Phillip Harth, *Swift and Anglican Rationalism* (Chicago: University of Chicago Press, 1961), especially 46–51.

5. "Swift, God, and Power," *Walking Naboth's Vineyard: New Studies in Swift*, ed. Christopher Fox and Brenda Tooley (Notre Dame: University of Notre Dame Press, 1995), 79.

6. *The Prose Works of Jonathan Swift*, Vol. I, *A Tale of a Tub*, ed. Herbert Davis (Oxford: Basil Blackwell, 1957), 34–35.

7. *Swift: The Man, His Works, and the Age*, Vol. 2, *Dean Swift* (Cambridge, MA: Harvard University Press, 1983), 69n3.

8. Morgan, "Last Week I Saw a Woman *Flay'd*': Swift's Meta-Social Discourse and the Implication of the Reader," *Swift Studies* 1 (1999): 59.

9. See, for instance, Lady Mary Wortley Montagu's letter to her daughter in which she argues that Swift's impiety can only be the result of madness (*Complete Letters of Lady Mary Wortley Montagu*, ed. Robert Halsband, 3 vols. [Oxford: Clarendon Press, 1965–67], 3:57).

10. Swift, "The Preface of the Author," *The Battel of the Books*, reprinted in *The Writings of Jonathan Swift*, eds. Robert A. Greenberg and William B. Piper, (New York: W. W. Norton and Co., 1973), 375.

11. Swift, "On the Testimony of Conscience," *Irish Tracts and Sermons*, 151.

12. "Causes of the Wretched Condition of Ireland," *Irish Tracts and Sermons*, 202.

13. Rawson, *God, Gulliver, and Genocide: Barbarism and the European Imagination, 1492–1945* (Oxford: Oxford University Press, 2001), 224–25.

14. See Swift's preliminary "Upon Giving Badges to the Poor," dated September 26, 1726. Reprinted as Appendix C of *The Prose Works of Jonathan Swift,* Vol. 13, *Directions to Servants etc. 1733–1742* (Oxford: Basil Blackwell, 1959), 172–73.

15. Swift, "A Proposal for Giving Badges to Beggars in All the Parishes of Dublin," *Directions to Servants,* 138.

16. "Swift is literature's great ventriloquist, and we have come to recognise that understanding his works is a matter of distinguishing the master's voice from those of his puppet personae" ("Swift and the Beggars," 219).

17. Barnett, "Deconstructing *Gulliver's Travels:* Modern Readers and the Problematic of Genre," reprinted in *Jonathan Swift,* ed. Nigel Wood (London: Longman, 1999), 256.

18. Foucault, "What Is an Author?" reprinted in *Language, Counter-Memory, Practice,* ed. Donald F. Bouchard (Ithaca, NY: Cornell University Press, 1977), 123.

19. "There looms, within abjection, one of those violent, dark revolts of being, directed against a threat that seems to emanate from an exorbitant outside or inside, ejected beyond the scope of the possible, the tolerable, the thinkable. It lies there, quite close, but it cannot be assimilated. It beseeches, worries, and fascinates desire, which nevertheless does not let itself be seduced. Apprehensive, desire turns aside; sickened, it rejects" (Julia Kristeva, "Approaching Abjection," *Powers of Horror* [New York: Columbia University Press, 1982], 1).

"Wild Work in the World": The Church, the Public Sphere, and Swift's Abstract of Collins's *Discourse*

Brian A. Connery

When there is a controversy in an account, the parties must by their own accord, set up for right Reason, the Reason of some Arbitrator, or judge, to whose sentence they will both stand, or their controversie must either come to blowes, or be unde-cided, for want of right Reason constituted by Nature; so is it also in all debates of what kind soever: And when men think themselves wiser than all others, clamor and demand right Reason for judge; yet seek no more, but that things shall be determined by no other man's reason but their own, it is as intolerable in the society of men, as it is in play after trump is turned, to use for trump on every occasion, that suite whereof they have most in their hand.

—Thomas Hobbes, *Leviathan* 1.5; 32–33

Many a long dispute among divines may thus be abridged: It is so. It is not so. It is so. It is not so.

—Benjamin Franklin, *Poor Richard's Almanac*, London, 1743

ANTHONY COLLINS'S 1713 PUBLICATION OF *A DISCOURSE OF FREE-THINKING; Occasioned by the Rise and Growth of a Sect Call'd Free-Thinkers* signaled the beginning of an inevitable new stage in the campaign to undermine the Church Established undertaken by the informal college of the Grecian Coffeehouse, commonly known as the athe-ists, deists, and freethinkers. As the Church had persistently dissoci-ated itself from the enthusiasm of dissenters after the Restoration, it had increasingly engaged in and responded to rational inquiry. It thus became increasingly susceptible to demands, by those accusing it of priestcraft, for the completion of the Reformation by the ratio-nal elimination of its remaining vestiges of superstition and by its legitimation by reason to claims to priestly authority. Reason was being deployed increasingly by the clergy in propagating and refin-ing doctrine—witness the controversy about the Trinity, commencing with the publication of *A Brief History of the Unitarians* in 1687—and, after the expiration of the Licensing Act in 1679, reason was deployed increasingly by the laity *against* the allegedly mystificatory practices of the clergy upon which, supposedly, the authority of the Church mistakenly rested. A quick summary of the representations in print of a Harringtonian resurgence, a Whig ascendancy, and a decline in authority of the Church Established would include John Locke's *A Letter Concerning Toleration* and the Act of Toleration (1689), Locke's *The Reasonableness of Christianity* (1695), John Toland's *Christianity not Mysterious* (1696), and the Earl of Shaftesbury's *An Inquiry Concerning Virtue* (which posited the case of a "moral atheist") in 1699. The rationalists' critique altered strategy, turning to antipriestcraft tracts and Erastian arguments for the subservience of the Church to the legislature in John Toland's *The Art of Governing by Parties* (1701), John Dennis's *The Danger of Priestcraft* (1702), Matthew Tindal's *Rights of the Christian Church Asserted* (1706), and Collins's *Essay concerning the Use of Reason in Propositions, the Evidence whereof depends on Human Testimony* (1707).

It was, of course, within this context that Swift's *Tale of a Tub* (1704) was published, and it was exactly this context that produced the misreadings of Swift's first major work associating him with the deists and alleged atheists. The primary means of attack upon the Church—or the primary rationale for the application of reason to the doctrine of the Church—was an examination of the ways in which "corruptions" had been introduced to the Church (Harrison, 95)—exactly the subject of the primary narrative in the *Tale*. Moreover, the deists, having invented something very much like what we might regard as comparative religion, were remarkably fond of the ancients, and regularly used classical authors as examples of their points, especially concerning the possibility of morality without Christianity. Given the *Tale*'s decided preference for the ancients over the moderns, its general sense of the degeneration of learning and virtue over time, and its antipathy to enthusiasm and deployment of reason—it naturally appeared to many in the reading public that the author of the *Tale* was at least sympathetic in many ways to the arguments and viewpoints of the deists and freethinkers.[1] It is, consequently, little wonder that in the popular press—as well as in work by Shaftesbury and the Bishop of Wake—the catalogs of freethinkers and deists regularly included Swift along with Toland, Tindal, and Collins.[2] In spite of a flurry of writing and publication designed to demonstrate his orthodoxy and thus to rehabilitate his public image, the association between Swift, the *Tale,* and freethinking persisted. Indeed, the author of *The Britain*'s response to Collins's 1713 *Discourse,* immediately linked it to the *Tale:* "All the difference I can see between the *Free Thinker* and the *Tale of a Tub* is, that the one would Reason us, and the other laugh us out of our Religion" (quoted by Phiddian, 72).

It was largely this context—the increasing Whiggish attacks on the authority of the Church—which had prompted Swift's *Sentiments of a Church of England Man* in 1708, an early effort at image rehabilitation, during which year he also composed but did not publish an answer to Tindal's *Rights of the Christian Church,* published his famous *Argument against abolishing Christianity,* and was probably considering, if not composing, the Apology, which would be inserted in the fifth edition of the *Tale* in 1710. Collins, at that time a young protege of Locke and then of Tindal, was working on *Priestcraft in Perfection,* which would be published in 1709, while Swift was working on his *Project for the Advancement of Religion.*

The effect of the Licensing Act's expiration was not unremarked in the course of these at least nominally religious disputes. After the Act's expiration, though work was no long vetted prior to publication, prosecutions occurred after the fact for libel and sedition or seditious libel. 1698 saw the passage of the Act for the More Effectual Suppressing of Blasphemy and Profaneness, remarked upon with passing outrage in Swift's *Abolition of Christianity,* which in effect enabled the prosecution of heresy under the head of blasphemy.[3] The freethinkers and deists were, not surprisingly, the occasional targets of such prosecutions—Tindal's work was burned by the hangman—and strenuous proponents of a freer press, beginning with Charles Blount's *A Just Vindication of the Learned.* Tindal, in his 1698 *Letter to a Member of Parliament shewing that a Restraint on the Press is Inconsistent with the Protestant Religion,* claims, perhaps extravagantly, that "the Reformation is wholly owing to the press" and that "the discovery of printing seems to have been designed by Providence to free men from the Tyranny of the Clergy."[4] This position certainly strengthened the alliance between freethinkers and Whigs, who had needed to maintain a free press throughout the 1680s in order to maintain its opposition (Crist, 50). Indeed, Tindal's *Rights of the Christian Church* linked the spiritual tyranny by the clergy with the political tyranny of ideas, and in *Restraint of the Press* he indicated that publications were suppressed in order to protect the status quo from reform: the purpose of censorship is "to prevent the defects in either the Government or the Management of it from being discovered and amended" (24). Within works ostensibly about matters political and/or theological, the Grecian Coffeehouse writers consistently complained about the suppression of ideas, as in Tindal's *Christianity not Mysterious:* "A Man dares not openly and directly own what he thinks in Divine Matters, though it bc never so true and beneficial" (iv). What Jürgen Habermas recognizes—and what the Whigs and the freethinkers must also have recognized—is that a free press is not just a means of publicizing information and opinion but an enactment of a deeper principle: for the freethinkers, publication broke the monopoly of the clergy on religious discourse.[5] While the critique of the Church Established had been presented in a number of different ways and from a number of different angles, the cumulative effect was—and was designed to be—the reduction of the authority of the church, both in relation to the legislature (the Erastian argument) and in the clergy's relation to the laity. As Phillip Harth has demonstrated, when Hooker had begun to stress the necessity of the application of reason to the interpretation of scripture, as a defense against enthusiasm, his purpose had been, in fact, "to limit the competence of private judgment and to stress the need for public authority" (38–39). Now reason was being proposed as the instrument of the laity against the mystificatory practices of the clergy (and government), and Tindal's *Rights of the Christian Church* had proposed, along the lines of Harrington's *Oceana,* that as in government, the clergy's authority came from the laity—not from the sacerdos of an apostolic succession (Champion, 136).

Collins's *Discourse* may be regarded—as it is by Frederick C. Beiser—as a decisive moment in this movement: Locke and Tindal had provisionally established that reason was competent in matters of religion. Collins's work was designed to complete the argument that reason had the right to exert its competence.

One could tell the story of "the Church in danger, 1680–1713," in any number of ways. I have told it in this way because I think that this history addresses the dangers that Swift saw generally (as suggested in other works of this period) and specifically the dangers he saw in Collins—which can help to account for both the mode and the content of his response. But the Sacheverell case, exploding in 1709 and precipitating the change to a Tory majority and the introduction of a new ministry, is suggestive of another powerful factor. While the assault upon the church's authority was kept up by Toland, Tindal, and Collins, the Church was also rupturing from within, as in the squabbling between High and Low Church, in the aforementioned controversy about the trinity, and in the controversy swirling around Samuel Clarke's raising the question of the immateriality of the soul in 1707. In 1710, Collins published *A Defense*

of the Divine—a peculiar ironic attack on a sermon by Swift's Archbishop King, of Dublin, in which Collins notes the contradictions in divine character implied by King's attempted explanation in a published sermon of the concepts of Divine omniscience and human free will. Indeed, in 1711, *A Representation of the Present State of Religion, Unanimously Agreed upon by a Joint Committee of Both Houses of Convocation of the Province of Canterbury* attributed the "late excessive growth of infidelity, heresy, and profaneness" to two "evils"—a free press and the end of the danger of Popery. The perceived end of the danger of Popery was considered an evil exactly because the absence of this external threat left the Church free to explore and to aggravate its internal differences. The free press was regarded an evil, at least in part, because it offered publicity as the Church did so (Stromberg, 5).

Exactly such public theologizing was an invitation for further dialogues with freethinkers as well as with schismatics. King seems to have recognized this, concluding, as he does in the previously mentioned sermon on predestination and foreknowledge, by remarking that "we ought . . . not unseasonably disturb the Peace of the Church, much less should we endeavor to expose what she Professes. . . . On the contrary, we are obliged . . . to discourage all who make them, as Enemies of peace, and False Accusers of their Brethren" (quoted in Fauske, 38). As Collins's response suggests, such pleas were ineffectual: the sermon itself opened up the opportunity for attack that the conclusion had attempted to foreclose.

Indeed, as Swift would have readily recognized, having labored mightily with the *Examiner* to ignore his Answerers, the clergy's attempts to engage with dissenters and freethinkers in defenses and discussions seemed consistently to exacerbate divisions and weaken the Church's authority rather than to resolve disputes or to legitimate the Church's authority. As J. G. A. Pocock and others have suggested, orthodoxy itself is dynamic, and we must remember that the English enlightenment occurred *within* the clerical culture as well as being a product of the dialogue between clergy and freethinkers.[6] As the ironies in *Abolition of Christianity* suggest, the orthodoxy that Swift consistently defends in the Church is an orthodoxy that no longer exists as he defends it. Just as he was fond of suggesting that he was an old style Whig, dedicated to the revolution settlement but not aligned with the "new party," so too he is an "old style" Church of Ireland man. What this means is that in a typically Swiftian manner, his writings about religion reflect not only on those whom he fairly explicitly identifies as heterodox enemies to religion but also on those who defend or support the new orthodoxy of religion.

Specifically, the increasingly rationalist reformation and discussion of Christianity, along with the concomitant post-Restoration development of creeds, propositions, catechisms, and articles, had privileged, especially within the developing public sphere, the propositional nature of religion and displaced the piety and communion with God, now associated with enthusiastic sects.[7] Mark Goldie observes that post-Restoration emphasis upon conformity "neglected such matters as holy living, preferring credal and ritual formation to moral reformation" as noted by Locke in his *Third Letter Concerning Toleration,* which railed against the way in which the issue of "coercive uniformity" had displaced the church's attention to "pastoral care and moral discipline" (Goldie, 213). Strains of Calvinist doctrinal discussion in particular had abetted this transformation of religion from a lived experience and communion with Christ to a matter of doctrine. As Peter Harrison argues, denominating this trend as "propositionalism," the "truth or falsity of a religion [became] the truth or falsity of the propositions which constituted it (Harrison, 26). The more that religion became propositional, the more reason seemed the appropriate tool for examining it; and the more reason was applied, the more propositional religion became. In short, as Pocock succinctly suggests, the very act of discussion in the terms in which it was conducted transformed Christ from one with whom one has communion to one about whom one has opinions. Arguments for religious freedom, therefore, have always already packed within them the assumption of a Christ about whom one should be free to form opinions (Pocock, 49). It is exactly this to which Swift objects in the *Examiner* when criticizing the Whigs' reduction of religion to "a System of *Speculative Opinions* which no Man should be bound to believe"[8] and it is, in part, this phenomenon to which Swift refers ironically in the *Abolition of Christianity* when his speaker carefully distinguishes "nominal" from "real" Christianity.[9]

Swift's rejection of the privileging of propositions—and all that it entails—is yet another factor that made and continues to make him seem a fellow traveler with deists and freethinkers. "Matters indifferent" had become the focus of the political and theological discussions of toleration and conformity. For dissenters, it was exactly because such matters were "indifferent" that the Church Established should admit of alteration; for defenders of the Church Established like Swift, it was exactly because such matters were "indifferent" that dissenters should conform without raising qualms of conscience, for the sake of social stability and public morality, as ensured by the Church Established. For Swift, indifferent matters should not even be discussed because they focus attention upon difference rather than upon agreement. In his "Thoughts on Religion," Swift suggests that clergy do more harm than good by introducing speculative theology into their ministry: "I believe that thousands of men would be orthodox enough in certain points, if divines had not been too curious, or too narrow in reducing orthodoxy within the compass of subtleties, niceties, and distinctions with little warrant from Scripture, and less from reason or good policy" (*PW*, 9:262). It was, of course, about exactly such matters that the dissenters, freethinkers, and deists wished to think for themselves and so attacked the pronouncements of the clergy. The freethinkers objected to such priestly "interference" as tyrannous; Swift objected to such priestly "interference" as ill-advised, impolitic, and unnecessary.[10] For Swift, the Church's institutional authority was primary, the doctrine secondary; the potential refinement of the doctrine did not and could not justify the potential danger to the Church's institutional authority it entailed.

Swift's writings, consequently, repeatedly advise both the clergy and the laity to steer clear of speculative theology. Famously, his sermon "On the Trinity" brackets the discussion of this "mystery" with warnings that "Men should consider, that raising Difficulties concerning the Mysteries in Religion, cannot make them more wise, learned, or virtuous; better Neighbors, or Friends, or more serviceable to their Country; but, whatever they pretend, will destroy their inward Peace of Mind, by perpetual Doubts and Fears arising in their Breasts" (*PW*, 9: 166–67). His *Letter to a Young Clergyman* repeatedly advises against introducing theological mysteries to the congregation: "I defy the greatest Divine, to produce any Law either of God or Man, which obliges me to comprehend the Meaning of *Omniscience, Omnipresence, Ubiquity, Attributes, Beatifick Vision,* with a Thousand others so frequent in Pulpits" (*PW*, 9: 66). And again: "As I take it, human Comprehension reacheth no further: Neither did our Saviour think it necessary to explain to us the Nature of God; because I suppose it would be impossible, without bestowing on us other Faculties than we possess at present" (*PW*, 9:73). And so: "I do not find that you are any where directed in the Canons, or Articles, to attempt explaining the Mysteries of the Christian Religion. And, indeed, since Providence intended these should be Mysteries; I do not see how it can be agreeable to *Piety, Orthodoxy,* or good *Sense,* to go about such a Work" (*PW*, 9:77). Moreover, the clergy need not respond to atheists, deists, freethinkers and the like. First, because "Persons under those Imputations are generally no Frequenters of Churches" and secondly, "Neither do I think it any Part of *Prudence,* to perplex the Minds of well-disposed People with Doubts, which probably would never have otherwise come into their Heads" (*PW*, 9:77–78). Here, Swift is very much in line with standard Church strategy of *not* trying to increase its congregations by converting dissenters and others but of trying to *conserve* its present congregation by not *losing* them. The proper response of clergy and laity—to both mysteries and to free thinkers—is not to get involved in the conversation. In short, regarding theological propositions and speculations, Swift, at his most moderate, follows a don't-ask-don't tell policy, while preferring a policy of don't-talk-don't-listen: "Every man, as a member of the commonwealth, ought to be content with the possession of his own opinion in private, without perplexing his neighbor or disturbing the public" ("Thoughts on Religion," *PW*, 9:261) Thus can one's responsibilities to God and to Caesar be both fulfilled.

Swift's explicit and nonironic responses to attacks upon the clergy are few and startlingly brief, especially in light of his frequently deploring both publicly and privately the erosion of respect for and authority of the clergy. When Tindal vehemently demands a shift in power from the clergy to the laity ("'Tis absolutely necessary, for the preservation of Religion in its Purity and Simplicity, that all the Power Man is capable of, shou'd belong to the Laity, because they can have no Motive, no Temptation to abuse it, by corrupting Religion to advance their temporal Interest" (*Rights*, 190)), Swift's Church of England man answers only that priests are human, and therefore likely susceptible to ambitions like others (*PW*, 4:10).

In his concern for the Church Established as a social institution, Swift was, in fact, consistent with the views of many of the rationalists, deists, and freethinkers. Harrington, Locke, Toland, and Shaftesbury agreed with the institution of an established religion, since they saw the business of government and religion as fused; the Church's function was to shame vice and dishonesty, to promulgate virtue and morality, and thus to promote civil order and stability (Champion 179; 207–8). Within this view, the state provides secular authority and power to the church, while religious authority supports the state. Nor was there very much disagreement regarding the Church's function as a social agent.

The failure to relinquish claims to divine sanction, of course, suggests to reform-minded adversaries Romish tendencies, the trust in Church theologians being, as Calvin had argued, the surest precipice to destruction. But Swift's rationale for accepting the premise of divine sanction was *not* based upon either an argument for the apostolic transmission of authority or upon any notion of infallibility; instead, he repeatedly invokes a Hobbesian arbitrary-absolutist pragmatism and a Harringtonian sense of the fit between country and Church.[11] The Church of England man declines to become involved in disputes about church history and divine sanction: He "hath a true Veneration for the Scheme established among us of Ecclesiastical Government; and although he will not determine whether Episcopacy be of Divine Right, he is sure it is most agreeable to primitive Institution; fittest, of all others, for preserving Order and Purity, and under its present Regulations, best calculated for our Civil State" (PW, 2:5). The stability of the church—and consequently of government—is more important to the Church of England man than is the truth of its propositions or the propriety of its rites and ceremonies because the stability of the Church ensures the Church's capacity to fulfill its primary functions as a social institution. The Church of England man would consent to alterations in rites, ceremonies, and forms of prayer were the clergy or legislature to so direct but expects that any such concessions to dissent will lead only to more demands rather than to unity and stability (PW, 2:5–6). He disregards the potential "Danger of Schism as a Spiritual Evil" and explores the temporal one: "I think it is clear, that any great Separation from the established Worship, although to a new one that is more pure and perfect, may be an Occasion of endangering the publick Peace; because it will compose a Body always in Reserve, prepared to follow any discontented Heads, upon the plausible Pretexts of advancing *True Religion,* and opposing Error, Superstition, or Idolatry" (PW, 2:11–12). For Swift, the Church, as an institution, was primary; its doctrine, secondary. Robert South and Bishops Samuel Parker and Gilbert Burnet, as well as Jeremy Collier, all insist that irrespective of its truth or falsehood, belief in religion and in rewards and punishments in the afterlife was essential to maintenance of social order (Hill, 58–59). The theological propositions of the church were, from this perspective, not very important. Swift's writings on the Church often seem to echo Harrington's *System of Politics:* "As not this language, nor that language, but some language; so not this religion, nor that religion, yet some religion is natural to every nation" (quoted in Champion, 179). So, in supporting the Sacramental Test, Swift presents himself as "one who is altogether indifferent to any particular system of Christianity" as long as the system is most appropriate for the country in which it predominates (Fabricant, 155). Like the freethinkers, Swift looks to the ancients for authority on this matter, citing Plato's proto-Harringtonian prescription that "men ought to worship the Gods, according to the Laws of the Country" and Socrates' disowning of the crime of "teaching new Divinities" (*PW*, 2:12). Again, the Church is more endangered by schism than it is by its own doctrinal shortcomings; repeatedly Swift acknowledges the possibility of improving the established religion but will not allow such improvement to be prompted by the laity, which would undermine the authority of the church and consequently prevent it from functioning effectively as a social institution to promote stability and morality. In his *Thoughts on Religion,* Swift hypothesizes the Church as a self-correcting institution, theorizing that there is a sort of tipping point that prompts self-correction: "There is a degree of corruption wherein some nations, as bad as the world is, will proceed to an amendment; until which time particular men should be quiet" (*PW*, 9:261). Repeatedly, Swift argues that "few States are ruined by any Defect in their Institutions, but generally by the Corruption of Manners; against which, the best Institution is no long Security, and without which a very ill one may subsist and flourish" (*Church of England Man, PW*, 2:14; see also *A Project, PW*, 2:57).

Swift seems to differ from the freethinkers on two major points: (1) He could not bring himself to see the Church as authorized entirely by and thus under the full administration of the sovereign. Whether or not this is a function of his nominal belief in apostolic succession (which he denies) or whether it's his sense that it's exactly the sacerdotal authority of the Church which justifies its integration into government and which is, in fact, its major contribution and effect, is a question he never directly addresses. (2) He sees the attempt to adjust the Church Established as itself an affront to the church's authority and an enactment of rebellion that challenges, for him, the very idea of an established church. As Harrington, Shaftesbury, Toland, and Swift agreed, the very function of an established church is to serve as a final authority,[12] and the divine sanction of Christ was exactly the strongest basis for its nomination to this position. Like the freethinkers, Swift admired the ancients and found them a useful complement to Christianity: "I am deceived, if a better Comment could be anywhere collected upon the moral Part of the Gospel, than from the Writings of those excellent Men. Even that divine Precept of loving our Enemies, is at large insisted by Plato." Indeed, in an argument that sounds more like Herbert of Cherbury or like Toland's developing pantheism than like a high-flying Tory, "it is a gross Piece of Ignorance among us to conceive, that in those polite and learned Ages, even Persons of any tolerable Education, much less the wisest Philosophers, did acknowledge or worship any more than one Almighty Power, under several Denominations, to whom they allowed all those Attributes we ascribe to the

Divinity" (*Letter to a Young Clergyman, PW,* 9:73). What the ancients lacked is exactly what the freethinkers would take away from the Church Established, however, in attempting to enshrine Reason as the final authority: "The true Misery of the Heathen World [was] the Want of a Divine Sanction; without which the Dictates of the Philosophers failed *in the point of authority*" (*PW,* 9:73; my emphasis). Even the latitudinarian Tillotson says, very clearly, linking the authority of the apostolic succession to that of the state, "I cannot think (till I be better informed, which I am always ready to be) that any pretence of conscience warrants any man, that is not extraordinarily commissioned, as the apostles or first publishers of the gospel were, and cannot justify that commission by miracles as they did, to affront the established religion of a nation (though it be false) and openly to draw men off from the profession of it, in contempt of the magistrate and the law" (quoted in Harth, 130). So too, in his sermon "On Doing Good," Swift does not distinguish either forms of government or of creeds in his general explanation of the conjunction of church and state: "All government is from God, who is the God of order, and therefore whoever attempts to breed confusion or disturbance among a people doth his utmost to take the government of the world out of God's hands and to put it into the hands of the Devil. . . . No crime . . . can equal the guilt of him who doth injury to the public" (*PW,* 9:238).

To paraphrase Tom Stoppard, inverting Voltaire, Swift may have, in fact, agreed with many of the ideas of the deists and freethinkers, but he would fight to the death against their right to speak them As regards toleration, Swift seems to grant it grudgingly—but only under the conditions that dissenters be deprived of all public power including public speech, clearly a form of power:

> Liberty of conscience, properly speaking, is no more than the liberty of possessing our own thoughts and opinions, which every man enjoys without fear of the magistrate: But how far he shall publicly act in pursuance of those opinions, is to be regulated by the laws of the country. Perhaps, in my own thoughts, I prefer a well-instituted commonwealth before a monarchy; and I know several others of the same opinion. Now, if upon this pretense, I should insist on liberty of conscience, form conventicles of republicans, and print books, preferring that government, and condemning what is established, the magistrate would, with great justice, hang me and my disciples. It is the same case in religion, although not so avowed, where liberty of conscience, under the present acceptation, equally produces revolutions, or at least convulsions and disturbances in a state; which politicians would see well enough if their eyes were not blinded by faction. . . . *Thoughts on Free Thinking,* (*PW,* 9:263)

The publication of Collins's *Discourse* occurred in the aftermath of Swift's work as the *Examiner*, his most extended foray into the public sphere, and close upon his efforts to defend the peace. Even prior to this, in the work collected in the *Miscellany* of 1711, it was clear that Swift believed that the government should take a strong hand, if not in preventing the publication of work that could scandalize or disorder the Church, at least in prosecuting it after the fact. The *Project for the Advancement of Religion and the Reformation of Manners* (1709) is largely offered as a plan that the queen might put into effect without the legislature but concludes with suggestions about some laws, including censorship:

> It cannot easily be answered to God or Man, why a Law is not made for limiting the Press; at least so far as to prevent the publishing of pernicious Books, as under *Pretence* of *Free-thinking*, endeavor to overthrow those Tenets in Religion, which have been held inviolable almost in all Ages by every Sect that pretends to be Christian; and cannot therefore with any Colour of Reason be called *Points* in *Controversy*, or *Matters* of *Speculation*, as some would pretend. The Doctrine of the Trinity, the Divinity of Christ, the Immortality of the Soul, and even the Truth of all Revelation are daily exploded, and denied in Books openly printed; although it is to be supposed, that neither Party avow such Principles, or own the supporting of them to be anyway necessary to their Service. (*PW*, 2:60)

The Church of England man declares that he "thinks it a Scandal to Government . . . that such an unlimited Liberty should be allowed of publishing Books against those Doctrines in Religion, wherein all Christians have agreed" because "these undermine the Foundation of all Piety and Virtue" (*PW*, 2:10–11). Even Locke, in his *Letters on Toleration*, had included in a list of ideas "absolutely destructive to society" the notion that "one is bound to broach and propagate any opinion he believes himself." This, he suggested, was both a political and a moral error if one did not consider the social consequences (Rogers, 110). Swift, too, regularly distinguished between liberty of conscience and liberty of opinion: the Church of England man remarks that the difference is often overlooked: "Atheists, Libertines, Despisers of Religion, and Revelation . . . are not so over nice to distinguish between an unlimited Liberty of Conscience, and an unlimited Liberty of Opinion" (*PW*, 2:3). Swift's sermon *On the Testimony of Conscience* explains the distinction: "Liberty of Conscience . . . properly speaking, is no more than a Liberty of knowing our own Thoughts, which no one can take from us. . . . Liberty of Conscience is now-a-days not only to be understood to be the Liberty of believing what Men please, but also of endeavoring to propagate the Belief as much as they can, and to overthrow the Faith which the Laws have already established" (*PW,* 9:15).[13] In regard specifically to Collins's *Discourse,* Clive Probyn remarks, "Swift's ground for dismay at free-thinkers publishing their works is the conviction that a man's conscience is free but the society should determine the limits on the toleration of public heterodoxy" (See "Haranguing upon Texts" 190–91). Similarly, the laxity of government control of the press is touched on ironically in the *Abolition of Christianity:* "Is not every Body freely allowed to believe whatever he pleaseth; and to publish his Belief to the World whenever he thinks fit; especially if it serve to strengthen the Party which is in the Right? Would any indifferent Foreigner, who should read the Trumpery lately written by *Asgill, Tindal, Toland, Coward,* and Forty more, imagine the Gospel to be our Rule of Faith and confirmed by Parliament? (*PW,* 2:29). Ideally, expression of heterodox ideas would be self-suppressed, since, in fact, the authority of tradition and common sense should render anyone uncertain of opinions to the contrary. As the *Tale* asks, "What Man in the natural State, or Course of Thinking, did ever conceive it in his Power, to reduce the Notions of all Mankind, exactly to the same Length, and Breadth, and Height of his own? (*PW,* 1:105). Skepticism, in particular, should be self-suppressed: "The want of belief is a defect that ought to be concealed when it cannot be overcome" (*Thoughts on Religion, PW,* 9:261).

The two forms of censorship—self-censorship and governmental censorship—become a major theme in *Remarks upon a Book entitled the Rights of the Christian Church Asserted,* published in the 1711 *Miscellany* in response to Tindal's book also published in 1711. The introductory remarks in this piece focus upon both forms of censorship: "there are but two Things wonderful in his Book: First, How any Man in a Christian Country could have the Boldness and Wickedness to write it. And, how any Government would neglect punishing the Author of it, if not as an Enemy of Religion, yet a profligate Trumpeter of Sedition." Swift himself seems startled by the vehemence of his denunciation, which is immediately followed by the self-reflection, "These are hard Words, got by reading his Book" (*PW,* 2:98). When Tindal decries the power of the clergy, Swift responds, "I would appeal to any Man, whether the Clergy have not too little Power, since a Book like his, that unsettleth Foundations, and would destroy all, goes unpunished &c." (*PW,* 2:95). When Tindal remarks upon the corruptions of religion, Swift responds, "That which hath corrupted Religion is the Liberty unlimited of professing all Opinions" (*PW,* 2:96). When Tindal suggests apocalyptically that "could [our clergy] like the Popish Priests, add to this a Restraint on the Press, their Business would be done," Swift rejoins, "So it ought: For Example, to hinder his Book . . ." (*PW*, 2:97).

Consistently, Swift finds the offense of these works to be against the public good: as the king of Brobdingrag would suggest fifteen years later, "He knew no Reason why those who entertain Opinions prejudicial to the Publick should be obliged to change, or should not be obliged to conceal them. And, as it was Tyranny in any Government to require the first, so it was Weakness not to enforce the second; For, a Man may be allowed to keep Poisons in his Closet, but not to vend them about as Cordials" (*PW*, 11:131). Underlying Swift's demands for self-censorship and government censorship is the absolute and fundamental belief (a belief that all his writings assume, as their raison d'être) that words and ideas have real consequences. Swift sees censorship much as many late twentieth-century social reformers see gun control: a citizen with a dangerous idea is liable to hurt him or herself as well as others.

Thus, Swift demands accountability from such authors: "If [Free-Thinkers] publish [their thoughts] to the world, they ought to be answerable for the effects their thoughts produce in others" (*Thoughts on Free-Thinking*, *PW*, 4:49). The increasing propositionalism of religion is, itself, a function of and a factor in the increasing obscuration of the relation between ideas and actions. In *Abolishing Christianity*, "real" Christianity is distinguished from the current nominal form of (propositional) Christianity by having had "in primitive Times (if we may believe the Authority of those Ages) . . . an Influence upon Mens Beliefs *and Actions*" (*PW*, 2:99; my emphasis). Of Tindal's *Rights of the Christian Church*, Swift remarks, "This great Reformer, if his Projects were reduced to Practice, how many thousand Sects, and consequently Tumults &c. Men must be governed in Speculations, at least not suffered to vent them, because Opinions tend to Actions, which are most governed by Opinions &c." (*PW*, 2:99)

What Swift objected to about Collins's *Discourse*, then, was not the matter so much as it was the very fact of its existence. While he had been vocal for prosecution of authors and printers of objectionable matter, he also recognized that such attention amounted to considerable publicity: in regard to Tindal's *Rights of the Christian Church*, he had said,

It may still be Wondered how so heavy a Book written upon a Subject in Appearance so little instructive or diverting, should survive to three

Editions, and consequently find a better Reception than is usual with such bulky spiritless Volumes. . . . To which I can only return, that as burning a Book by the common Hangman, is a known Expedient to make it sell: So, to write a Book that deserveth such Treatment, is another; And a third, perhaps, as effectual as either, is to ply an insipid worthless Tract with grave and learned Answers, as Dr. *Hicks,* Dr. *Potter,* and Mr. *Wotton* have done. Designs and Performances, however commendable, have glanced a Reputation upon the Piece; which oweth its Life to the Strength of those Hands and Weapons that were raised to destroy it; like flinging a Mountain upon a Worm, which instead of being bruised, by the Advantage of its littleness, lodgeth under it unhurt. (*PW,* 2:29)

Like Tindal's *Rights of the Christian Church,* Collins's *Discourse* was roundly answered by defenders of the emerging orthodoxy— including Daniel Defoe, Richard Bentley, George Berkeley, Thomas Cockman, the anonymous author of *Free Thoughts,* Benjamin Hoadly, Benjamin Ibbot, the anonymous author of *A Letter to Free Thinkers,* William Oldsworth, Richard Steele, Henry Sacheverell, John Addenbrooke, Francis Hare, Samuel Pycroft, William Whiston, and Daniel Williams.[14] The effect was exactly that which Swift had observed regarding Tindal's work. What seems clear to Swift—and thoroughly unclear to the other answerers, except for Ibbot who, using Socrates as an example, argues simply that authority is necessary, skepticism dangerous (Beiser, 17)—is that discussion of Collins's work legitimates the work as an object of discussion, the press and public sphere as the media and discursive arena in which the discussion should be staged (as well as, in the instances of answers offered in sermons, opening up a clear channel between the pulpit and the press, thereby rendering the pulpit part of the public sphere), and reason as the appropriate tool for determining the truth of the matter. With perhaps the exception of Steele, the answerers implicitly seem to agree with Bishop Francis Atterbury's claim, which must have chilled Swift's heart, that the Church of England "desires nothing more than to be tried at the bar of unbiased reason, and to be concluded by its sentence."[15] Collins could wish nothing more. Indeed, he welcomes it.

Beginning in 1680 with Charles Blount, widely recognized as the primary seventeenth-century publicist for deism, the primary strategy of the antipriestcraft writers was to gesture toward the multiple disagreements among the clergy: "If Preachers, Teachers, and Pastors . . . disagree about Matters, which they preach up as necessary points of Faith, they deservedly lose all Credit and Authority" (Blount, 10). Collins reiterates the point: "The Priests dispute every

Point in the Christian Religion, as well as almost every Text in the Bible; and the force of my Argument lies here, that whatever point is disputed by one or two Divines, however condemned by the Church, not only that particular Point, but the whole Article to which it relates, may lawfully be received or rejected by any Free-Thinker" (*Discourse*, 35). In short, what is at stake here is the church's authority.

That Collins's pamphlet precipitated such an avalanche of clerical discourse, then, would no doubt be relished by Collins and his associates as a demonstration of further instances of disagreement and wrongheadedness. From Collins's and Tindal's perspectives, the more the clergy wrote, the clearer the case became for freethinking, and the more that the clergy talked against freethinking, the more evidence there was of priestcraft. The preface to *The Rights of the Christian Church* professes that the book is designed to show "that they who raise the greatest Noise about the Danger of the Church, are the greatest Enemies to it, by asserting such Notions as undermine both Church and State, and are in direct opposition to the Principles of the Reformation."[16]

Steele's response in the *Guardian* recognizes the strategy: "Whatever Clergymen in Disputes against each other, have unguardedly uttered, is here recorded in such a manner as to affect Religion it self, by wresting Concessions to its Disadvantage from its own Teachers" (*Guardian*, no. 3, 47). Nonetheless, not only did the answers provide publicity for Collins, but because the Church neither spoke with one voice nor stayed on message, the heterogeneity of the consequent flood of clerical discourse would provide more material for Collins's destructive pen and, conceivably, more evidence for his argument. It was, after all, Collins who had famously remarked that nobody doubted the existence of God until Samuel Clarke tried to prove it (Stromberg, 10), a maliciously witty expression of the same point that Swift makes in *A Letter to a Young Gentleman:* "Neither do I think it any Part of *Prudence,* to perplex the Minds of well-disposed People with Doubts, which probably would never have otherwise come into their Heads" (*PW,* 9:78).

As an indication of the difference between what I've nominated Swift's "old" orthodoxy and the "new" orthodoxy, it was Richard Bentley, one of Swift's targets in the *Tale of a Tub,* who emerged as the champion of the church in the 1713 Collins controversy, based largely upon his corrections of many of Collins's mistranslations from Greek and Latin and his refutations of misunderstandings and misstatements about practices in antiquity. But at the very outset of his answer, Bentley characterizes *himself* as a freethinker and praises freethinking as fundamental to Christianity and the Reformation.[17] He consequently dismisses Collins's five arguments to prove the necessity of freethinking since, he says, they "prove what none deny." Instead, he chooses, as he says, "only [to] make some *remarks* upon his ignorance and unfairness" (Bentley, 300–301). Bentley's performance is largely that of a professional scholar exploding and scoffing at the errors of a dilettante, reminiscent of his attack on Sir William Temple, Swift's patron and mentor, in the affair of the *Epistles of Phalaris*. To a sensitive reader, Bentley seems increasingly the bully as his answers plod through dry demonstrations of conjugations and etymologies, broken up only by sporadic self-congratulating failures at wit: "I'll try if I can make him amends, when I rub in his nose, as I have done several already, some more of his *own translations*" (Bentley, 472). Along the way, he does manage to offer a brilliant explanation in lay terms of how, through the practice of philology, increases in the number of scriptural variants make possible greater certitude about the correct version and interpretation, thus enhancing rather than damaging scriptural authority. Thus, as Atterbury predicted, the Church stood and was victorious at the bar of reason. However, from Swift's perspective, Bentley may win the battle, but he cedes the war as he validates the grounds and necessity of freethinking and of earning authority through reason and the demonstration of fact. His case discounts Collins's conclusions by discounting his evidence but he accepts Collins's method.

In fact, the idea of freethinking seems so commonsensical to him that Bentley decides that the major thrust of Collins's work is a covert dogma: "Under the specious shew of *free-thinking*, a *set* and *system of opinions* are all along inculcated and dogmatically taught" (Bentley, 290) Not surprisingly, having achieved wide renown with his Boyle lectures against atheism, Bentley discovers that the dogma is atheism: "For under all this pretence to *free-thinking*, he and his friends have a set of principles and *dogmata*, to which he that will not *assent* and *consent* . . . shall be excluded from the sect. That the soul is material and moral, Christianity an imposture, the Scripture a forgery, the worship of God superstition, hell a fable, and heaven a dream, our life without providence, and our death without hope like that of asses and dogs, are part of the glorious gospel of these truly *idiot evangelists*.[18] Failing to recognize the connection between ideas and actions, Bentley apprehends Collins's discourse as mere religious propositionalism and attempts to identify and refute the propositions he believes the book attempts to address.

Bentley's responses defeated Collins but failed to come to grips with his questioning of religious authority and his demonstration of divergent opinions and heterodoxy on the Trinity within the Church, issues with which philology was not equipped to deal. Bentley simply responds to this by noting that the Protestant Church does not anathematize the heterodox, thus seeming to support toleration and to support Collins. Indeed, though Bentley went systematically through Collins's work, he never completed his own final section, which would have addressed Collins's remarks on English clergy. His nephew, editor, and sole executor tells us that the work was in progress, having been requested by the queen, "but a dispute then unhappily arising about his fees as professor, in which he thought himself extremely ill used, he threw the book by with indignation; nor could he after having excused himself to her royal highness, be ever prevailed upon to resume it again" (Bentley, 472).

Swift, on the other hand—characteristically—saw the rhetorical situation of answering Collins as a double bind, recognizing that the *Discourse* was a rhetorical Trojan Horse that threatened to make any answer into a legitimation of itself. As Collins argued, even the suppression of free thought must be freely thought about: "whoever affirms that I ought to be restrain'd from thinking, is in virtue of that *Affirmation,* oblig'd to assign some Argument or other which ought to lay a restraint upon me" (Collins, *Free-Thinking,* 27). But as soon as we begin freely thinking about the suppression of free thought, Collins has won the day.

Moreover, a proper answer, by convention, would reprint Collins's text (as Bentley's did) and/or compel the answerer's reader to compare texts side by side—and thereby both disseminate and legitimate Collins's work. This is the form that Swift had attempted, unsuccessfully and unsatisfactorily, with Tindal and Burnet. Straight rebuttal would produce more fodder for Collins's destructive pen and, conceivably, inadvertently more evidence for his argument.

The rhetorical problem, as Swift understood it then, was to dismiss freethinking *without thinking about it*—which is exactly what Swift's *Abstract* is designed to make happen. His strategy is to deflect attention from the question of the Church's authority, to reject the invitation to reason with Collins, and to deny Collins's book as a legitimate subject for discussion, while stripping the free-thinkers of authority by making them ludicrous.

The solution is the form of the mock-abstract. The function of an abstract, unlike that of an answer, is to make a reading of the original document redundant—hence, the *Abstract of Mr. Collins's Discourse* is intended as a preemptive maneuver to steer the reader away from Collins's own work. By ventriloquizing Collins, in the voice of "a friend," Swift avoids at least the appearance of dialogue and some of the pitfalls it entails, while assuming complete control of the discussion. The mock-abstract also largely escapes the demands of rational argument; Swift returns to the strategy, dubbed "nonsensification" by Frank Ellis, employed in the *Tale* and defended in his 1710 Apology: "To expose the abuses in religion in the most ridiculous Manner . . . is perhaps the most probable way to cure them, or at least to hinder them from farther spreading" (*PW*, 1:2).[19]

From the outset of Swift's pamphlet, the question of freedom of the press is raised. In his prefatory remarks, the self-identified Whig author confides that he does not fear prosecution for his work: "Though our Friends are out of Place and Power, yet we may have so much Confidence in the present Ministry to be secure, that those who suffer so many *Free Speeches* against their Sovereign and themselves to pass unpunished, will, never resent the expressing the *freest* Thoughts against their Religion, but think with Tiberius, That if there be a God, he is able enough to revenge any Injuries done to himself, without expecting the *Civil Power* to interpose" (*PW*, 4:27). Throughout the abstract, Swift's most noticeable revisions are his emphatic and repeated amplifications of Collins's definition of free-thinking to include its dissemination and propagation. In fact, the first major addition made by Swift is in Collins's definition of free-thinking, adding the discursive element of freethinking that Collins more often than not suppresses. Collins defines his project as follows: "By Free-Thinking, then I mean, the Use of the Understanding, in endeavoring to find out the Meaning of any Proposition whatsoever, in considering the nature of the Evidence for or against it, and in judging of it according to the seeming Force or Weakness of the Evidence." (*Free-Thinking*, 5). Swift amplifies Collins's definition by including the dissemination and propagation of freethinking: "There is not the least hurt in the wickedest thoughts, provided they be free; nor in telling those Thoughts to every Body, and endeavoring to convince the World of them; for all this is included in the Doctrine of Free-thinking." (*PW*, 4:30). And again: "And here I must take leave to tell you, although you cannot but have perceived it from what I have already said, and shall be still more amply convinced by what is to follow; that *Free Thinking* signifies nothing, without *Free Speaking* and *Free Writing*. It is the indispensable Duty of a *Free Thinker*, to endeavor *forcing* all the World to think as he does, and by that means make them *Free Thinkers* too" (*PW*, 4:36). Indeed, throughout his version of Collins's *Discourse*, the speaker associates "Free Speaking" and "Free Writing" almost reflexively with "Free Thinking."

It is exactly the question of the capacity of human beings to engage in freethinking that gives rise to the most famous line of Swift's abstract. After outlining the nature and projected advantages of freethinking, Collins turns to answer objections, the first of which he identifies as follows: "It is objected, That to suppose Men to have a right to think on all Subjects, is to engage them in Enquirys, for which they are no ways qualified; the Bulk of Mankind really wanting a capacity to think justly about any Speculation. . . ." (*Free-Thinking*, 99). This, the abstracter renders as "But to this it may be objected, that the Bulk of Mankind is as well qualified for *flying* as *thinking*, and if every Man thought it his *Duty* to *think freely*, and trouble his Neighbor with his thoughts (which is an essential Part of *Free-thinking*,) it would make wild work in the World" (*PW*, 4:38). Collins's solution is an absolute toleration of diversity of creeds and opinions, and he points to the ancients as examples; in his view, diversity of opinions results in "wild work in the world" only when it meets with intolerance and persecution, which inflates the importance of things indifferent. In Swift's view, the reduction of all religion to speculative points and matters of opinion dissipates the authority of the Church, and since it is a Church established, concomitantly undermines the authority of the state.[20]

Nonetheless, Collins agrees, and the abstracter dutifully reports, that should a man be incapable of thought, he may let it alone. Moreover, "supposing the Bulk of Mankind do want the Capacity to *think freely* on matters of Speculation, I do then allow, that *Free-Thinking*, can be no Duty; *and the Priests must likewise allow, that Men can be no way concern'd about Truth or Falsehood in speculative matters, and that the Belief of no Opinions can be justly requir'd of them*" (*Free-Thinking*, 100; my emphasis). Collins's point is clear: the clergy have initiated the exploration of speculative matters, and if the speculative matters are, in fact, important, the laity must be allowed to participate in the speculation and their speculation must be tolerated. His pamphlet wittily notes that the Jews tolerated Jesus's discussion with the elders in the temple, contemplates the possible consequences of Quaker William Penn, hypothetically, interrupting services at St. Paul's in order similarly to engage the presiding clergy in discussion, and proposes a sort of exchange program in which shamans, griots, and priests from heathen countries would be imported to England while Swift, Sacheverel, and other prominent High Church clergy would be sent to the colonies. If the speculative matters are, in fact, important, the laity must be allowed to participate freely in a universal dialogue and their speculation must be tolerated. Swift's position, on the other hand, is that these matters simply shouldn't be discussed publicly by the laity *or by the clergy*.

While the major object of Swift's attack is the public dissemination of ideas like those of Collins, Swift's handling of Collins's text maintains rather than suppresses the clergy's implication in the relocation and consequent deformation of religion into the public sphere. In a typically Swiftian manner, having created a world that seems divided between freethinkers and clergy, the satire of the *Abstract*, rather than attacking one side and vindicating the other, directs criticism against both. Collins's tract quotes extensively—and certainly not altogether unjustly—from a variety of clergymen in order to let their inconsistencies and folly undermine their authority. So, Swift's abstract quotes Collins quoting the clerics, amplifying the foolishness of Collins's conclusions but—significantly—preserving the foolishness of the clergy.[21] Swift *does* make most of the clergymen sufficiently foolish that they are clearly singular and thus not representative of the Church itself.

In particular, Swift gives full force to Collins's point about the clergy's use of the dialogue as a favored form for their work. Citing Lesley's *Dialogue between a Deist and A Christian,* and *Dialogues between a Socinian and A Christian,* Collins writes, "An Eighth Instance of the Conduct of the Clergy by which they make *Free-Thinking* necessary, is, Their *daily publishing of Books* concerning the *Nature of God,* and the *Truth* and *Authority* of the *Scriptures,* wherein they suggest the Arguments of *Unbelievers;* and more particularly, *Treatises in Dialogue,* where they actually introduce *Atheists, Deists, Scepticks,* and *Socinians,* speaking in behalf of their Opinions, and that (unless you will suppose the Priest to be unfair Writers in Controversy) with the same Strength, Subtilty, and Art, those Men show either in their Books or Conversation" (*Free-Thinking,* 91).

Collins's point is clear: the clergy have introduced these controversies into the public sphere; they have even represented the views of skeptics, atheists, and deists in their full strength and subtlety. They have, in effect, compelled their readers to consider in such controversies and to utilize freethinking. The point for Swift is equally obvious: such writings, especially in dialogue form, which offer dignity instead of ridicule to dangerous views, should not be published.

Swift's abstract of this section underlines Collins's conceit that the clergy's own representations of their opponents is subversive, but the more practical point that the clergy should simply not take these risks remains:

There is another thing that mightily spreads *Free-Thinking,* which I believe you would hardly guess: The Priests have got a way of late of Writing

Books against *Free-Thinking;* I mean Treatises in Dialogue, where they introduce *Atheists, Deists, Skepticks,* and *Socinians* offering their several Arguments. Now these Free Thinkers are too hard for the Priests themselves in their own Books; and how can it be otherwise? For if the Arguments usually offered by *Atheists,* are fairly represented in these Books, they must needs convert every Body that reads them; because Atheists, Deists, Scepticks, and Socinians, have certainly better Arguments to maintain their Opinions than any of the Priests can to maintain the contrary. (*PW,* 4:37)

As Judith Mueller points out, "Any dialogue, by introducing multiple perspectives, runs the risk of readers adopting the wrong perspective" ("Ethics," 486). Any confidence in the reader's abilities to distinguish the good arguments of the priests from the bad ones of the skeptics is contradictory to everything else about the abstract as well as the complete works of Jonathan Swift. Significantly, Bishop Berkeley seems not to have understood the point: his answer to Collins is in the form of a dialogue; similarly, Bentley responds to this section only with bewilderment, indicating he can find nothing wrong with a dialogue as long as the atheist loses: "But what, I pray is the pretended crime? Or where does the wrong conduct lie? I had thought that to propose objections with their full force had been a certain sign both of fairness in the writer, and assurance of a good cause. If they make atheists talk with great strength and subtilty, do they not refute them with greater strength, and overcome subtilty with truth?" (Bentley, 376).

In a more egregious instance, Collins, with a good deal of delight, points out that it was a clergyman who, with support and subsequent applause from many other clergy who would eventually become eminent, provided the English-speaking world with a translation of the complete atheology:

There is but one compleat Antient *System of Atheism* (*viz.* EPICURUS's System written by Lucretius) left us upon Record, and the Priests will not suffer that to lie hid in a learned Language; but one of them, the late Reverend Mr. CREECH, has translated it into *English* Verse, for the Benefit and Entertainment of the *English* Reader. And there are more Recommendations of divines prefix'd before his Performance, than ever I saw before any *Religious* or *Devout* Author whatsoever; and those all eminent and high Divines, such as the Reverend Dr. Edward BERNARD, the Reverend Dr. DUKE, the Reverend Dr. ADAMS, Provost of *King's College* in *Cambridge,* and the Reverend Mr. *Joshua BARNES,* and divers others; in whose company appears also the Right Modest and Orthodox Matron *Mrs. A. BEHN.* (*Free-Thinking,* 91–92)

Swift modestly reduces the glee and the amplitude of the passage above—but does not suppress it: "Mr. *Creech,* a Priest, translated *Lucretius* into *English,* which is a compleat System of Atheism; and several Young Students, who were afterwards Priests, write Verses in Praise of this Translation. The Arguments against Providence in that Book are so strong, that they have added mightily to the Number of *Free-Thinkers*" (*PW,* 4:37.)

Swift does suppress Collins's pointed attack on Stillingfleet: "There are not only Priests on both sides of the Question [of Episcopacy], but one eminent Priest, Dr. STILLINGFLEET, is himself on both sides: when he was a Presbyter, he wrote a *Book* to prove the *human institution* of *Episcopacy;* and when he was a *Bishop,* he wrote to prove it of *Divine Institution*" (*Free-Thinking,* 71–72). Swift does not, however, suppress Collins's attacks on clergymen who have written in inadvertently subversive ways of such speculative mysteries as the Trinity, afterlife, and so on. Indeed, Swift's "abstract" of the passage on Whiston seems to heighten the sense of the danger of such publications rather than to mitigate them, and gives voice to Swift's own disposition towards them: "Mr. Whiston [writes Swift's abstracter] has publish'd several Tracts, wherein he absolutely denies the Divinity of Christ: A Bishop tells him, *Sir, in any Matter where you have the Church's judgement against you, you should be careful not to break the Peace of the Church, by Writing against it, though you are sure you are in the right.* Now my Opinion is directly the contrary; and I affirm, that if Ten Thousand Free Thinkers thought differently from the received Doctrine, and from each other they would be all in Duty bound to publish their thoughts (provided they were all sure of being in the right) though it broke the Peace of the Church and State, Ten thousand times" (*PW,* 4:36). Here, the clergy who write and publish speculative theology are held as indistinguishable in effect and consequences from the freethinkers they encourage. And the consequences—the breaking of the peace of church and state—are rendered clear.

Swift's abstracter delivers one section of Collins's *Discourse* almost verbatim—enhancing it only to make it more forceful. Collins wonders about the priorities of the clergy: "Are not the Streets of the City of *London* (like those of *Rome, Paris,* or *Venice*) full of common whores, who are in effect publicly tolerated in their Wickedness? And are not the Men who have dealings with them free from all Punishment and almost from Censure? And yet few or no Complaints are made, of the Wickedness in the open street, either from the *Pulpit* or the *Press . . .*" So Swift's abstracter amplifies: "Priests . . . never once preach to you to love your Neighbor, to be just in your Deal-

ings, or to be Sober and Temperate: The Streets of London are full
of Common Whores, publickly tolerated in their Wickedness; yet the
Priests make no Complaints against this Enormity, either from the
Pulpit or the Press: I can affirm, that neither you nor I Sir, have ever
heard one Sermon against Whoring since we were boys. No, the
Priests allow all these Vices, and love us the better for them, provided we will promise not to *harangue upon a Text,* nor to sprinkle a
little Water in a Child's Face, which they call Baptizing, and would
engross it all to themselves" (*PW,* 4:40–41). Exactly here we find
what could easily serve as the satiric norm of this parody—and Swift
needs to change hardly a word. Swift here makes Collins's point for
him *more* forcefully, and here, if we believed in such things, we might
find the satiric norm of this parody. Swift follows Collins in criticizing the clergy for engaging in points of speculative theology while
neglecting the simple morality compelled by Christianity, a morality
that would justify its affiliation with the state as an institution preserving stability and order. While the clergy are haranguing upon
texts, the laity are sunk in a morass of vice and immorality. The
propagation of speculative propositions has displaced pastoral care:
The clergy's responsibilities, according to Swift's *Letter to a Young
Gentleman,* "are first to tell the People what is their Duty; and then
to convince them that it is so" (*PW,* 9:70). That is, the discursive
function of the clergy is not to harangue upon texts but to tell the
congregation what to do

   Swift's cause was a lost one. Joseph Levine concludes his short history of the controversy between deists and Anglicans by remarking,
"In the end it was the Christian moderns, perhaps even more than
the radical deists, who contributed most to the ultimate decline of
Christian conviction. By introducing an incipient idea of progress
and a historicist reading of Biblical history, and by criticizing all the
ancient sources . . . they gradually undid the universalist claims of
both revealed religion and the pagan authors, and so left the way
open to that historical relativism that is the characteristic mode of
modern thinking about the past."[22] Swift's paragraph of paraphrase
of Collins's optimistic projections of religious pluralism is prophetic:
"A great deal of Free-Thinking will at last set us all right, and every
one will adhere to the Scripture he likes best; by which means Religion, Peace, and Wealth will be forever secured in Her Majesty's
Realms" (*PW,* 4:32–33). As Collins predicted, and as Swift feared,
and as Habermas recounts, the public controversy about religion,
supported and prolonged by the clergy's public engagement with

the deists and freethinkers, eroded religious authority further, thereby making the case for greater religious freedom, which, in turn, produced more religious controversy. Unlike the religious controversies which had precipitated the civil war, however, the cause of liberty was now represented by reason, rather than by enthusiasm, and it was the church's own faith in reason which proved its undoing.[23]

Over the short term, Swift's pamphlet was a failure, receiving no critical notice. It appeared neither in the *Miscellany* of 1727 nor in the Faulkner edition of Swift's works, and was not reprinted until John Nichols's 1776 collection, *A Supplement to Dr. Swift's Works* (Ellis, 84). Still, the *Post Boy* of March 26–28, 1713, reports that the judge and jury at the Derby assizes condemned Collins's *Discourse* and that the volume was burned leaf by leaf by the hangman (Phiddian, 65). This was, no doubt, largely the consequence of Bentley's refutations, the first two volumes of which went into several editions, though the third volume, as mentioned above, remained incomplete

During the subsequent Bangorian controversy, Collins wrote to a friend, "I was extremely pleas'd with Bishop Hoadly's controversy, as it as upon the true and only point worth disputing with ye priests, *viz.* Whether the laity are the calves and sheep of the priest." He remarks further on the way in which the clergy engaged in this controversy have all publicly undermined the authority of the Church: "And I am not less pleased to see them manage their controversy with ye same vile arts against one another as they always use towards the laity. It must open the minds of a few and convince them, that the priests mean nothing but wealth and power and have not the least portion of those qualities for which the superstitious world admires them" (quoted in O'Higgins, 19).

Collins's subsequent *Discourse of the Grounds and Reason of the Christian Religion* in 1724 was prefaced by "an Apology for free debate and liberty of writing" which, ironically, defended the rights of those who had answered his previous work, in particular, Whiston: "In matters of opinion it is every man's natural right and duty to think for himself. . . . Another man has no more right to determine what Mr. WHISTON's opinions shall be, than Mr. Whiston has to determine what another man's opinions shall be" (*Grounds and Reasons*, v). In this preface, Collins does *not* suppress his belief in the public sphere, and seems, in fact, to adopt Swift's abstract's very language in insisting upon the necessity of public advocacy: "As it is every man's natural right and duty to think and judge for himself in matters of opinion, so he should be obliged *freely* to *profess* his opinions, and to endeavor, when he judges proper, to *convince* others, also of their truth" though qualifying this proposition, with perhaps a sardonic wink to Swift, "provided those opinions do not tend to the disturbance of society." And perhaps a wink to Bentley here: "For unless all men be allow'd *freely* to *profess* their opinions, the means of information in respect to opinions, must in great measure be wanting, and just inquiries into the truth of opinions almost impracticable" (*Grounds and Reasons,* vi). Collins seems to have learned the lesson Bentley taught so patiently in his earlier refutation about the way in which philology's accuracy was enhanced by the proliferation of variant texts and interpretations.

It remained for Hume to announce that Christianity could not be founded upon reason, and for John Wesley and William Law to imply that reason is irrelevant to the most important parts of religion, and for Butler, seconded by Berkeley, to indicate that religious truths cannot be proved. Nonetheless, Stromberg reports that Henry Dodwell's *Christianity not founded on an Argument,* published in 1743, was met with outrage by many Anglicans who believed, based on the work of Bentley and others, that Christianity *was* founded on an argument, a rational and positive demonstration of its historical truth and accuracy" (quoted in Stromberg, 10). In passing, Dodwell also insisted that the idea of a "religious dialogue" was oxymoronic (Prince, 15).

Collins's influence was relatively short lived in England, but he was read with interest by Voltaire. Bentley's influence persisted, although not with altogether salutary results. In his *Autobiography,* Benjamin Franklin recounts his own early religious quest:

> My Parent's had early given me religious Impressions, and brought me through my Childhood piously in the Dissenting Way. But I was scarce 15 when, after doubting by turns of several Points as I found them disputed in the different Books I read, I began to doubt of Revelation it self. Some Books against Deism fell into my Hands; they were said to be the Substance of [Bentley's] Sermons preached at Boyle's Lectures. It happened that they wrought an Effect on me quite contrary to what was intended by them: For the Arguments of the Deists which were quoted to be refuted, appeared to me much Stronger than the Refutations. In short I soon became a thorough Deist.[24]

NOTES

1. Claude Rawson sums up one of the frequent difficulties of reading Swift: "a paradox . . . of an aggressively slippery identity of views between Swift and the things

or people he rejects." See "Mandeville and Swift," in *Eighteenth-Century Contexts: Historical Inquiries in Honor of Phillip Harth,* edited by Howard D. Weinbrot, Peter J. Schakel, and Stephen E. Karian (Madison: University of Wisconsin Press, 2001), 60–80. As I hope to show in this essay, such distinctions are difficult because Swift, in fact, rejects many ideas with which he identifies, because when considering any controversy Swift characteristically rejects *both* sides (though sometimes in different degrees), and because we, as readers, too often identify too absolutely with Swift's preferred enemies. In regard to the *Tale* and specifically to the *Abstract of Mr. Collins's Discourse,* Clive Probyn and Michael DePorte have both explored the possibility of Swift's sympathies for freethinkers. Probyn suggests, "There is a close and nervous similarity between what Swift sees in Collins and what some readers saw Swift doing in the religious satire of *Tale of a Tub*." See " 'Haranguing upon Texts': Swift and the Idea of the Book," *Proceedings of the First Münster Symposium on Jonathan Swift,* edited by Hermann J. Real and Heinz J. Vienken (Munich: Wilhelm Fink Verlag, 1984), 187–97; Michael V. DePorte "Contemplating Collins: Freethinking in Swift," in *Reading Swift: Papers from the Third Münster Symposium on Jonathan Swift,* edited by Hermann J. Real and Helgard Stöver-Leidig (Munchen: Wilhelm Fink Verlag, 1998), 103–16.

2. For a particularly good account of this, see Frank Boyle, "Profane and Debauched Deist: Swift in the Contemporary Response to *A Tale of a Tub*." *Eighteenth-Century Ireland* 3 (1988): 25–38.

3. It is a prosecution on the basis of this law, I believe, to which Swift refers—obviously disapproving of the leniency of the law compared to its predecessors—in *Abolition of Christianity:* "Two young Gentlemen of great Hopes, bright Wit, and profound Judgment, who upon a thorough Examination of Causes and Effects, and by the meer Force of natural Abilities, without the least Tincture of Learning; having made a Discovery, that there was no God, and generously communicating their thoughts for the good of the Publick; were some Time ago, by an unparalleled Severity, and upon I know not what obsolete law, broke only for Blasphemy. And, as it hath been wisely observed; if Persecution once begins, no Man alive knows how far it may reach, or where it will end" (*PW,* 2:28).

4. Matthew Tindal, *A Letter to a Member of Parliament shewing that a restraint on the press is inconsistent with the Protestant religion and dangerous to the liberties of the nation,* London, 1698. Printed by J. Danby. Sold by Andrew Bell.

5. See David Zaret, "Religion, Science, and Printing in the Public Sphere in Seventeenth-Century England," in *Habermas and the Public Sphere,* edited by Craig Calhoun (Cambridge: MIT Press, 1992), 221: "Encouragement of popular participation in religious debates was both a means of disseminating reformed doctrine and a principle topic of controversy that divided reformers from religious conservatives. . . . Fed by a vernacular religious literature, lay religious intellectualism pointed to a future in which a rough equality between cleric and layman would replace traditional lay subservience in religious matters."

6. See B. W. Young, *Religion and Enlightenment in Eighteenth-Century England: Theology and Debate from Locke to Burke* (Oxford: Clarendon, 1998); J. G. A. Pocock, "Within the margins: The Definition of Orthodoxy," in Roger Lund (ed.), *The Margins of Orthodoxy: Heterodox Writing and Cultural Response 1660–1750* (Cambridge: Cambridge University Press, 1995), 33–53.

7. Jürgen Habermas's initial account of the construction the public sphere in seventeenth-century England attributes considerable impact from religious discussion: "With the privatization of religion and of property and the emancipation of civil society's private people from the semi-public bonds of the Church and the in-

termediate powers of the estates, increased the importance of these people's private opinion even more." See *The Structural Transformation of the Public Sphere,* 91.

8. *Examiner,* no. 39, May 3, 1711; *PW, [?]:*143. The manner in which propositionalism seemed both to reduce religion to articles of a creed and then, for political expediency, to dismiss the theological function of the creed, attributed by Swift to the Whigs and certainly made use of them, can be seen in Edward Fowler, Bishop of Gloucester's *The Principles of Certain Moderate Divines of the Church of England (Greatly Misunderstood) Truly Represented and Defended* (1670): "We do not suffer any man to reject the Thirty-Nine Articles of the Church of England at his pleasure, yet neither do we look upon them as essentials of Saving Faith, or Legacies of Christ and his apostles; but in a mean, as pious opinions fitted for the preservation of unity; neither do we oblige any man to believe them, but only not to contradict them." Quoted by Roger Lund, "Introduction," in *The Margins of Orthodoxy: Heterodox Writing and Cultural Response 1660–1750,* ed. Roger Lund, (Cambridge: Cambridge University Press, 1995), 4.

9. It seems entirely likely to me that what I have termed the "old" orthodoxy is more characteristic of the Church of Ireland than the Church of England in the early eighteenth century. During that same year that Swift was writing his response to Collins, the Irish Convocation composed a *Representation of the Present Stile of Religion,* characterized by D. W. Hayton as a comprehensive denunciation of speculative theology, skeptical freethinking, aggressive Presbyterianism, moral dereliction, and popery." See D. W. Hayton, "The High Church Party in the Irish Convocation 1703–1713," in *Reading Swift: Papers from the Third Münster Symposium on Jonathan Swift,* edited by Hermann J. Real and Helgard Stöver-Leidig (München: Wilhelm Fink Verlag, 1998), 123.

10. The freethinkers and deists, like Swift, were also highly critical of the court Whigs and especially of Marlborough, though, again, they came to this position from another direction. See Margaret Jacob, *The Radical Enlightenment: Pantheists, Freemasons, and Republicans* (London: George Allen & Unwin, 1981), 151. In terms of public positions, however, as suggested in this essay, in many ways Swift shared more views with the freethinkers and deists than otherwise.

11. Both Carole Fabricant and Claude Rawson agree in seeing Swift's devotion to the Church as being based largely on its sociological rather than its theological function. Fabricant says, "While Swift, as we know, forcefully defended the Established Church on a number of occasions, the grounds of his defiance were invariably pragmatic and empirical, hence based neither on theological doctrine nor on the assertion of a divine destiny unique to Protestantism. Again and again, what Swift emphasized as the strongest argument for the Established Church was not the validity of its spiritual claims but its role of preserving peace and stability in society." See "The Voice of God and the Actions of Men: Swift among the Evangelicals," in *Reading Swift: Papers from the Third Münster Symposium on Jonathan Swift,* edited by Hermann J. Real and Helgard Stöver-Leidig (München: Wilhelm Fink Verlag, 1998), 150. Rawson finds Swift less straightforward but infers his tendencies in this direction: "Swift [in the *Abolition of Christianity*] denies [ironically] religion as the invention of power to keep the people in line. [He] typically repudiated the imputed cynicism of those who held this view, but wasn't altogether ready to deny its validity and remained committed to his own supposedly sanitized version of it." See "Swift and Mandeville," 62–63.

12. The best summary of Swift's understanding of this, to my knowledge, appears in Roger Lund, "Swift's Sermons, 'Public Conscience,' and the Privatization of Religion," *Prose Studies* 18.3 (1995): "As Habermas would have it, the resolution of such

conflicts was to be found in the expansion of the public sphere. But for churchmen like Swift, the chaos of conflicting claims could be settled only by the forceful authority of a single, legally established Church. For only an established Church could assert the absolute precedence of public concord over all expressions of private doubt or rational opinion, doubts and opinions which to Swift seemed often inimical to the public peace. In this respect, Swift's lack of charity with those who differed from him in articles may be regarded less as a matter of personal failure (or unsuitability for his clerical role) than as a natural corollary of his faith in the public function of religion" (158).

13. Exactly the same point is made in the sermon *On the Martyrdom of King Charles:* "If a [dissenter's] religion be different from that of his country and the government thinks fit to tolerate it, (which he may be very secure of, let it be what it will) he ought to be full satisfied, and give no offence, by writing or discourse, to the worship established, as the dissenting preachers are apt to do. But, if he hath any new visions of his own, it is his duty to be quiet and possess them in silence, without disturbing the community by a furious zeal for making proselytes" (*PW,* 9:227).

14. Responses included Benjamin Hoadly's *Queries Recommended to the Authors of the Late Discourse of Free Thinking, by a Christian* (London, 1713); William Whiston, *Reflexions on an Anonymous Pamphlet, Entituled a Discourse of Free Thinking* (London, 1713); the anonymous *A Further Discourse of Free-Thinking: In a letter to a Clergy-Man, with some Considerations on Mr. Pyecroft's Treatise upon the same subject* (London 1713). For a comprehensive listing of responses, see Robert Phiddian, "The Reaction to Collins's *A Discourse of Free-Thinking:* 'Not Politicks'?", 68–71. Phiddian notes, in support of his thesis that the seemingly theological debate is, in fact, largely political, that the predominant response was from Whigs—dissenters, moderns, latitudinarians. Phiddian argues that Swift's purpose in explicitly identifying Collins's pamphlet with Whig principles was to put the Whigs on the defensive, and that the Whig responses indicate their rejection of Collins; thus, the affair becomes Tubbical, distracting Whigs by creating an occasion for infighting. As I shall suggest, however, the response from Whigs, since it generally takes for granted foundational assumptions that Swift rejects, was disastrous for Swift's cause.

15. Quoted by Michael B. Prince, *Philosophical Dialogue in the British Enlightenment: Theology, Aesthetics, and the Novel* (Cambridge: Cambridge University Press, 1996), 15; also Roland N. Stromberg, *Religious Liberalism in Eighteenth-Century England* (Oxford: Oxford University Press, 1954), 10.

16. Tindal, *Rights of the Christian Church,* A3. The case for Swift's understanding of the clerical tendency to shoot themselves in their discursive feet through publishing speculations has been eloquently and persuasively made by David Bywaters: "My point is . . . that the satire of the 'Digression on Madness' is directed not specifically against philosophical atheism, but against philosophical speculation whatever its ostensible purpose, and especially against philosophically based refutations of atheism that the Anglican clergy had been turning out by the year since the Restoration" (593). The case for Swift's understanding of the clerical tendency to shoot themselves in their discursive feet through publishing speculations has been eloquently and persuasively made by David Bywaters: "My point is . . . that the satire of the 'Digression on Madness' is directed not specifically against philosophical atheism, but against philosophical speculation whatever its ostensible purpose, and especially against philosophically based refutations of atheism that the Anglican clergy had been turning out by the year since the Restoration." See "Anticlericism in Swift's *Tale of a Tub, Studies in English Literature, 1500–1900,* 36.3 (Summer 1996): 591.

17. Most answerers noted that it was hard to distinguish "free-thinking" from thinking of any sort. Collins defines it as follows: "By Free-Thinking, then I mean, the Use of the Understanding, in endeavoring to find out the Meaning of any Proposition whatsoever, in considering the nature of the Evidence for or against it, and in judging of it according to the seeming Force or Weakness of the Evidence."

18. Bentley, 300. He summarizes his sense of Collins's work subsequently: "Free-thinking here, for many pages together, is put for common use of reason and judgment, a lawful liberty of examining, and in a word, good Protestantism. Then whip about, and it stands for skepticism, for infidelity, for bare atheism. But his mask is too pellucid to cover his true face. He is still known for a mere atheist, though he talks of *free-thinking* in words that may become a Christian" (386). Bentley's discovery of crypto-atheism was not singular, but appears to me to be overly inferential at best. Nonetheless, the latest history of atheism in Britain devotes an entire chapter to Collins. See David Berman, *A History of Atheism in Britain from Hobbes to Russell* (New York: Croom Helm, 1988).

19. Roger Lund's comments on the *Tale* suggest that Swift's strategy was doomed from the outset by his resorting to wit: "As Tindal recognized, much to his delight, where the implementation of Christian wit was concerned, there was no way that a writer like Swift could finally win. Because wit had been so closely identified with heterodox assaults on religion, it was simply impossible for a Christian apologist, no matter how sincere (Swift's sincerity is, of course, always a matter of debate) to adopt the weapons of wit without giving comfort to the enemy" ("*A Tale of a Tub*, Swift's Apology," 107). Whether or not this was the case with the *Abstract* or not, I do not propose to resolve.

20. Swift's disagreement with Collins here also anticipates significantly the view of human nature as *rationis capax,* which has figured so heavily in interpretation of the fourth book of the *Travels.* Collins argues that the more thinking is free, the more likely is the discovery of truth, "unless it be suppos'd that Men are such absurd Animals, that the most unreasonable Opinion is as likely to be admitted for true as the most reasonable, when it is judg'd of by the Reason and Understanding of Men. In that case, indeed it will follow, That Men can be under no Obligation to think of these matters. But then it will likewise follow, That they can be under no Obligation to concern themselves about Truth and Falshood in any Opinions. For if Men are so absurd, as not to be able to distinguish between Truth and Falshood, Evidence and no Evidence, what pretence is there for Mens having any Opinions at all?" (33). Citing Chillingworth, he suggests that it would be a cruel God who would create such an absurd creature as this and then expect him to be able to ferret out the truth (34). The applicability here to some of the paradoxes of part 4 of *The Travels* is too obvious to require comment.

21. The way in which this attack upon the clergy conforms to Swift's own criticism of the clergy has been noted by Judith Mueller. See "The Ethics of Reading."

22. Joseph Levine, "Deists and Anglicans: The Ancient Wisdom and the Ideo of Progress," in Roger Lund, ed., *The Margins of Orthodoxy: Heterodox Writing and Cultural Response 1660–1750* (Cambridge: Cambridge University Press, 1995), 239.

23. See Beiser, 265. In this regard, it is telling that Collins, according to his biographer, admired the independence of thought of the seventeenth-century Puritans, along with their rejection of civil authority, but also admired the theology of the Anglican Great Tew Circle, the Cambridge Platonists, and the Latitudinarians. Thus, his views unite the politics of the enthusiasts and the theology of the rationalists. See O'Higgins, 41.

24. Benjamin Franklin, *Autobiography.* Many thanks to my colleague, Jane Eberwein, Distinguished Professor of English at Oakland University, for helping me to locate this account.

Swift and the Rabble Reformation: *A Tale of a Tub* and State of the Church in the 1690s

Christopher Fox

Nᴇᴀʀ ᴛʜᴇ ᴇɴᴅ ᴏꜰ ꜱᴡɪꜰᴛ'ꜱ *ᴛᴀʟᴇ ᴏꜰ ᴀ ᴛᴜʙ*, ᴡᴇ ᴀʀᴇ ɢɪᴠᴇɴ ᴀ ꜰɪɴᴀʟ ᴘɪᴄᴛᴜʀᴇ of the three brothers sketched by a narrator who claims to have lost his papers. Were he to find them they would include, he says, a full account of "how *Peter* got a *Protection* out of the *King's-Bench;* and of a Reconcilement between *Jack* and Him, upon a Design they had in a certain *rainy Night,* to trepan Brother *Martin* into a *Spunging-house,* and there strip him to the Skin. How *Martin,* with much ado, shew'd them both a fair pair of Heels. How a *new Warrant* came out against *Peter:* upon which, how *Jack* left him in the lurch, *stole his Protection, and made use of it himself.* How *Jack's* Tatters came into Fashion in *Court* and *City;* How *he got upon a great Horse, and eat Custard.*"[1] Commenting on this passage, Robert M. Adams noted some years ago that "we do not have to consult many footnotes to see in capsule summary a decade of English religious history from James II's Declaration of Indulgence (1687) to Sir Humphrey Edwin's curious performance as the first avowedly Presbyterian lord mayor of London (1697). Jack and Peter maneuver and connive to such effect that all Martin can do is make his escape in a rainstorm. Thus the establishment (Martin) is pushed aside by Presbyterianism (Jack) which makes use of a toleration stolen from the Roman Catholics (Peter)." Sir Humphrey Edwin here provides a signal illustration of the dangers of toleration and of the Presbyterians' new clout: "By the terms of the Test Act, Sir Humphrey was obliged, as a condition of his office, to show that he had attended the Anglican communion at least once in the past six months. He duly did so, and was properly sworn into office—he sat on the great horse and ate the ceremonial custard; but then, before he had been in place a month, proceeded on two consecutive Sundays (31 October and 7 November 1697) to don the robes of office, command the official sword-bearer to precede him, and thus in his official capacity to attend a conventicle at Salters' Hall." Swift's version of this event alone shows an established church in 1697 far from triumphant and under assault, particularly from the Presbyterians. Highlighting this episode, Adams proposes to look at the *Tale* "as if it were a book composed by a man who had some reason to doubt that there was going to be an eighteenth-century establishment." Given the threatening historical circumstances of the 1690s in which it was composed, *A Tale of a Tub,* Adams concludes, is "more a crisis book than a compromise book."[2]

I agree with this conclusion and with Adams's attempt to see the religious satire as a product of the 1690s rather than of a later period. But I would like to qualify Adams's argument, then build on it to explore in more detail what those specific historical circumstances were and how they might help us understand Swift's work.

I

First, the qualifications. The Presbyterian crisis Adams finds in the *Tale* is essentially an *English* one. Swift, of course, was astutely aware of the history of the English church's vexed relations with dissent in general and Presbyterianism in particular. He was an avid reader of that history in such writers as Clarendon, Burnet, Ludlow, and Heylin. He was interested in the Civil Wars in England during which his clergyman grandfather suffered sequestration and imprisonment under the hands of local Presbyterians and the County Committee (headed by Edward Harley, Sir Robert Harley's father). Swift also loved his Butler, who wrote

> As if *Presbytery* were a standard
> To size whats'ever's to be slander'd.[3]

The *Tale* itself alludes to other parts of the English history, including the 1679 Meal-Tub affair, "*an Account of a* Presbyterian *Plot, found in a Tub, which then made much Noise.*"[4] This conspiracy, involving papers said to have been hidden in a meal tub in the house of Mrs. Cellier, a Roman Catholic, had provoked such broadsheets as *State-Cases Put to Jack Presbyter* (1681) which opens:

> JACK, if you have one Grain of Sence
> That's free from Pride and Impudence,
>   Say something in your own Defence,
> But LYE NOT.
> Why dost thou make our Blood recoyl
> With Noise of *Plots* and *Popish* Guile,
> Whilst you're the Traitor all the while:
> And BYGOT.[5]

The same event had also sparked "Jack Presbyter" burnings in England like the one at the Globe Tavern in Cornhill "where a great fire was made, and Jack Presbyter brought out, leaning over a board nailed to a tub—that is, the Meal Tub—and holding in his right hand the Solemn League and Covenant, and in the left the Association. Between both was the inscription 'The Pope is an ASS to ME!'"[6]

Exclusive focus on this and other parts of the English history, however, leaves another story untold. As the *Tale of a Tub* reminds us, there are many different iterations of Jack: "Sometimes they would call Him, *Jack the Bald;* sometimes, *Jack with a Lanthorn;* sometimes, *Dutch Jack;* sometimes *French Hugh; . . . .* and sometimes, *Knocking Jack of the North."*[7]

The last, identified in Swift's own note as "*John Knox, the Reformer of Scotland"*[8] is not mentioned in Adams's discussion of the *Tale* or of the crisis in the church in the 1690s. Knox's Scots Presbyterians, nonetheless, play a prominent role in both. In the introduction to *A Tale of a Tub,* Swift's narrator remarks: "Of *Pulpits* there are in this Island several sorts; but I esteem only That made of Timber from the *Sylva Caledonia,* which agrees very well with our Climate. . . . The Degree of Perfection in Shape and Size, I take to consist, in being extreamly narrow, with little Ornament. . . ." A note added to this passage in the 1720 edition of the *Tale* tells us that "the Opinions of the greatest part of our Dissenters falling in with those of the Scotch Kirk by law established, makes the Author recommend this wood for pulpits; and their affected plainness and simplicity is exposed by the figure and size here prescribed."[9] Later in the *Tale,* the wind-worshiping Aeolists find the source of their inspiration in "the *Almighty-North"* or "the *Land of Darkness,"* identified by an eighteenth-century reader as "Scotland." A 1720 note to this reference adds that "our Dissenters in England, who pretend to a much larger share of the Spirit, than those of the establisht Church, own the Kirk of Scotland for their Mother Church, where the Gospel shines in its greatest purity and lustre."[10] The dissenters had good reason to do so. For the Scottish national Episcopal Church had been virtually replaced by the "Kirk by law established," first by mob action—or the "rabblings," as they were called—then by a 1690 Act of the Scottish General Assembly and finally by the Act of Union (which as John Spurr notes "allowed Scotland to retain the Presbyterianism and thus produced the anomaly of two established religions in one kingdom").[11]

In looking at Presbyterian Jack, Adams and subsequent scholars have missed the Scottish dimension of the *Tale.* The disestablishment of the Scottish episcopal church in the 1690s was a great victory for the Presbyterians and a devastating blow for those of Swift's persuasion who could envision only one established Church. On its opening page, *A Tale of a Tub* lists among "Treatises wrote by the same Author, most of them mentioned in the following Discourses. . . . *A Modest Defence of the Proceedings of the* Rabble *in all Ages.*"[12] Swift's Jack mimics activities of the "rabblers" in his own age who brought down the Scottish Episcopal Church and caused a key crisis in the 1690s.

Adams's attempt to recover circumstances surrounding the composition of the *Tale* in the 1690s also excludes any mention of the probable place where the work was begun or at least conceived, Kilroot, County Antrim. In his classic study of Swift and the Church of Ireland, Louis Landa remarks that we "must not overlook the possibility that a portion of *A Tale of a Tub* was written at Kilroot" or "with the experience of Ulster Presbyterianism fresh enough to give a dark and bitter tinge to that work."[13] Herbert Davis agrees, adding that "if the *Tale* is read with an eye to the actual conditions in Ireland, Swift's point of view will often be better understood."[14] Many have echoed these sentiments but few have followed them up. If Swift had wanted to find a church in crisis, he could not have picked a better place or time to go.

The Scottish and Irish stories are connected. Though largely neglected by scholars, both have something to say about the representation of religious crisis in Swift's work,

Let's take each in turn.

II

"We are surrounded on all hands by the most ungenerous and spiteful Adversaries," wrote an anonymous Episcopal clergyman from Scotland in 1696 in *An Enquiry into the New Opinions (Chiefly) Propagated by the Presbyterians of Scotland*. They "lay siege to the Foundations of our Faith, and it is with great difficulty that the publick Worship of God is not quite extinguished, as it is indeed despised and ridiculed: So grievous is our present Calamity."[15] In 1690, another clergyman had declared that "the Church of *Scotland* is at this time under the Claw of an inraged Lion; Episcopacy abolished, and its Revenues alienated; the Clergy routed, some by a form of Sentence, and others by violence and popular Fury; their Persons and Families abused, their Houses ransack'd, their Gowns torn to pieces, with many other Injuries and Indignities done them, which I forbear naming. . . . The Occasion of all these Disasters is, the prevailing strength of the *Cameronian* Party."[16] In 1692, yet another clergyman spoke with "Grief and Sadness" about "the present State of the Church of *Scotland*" which had at one time flourished "whereas now the Scene of Affairs is so much altered, that the Church is made level with the ground, and her adversaries take pleasure in the rubbish thereof; the Apostolic Order of Bishops totally subverted, and the greatest part of the Episcopal Clergy barbarously driven from their respective Churches" and replaced by those who "have all along trained up in Mechanick Employments, and have now leapt directly from the Shop into the Pulpit, where they exercise their Gifts."[17] In *The History of Scotch Presbytery* (London, 1692), we learn that this sect has "frequently disturbed, and now at last hath almost over-run the Church of *Scotland,* in that they have Ruined and Oppressed a Learned, Grave, and Orthodox Clergy, especially in the Southern Shires. . . ." The Scots Presbyterians, the writer adds, excuse or deny altogether the "shameful rabbling of the Clergy"; but it certainly "cannot be imagined that the Episcopal Clergy left their *Houses,* their *Livings,* and some of them their *Relations* and their *Country,* for no other Design than to tell Stories of the Presbyterian Persecution."[18]

These writers in the 1690s are responding to what has been called the "greatest upheaval in the history of the Church of Scotland."[19] This upheaval was initiated by the "rabblings" that began in south-west Scotland on Christmas Day, 1688 and continued for many months afterwards. As one historian notes, "When the Scottish revolution at last dawned in December 1688, its sword arm was provided not by the Prince's Dutch professionals but by the militant covenanting presbyterians of south-west Scotland. And the covenanters had their own private agenda, the first item of which was the destruction of episcopacy in Scotland."[20] One of many such reports on file in Lambeth Palace Library—"The Case of the Episcopall Clergie of Scotland"—summarizes the story in 1694: "During the Intervall after his M[ajesty's]ts [King William's] Arrival in Britain, and before his Accession to the Crown, the bigoted Party of Presbiterians in Scotland, without any order of Law, did in the way of Rabbling by a Mob, turn out the most part of the [episcopal] Ministers in the West and South of Scotland."[21]

The rabblings signaled the end of the Restoration attempt in Scotland to enforce church government on the episcopal model. Though "precise totals are unknown" most accounts agree that "somewhere between two and three hundred [episcopal] ministers were driven from their livings in the winter and spring of 1688–89."[22] Soon after, episcopacy was abolished in Scotland in July 1689 and an act was passed on June 7, 1690, to restore Presbyterian government to the Scottish church.[23]

That the rabblings began in southwest Scotland makes sense, for this was the Presbyterian covenanting stronghold that had twice rebelled against episcopal authorities (1666, 1679) during the time evoked most memorably in Sir Walter Scott's *Old Mortality*. As Bishop Burnet narrates the event in the *History of his Own Time*, "in the Western Counties" of Scotland, "the Presbyterians, who had suffered much in the course of many years, thought that the time was now come" to secure their liberty and revenge. "They generally broke in upon the Episcopal Clergy with great insolence and much cruelty. They carried them about the parishes in a mock procession: They tore their gowns, and drove them from their Churches and houses."[24] "To reward them for which," Swift ironically noted next to this passage, "King William abolished Episcopacy."[25]

As many private reports and published narratives indicate, the Episcopal Church was still reeling from these events well into the 1690s. Such titles as *The Case of the Present Afflicted Clergy In Scotland Truly represented* (London, 1690) and the *Account of the Present Persecution of the Church in Scotland* (London, 1690), collected and republished in 1693, told and retold the tale, as did works with more formidable titles like the *Protestations of the Scots Episcopal Clergy Against the Authority of the Presbyterian General Assemblies* (London, 1694). Historian Craig Rose says that the "impact of these events upon opinion within the English Church" in the 1690s "cannot be overstated."[26] It certainly can be seen in Swift. "The Scotch went further than the English . . . when the matter was all over,"[27] he wrote at one point of 1688. In the *Examiner,* Swift would ask "Whether the *Episcopal* Assemblies are freely allowed in *Scotland?*' and add that it is "notorious that abundance of their Clergy fled from thence some Years ago into *England* and *Ireland,* as from a Persecution."[28]

The rabblings themselves were mob activities that followed a certain ritual. A small, armed group variously known as "Society People" or "Cameronians"[29] would arrive unannounced and—as a 1690 account reports—"carry the [episcopal] Minister out of his House to the Church-yard, or some publick Place in the Town, or Village, and there expose him to the People as a Condemned Malefactor, g[i]ve him strict charge never to Preach any more in that place, but to remove himself and his Family out of it immediately; and For the conclusion of this Tragedy, they caus'd his Gown to be torn over his head in a hundred pieces. . . ."[30] In one rabble action, Mr. Robert Bell, minister at Kilmanock, was taken from his manse on a "very frosty Day." The rabblers "kept him four or five Hours bare-headed, exposed to the Cold" and "caused his own Sexton to tear his Gown in pieces from his Shoulders; took the English Liturgy from his Pocket, and burnt it with much Ceremony in the Market-place; calling him Papist, and it the Mass-book in English." Else-where, when the rabblers could not find the Minister of Gawdor himself, they grabbed "his Gown" instead and took it in a "Proces-sion to the Church-yard, made a long Harangue, concerning their Zeal for God's Glory, and the Good Old Cause"; then, after "a long Prayer" they "rent the Gown."[31] Another Episcopalian minister, who had hidden his vestments, was marched to "the most publick place in the Village" where he was told to put on his morning gown—for "it was necessary for a Gown should be torn; that was an essential Formality"—and "then rent it to pieces."[32]

As these examples suggest, the "essential Formality" in the rab-bling was the ritual tearing of the gown. This humiliation is noted with outrage in nearly all the rabble accounts of the 1690s. It is also Jack's main activity in *A Tale of a Tub*. "*Ah, Good Brother* Martin," Jack asks: "*do as I do, for the Love of God; Strip, Tear, Pull, Rent, Flay off all, that we may appear as unlike the Rogue* Peter, *as it is possible.*" Attempting to return the coat his father gave him to its primitive state and "being Clumsy by Nature, and of Temper, Impatient; withal, beholding Millions of Stitches, that required the nicest Hand, and sedatest Constitution, to extricate; in a great Rage," Jack, we hear, "tore off the whole Piece, Cloth and all. . . ." As a result, "a Meddley of *Rags,* and *Lace,* and *Rents,* and *Fringes,* unfor-tunate *Jack* did now appear: He would have been extremely glad to see his Coat in the Condition of *Martin's,* but infinitely gladder to find that of *Martin's* in the same Predicament with his." By the end of the story, "*Jack* and his Tatters" are inseparable: what "little was left of the main Substance of the Coat, he rubbed every day for two hours, against a rough-cast Wall, in order to grind away the Rem-nants of *Lace and Embroidery. . . .*"[33]

Martin for his part begs his brother not to damage the coat be-cause it is the only one they had and "*to consider, that it was not their Business to form their Actions by any Reflection upon Peter's, but by observ-ing the Rules prescribed in their Father's* Will." But Jack, Swift says, en-tered "upon the Matter with other Thoughts, and a quite different Spirit":

> For, the Memory of *Lord Peter's* Injuries, produced a Degree of Hatred and Spight, which had a much greater Share of inciting Him, than any Regards after his Father's Commands. . . . Having thus kindled and en-flamed himself as high as possible, and by Consequence, in a delicate

Temper for beginning a Reformation, he set about the Work immediately, and in three Minutes, made more Dispatch than *Martin* had done in as many Hours. For (Courteous Reader) you are given to understand, that *Zeal* is never so highly obliged, as when you set it a *Tearing*: and *Jack*, who doated on that Quality in himself, allowed it at this Time its full Swinge. Thus it happened, that stripping down a Parcel of *Gold Lace*, a little too hastily, he rent the *main Body* of his *Coat* from Top to Bottom. . . .[34]

Examining Jack's antics, modern readers have read the coat here metaphorically. Phillip Harth for example argues that both Martin and Jack "set about the task of carrying out their father's injunctions, as revealed by the will, and of removing the ornaments which have been added to their coats. In other words, the reformers set about recovering the pure religion of early Christianity by getting rid of the accretions which have been added to the fabric of religion." Martin "brings reason and moderation to the task of fulfilling his father's directions and restoring his coat to its original simplicity. Jack, on the other hand, proceeds with such fervor that he only succeeds in tearing and bedraggling his coat until, angered by the result and by Martin's attempts to reason with him, he runs mad from spite and vexation."[35]

This reading makes sense. But the ripping of the coat in the *Tale* can also be read literally, as it was in Swift's day, to refer to the rabblings. When Swift states that Jack "rent the *main Body* of his *Coat* from Top to Bottom," an eighteenth-century reader glossed this passage as "Removing Episcopacy, and setting up Presbytery in its room."[36] That is exactly what happened in Scotland in the 1690s. Given the notoriety of the rabblings during the time Swift was writing his religious satire, it is not surprising that when he shows Jack ripping his coat—for "*Zeal* is never so highly obliged, as when you set it a *Tearing*: and *Jack*, who doated on that Quality in himself, allowed it at this Time its full Swinge"—a contemporary would have noted the reference to recent events in Scotland. In these scenes, Jack the ripper becomes Jack the rabbler.

That possibility is strengthened by a recent discovery in Ximenes Book Store in New York City. Cleaning out the store in 1995, Stephen Weissman found a one page handwritten table of contents for a bound group of pamphlets that had been broken up to sell off in single copies. He sent the manuscript to A. C. Elias, Jr. who found it to be "definitely in Swift's hand."[37] One pamphlet listed is the "*Scotch Presb. Eloquence.*"[38] Swift refers here to a work written directly in response to the rabblings, *The Scotch Presbyterian Eloquence: Or, The*

Foolishness Of Their Teaching Discovered From Their Books, Sermons, and Prayers. First published in 1692, this pamphlet began a long run that would include a second edition in 1693, two new printings in 1694, and more throughout the eighteenth century.[39]

Noting that in 1696 Swift was "returning to Moor Park after a two-year dose of Presbyterianism in Ulster, where the Anglican church might be legally established but the Dissenters still were dominant," Elias comments that the author of *The Scotch Presbyterian Eloquence,* who "calls himself 'Jacob Curate,' is clearly an Anglican clergyman surrounded by hostile Dissenters, as Swift had been in Ulster." The pamphlet, he suggests, reflects a situation Swift "may have felt at Kilroot: William III's disestablishment of the Anglican Church of Scotland in favor of the Presbyterian Kirk, with resulting mob persecution of the dispossessed bishops ('prelates') and parish ministers ('curates'), winked at when not actively encouraged by Kirk authorities." Elias also points to several parallels between the *Scotch Presbyterian Eloquence* and Swift's religious satire, stating that the pamphlet's "real significance—which remains to be traced in detail—derives from our knowing that Swift actually *did* own a copy, and preserved it, during the very period that he was writing the *Tale.*"[40]

Elias correctly connects the *Tale* to *The Scotch Presbyterian Eloquence* and to circumstances in both Scotland and Ulster in the 1690s. Published under the pseudonym of Jacob Curate and sometimes attributed to Robert Calder, the Minister of Nenthorn ousted in 1688, *The Scotch Presbyterian Eloquence* is more likely the work of Episcopalians Gilbert Crockatt and John Monroe. Along with offering a direct source of information about the rabblings during the time Swift was writing his religious satire, this pamphlet has some striking formal and thematic affinities to *A Tale of a Tub. The Scotch Presbyterian Eloquence* opens with a tubbian mock-dedication and is then divided, like the *Tale,* into a series of numbered "Sections."

The mock-dedication is directed to Lord "E. C.," identified as the Earl of Crawford, the staunch Presbyterian who presided over the body that disestablished the Scottish Episcopal Church.[41] The dedication commends his lordship for his constant "study of those extraordinary Books cited in this Pamphlet" and for listening every day "for many hours" to those "wonderful Preachers of whom I now Treat." "Malignants" (the Episcopal clergy, that is) "may accuse the Books and Sermons here cited of *Nonsense;* but for as ill natured as the World is grown, they must own, that your L[ordshi]p has been very long, and very intimately acquainted with the truest and best *Nonsense;* so that being a complete Master of it your self, it must be allowed that you are also a very good Judge." To whom, the narrator asks, "should I rather Dedicate this incomprehensible *Rhapsody of Humane Eloquence?* This Treasury of *Holy Aphorisms.*" "Your Lordship's unexpressible Merit (for which I want a Comparison) naturally led me to beg you to take the following *Flowers of Presbyterian Eloquence* into your Protection, as cordially as you do the Authors of them: If your L[or]ds[hip]'s unknown Modesty would allow it, I would tell the World in a few words, some of your natural and acquired Endowments: To your Courage and Conduct which are equal, you have added such a success as to raise the Church and State of Scotland to be the wonder and amazement of the World." In that important work, he is told, "the *West Country Rabble* were highly enriched" by "your Lordship's Protection" and Scotland has been miraculously delivered "from all the Popish Fopperies of Cassocks" and "close sleev'd Gowns." As in this passage, the rabblings are referred to throughout: later, we learn about the "five men and six Women, *Presbyterians*" who came to the home of William Ferguson, Minister of Kilpatrick. Because "he would not alter his manner of Praying and come out of his House, as they had charged him, they therefore *invaded his House*" and "*tore off his Cloaths. . . .*" What a "delicate Set of Reformers we have at this time in the *West* and *South of Scotland,*" the author of *The Scotch Presbyterian Eloquence* exclaims. With what "learning and manner of Preaching . . . our Rabble Reformation has been wrought."[42]

The sections of *The Scotch Presbyterian Eloquence* that follow drop the ironic mode of address of the opening dedication. They lack the verbal brilliance of *A Tale of a Tub,* but take on similar targets and in language that seems almost directly out of the *Tale.* At one point we hear that "such is the force that a loud Voice, and a whining Tone, in broken and smother'd Words, have upon the Animal Spirits of the Presbyterian Rabble, they look upon a Man as endowed with the Spirit of God . . . especially if he can drivel a little. . . . The Snuffling and Twang of the Nose, passes for the Gospel-sound." At another, we learn that the "most of their Sermons are Nonsensick Raptures, and abuse of Mystic Divinity, in canting and compounded Vocables, oftentimes stuffed with impertinent and base *Similes*" and that the real effect of this preaching is "to create a more religious madness in poor well-meaning People." In this "sort of Divinity," our "*Presbyterians* have quite out-done the senseless old Monks."[43]

These lines of attack (including the concluding throwaway comparison between Jack and Peter) would be familiar to readers of the *Tale of a Tub.* So would the image of the preacher in a pulpit that becomes a "Tub."[44] In the *Tale,* the best pulpits we recall are "made of Timber from the *Sylva Caledonia*"; and the Aeolist's tub has a se-

A true blew Priest a Lincey Woolsey Brother
One Legg a Pulpitt holds a Tubb the other
An Orthodox, grave, moderate, Prestbuterian
Half Surplice, Cloake half Priest half Puritan,
Made up of all these halfes hee cannot Pass.
For any thing intirely, but an Ass

The Scotch Presbyterian Eloquence, 4th edition, 1732. [Crockatt and Monroe?]
Reproduced courtesy of the British Library. Shelfmark 15 78 5319.

cret funnel attached to his buttocks through which the priest receives "new Supplies of Inspiration from a *Northern* Chink or
Crany." This northern (read: Scottish) wind is the source of the
"oracular *Belches*" delivered "to his panting Disciples."[45] The pulpit
become tub also appears in a cover illustration of *The Scotch Presbyterian Eloquence* (Figure 1). Jack here has also done some damage to
his coat. Dressed in half cloak, half surplice, he straddles a tub and
a pulpit and points to the remaining sleeve of his vestments and to
discarded trappings of the Catholic Church. Thrown out with these
works of time is the *Book of Common Prayer,* on the floor at his feet
under what is left of his gown. Beneath the illustration, the inscription reads:

> A true blew Priest a Lincey Woolsey Brother
> One Legg a Pulpitt holds a Tubb the other
> An Orthodox, grave, moderate, Presbyterian
> Half Surplice, Cloake half Priest half Puritan,
> Made up of all these halfes hee cannot Pass,
> For any thing intirely, but an Ass.[46]

Along with these lines of attack, *The Scotch Presbyterian Eloquence* also
adopts what would become Swift's favorite method, letting Jack
speak for himself.[47] (In this, *The Scotch Presbyterian Eloquence* like the
later *Tale* models itself at points on another pamphlet listed in
Swift's bound collection, Estrange's *Dissenters Sayings*.[48]) In section
11 of the *Tale,* Swift's narrator notes that Jack's "common Talk and
Conversation ran wholly in the Phrase of his Will, and he circum-
scribed the utmost of his Eloquence within that Compass. . . ."
After giving several pages of examples of Jack's sayings—allowing
Swift to satirize not only Jack's Bible language but also his refusal to
kneel at communion and his belief in predestination—the narrator
states: "THIS I have produced, as a Scantling of *Jack's* great
Eloquence. . . ."[49]

The last reference may or may not be a direct allusion to *The Scotch
Presbyterian Eloquence.* More important is the context itself. The rabblings and disestablishment of the Scottish Episcopal Church created a major crisis for the establishment in the 1690s. That crisis
plays a role in Swift's characterization of "*Knocking Jack of the
North.*"[50]

III

By the time he was writing the *Tale,* Swift had not just read about
Jack but had seen him close up, which gets us to the Irish side of the

story. "According to the available evidence," Phillip Harth argues, "Swift wrote his religious satire in 1695 and 1696, that is to say, during the time he held the prebend of Kilroot."[51] On January 13, 1695, Swift accepted Episcopal orders in Christ Church Dublin and later traveled north to Kilroot to take on his first Church of Ireland post.[52] The prebend of Kilroot included three County Antrim parishes on the northeast coast of Ireland—Kilroot. Templecorran, and Ballynure. The churches were in disrepair and there were few parishioners to be found.

From Kilroot, Ehrenpreis says, Swift had fine views of County Down across the bay.[53] What Ehrenpreis does not say is that, on a clear day from Kilroot Swift could have also seen the coast of Scotland, twenty-seven miles away. Nearby Carrickfergus, where Swift probably lived, was the site of William's landing five years earlier. According to Swift's acquaintance William Tisdall, Carrickfergus was "situated in the Neighbourhood of *Scotland,* in the very Center of the Northern Presbyterians."[54] "[T]he inhabitants are all protestants," the Duke of Schomberg had told William before his landing there, and "most presbiterians."[55] The inhabitants of Swift's parish at Kilroot were, said a contemporary, Richard Dobbs, "all Presbyterians and Scotch, not one natural Irish in the parish, nor papist." In Swift's adjacent parish of Templecorran, the inhabitants were reported by Dobbs to be "all Scotch, not one Irishman or papist" and "all Presbyterians except the parson and clark, who I think is his son."[56] Swift did not have to cross to Scotland to see Scots Presbyterians.

Kilroot is across the North Channel not simply from Scotland but from *southwest* Scotland, the place where the rabblings began. The whole area of northeast Ireland and southwest Scotland was the very center of an age old battle between Church and Kirk. Swift's own prebend had earlier been held by a Scots minister with Presbyterian sympathies, Edward Brice, who came to Kilroot from Dryburn in Stirling.[57] By the time Swift arrived in 1695, County Antrim already had a long history as the site, for instance, of the first ever known Revival meeting (the great Six Mile Water Revival in 1626 led by Scots minister, James Glendinning); or later, of Bishop Bramhall's crackdown on Presbyterians in the 1630s and Thomas Wentworth's notorious Black Oath, requiring rejection of the Solemn League and Covenant, administered to Scots at Carrickfergus in 1639.[58] Just as Wentworth's repression had earlier sent Scots back to their homeland (his only complaint was that he had not sent them all)[59] so, after the Restoration, an Episcopal crackdown in Scotland had stimulated new emigration into Ulster. As R. J. Dickson notes, Ulster

became "more and more Scottish as the seventeenth century pro-
gressed, partly because of the proximity of the two countries and
partly because of the greater sufferings of the Scottish presbyterians
when compared with the lot of their co-religionists in Ireland."[60] By
the time Swift arrived, Antrim had the densest population of Presbyterians in Ireland.

What would have been a greater shock was the number of *new*
ones arriving daily. In 1695–96, Swift was there to witness the largest
single immigration of Scots Presbyterians in the entire seventeenth
century. In the mid 1690s, the availability of cheap Ulster lands coupled with a "very famous run of famine years" turned a long stream
of Scottish immigration into a flood.[61] Whatever we call this famine—the Four Hungry Years, the Seven Ill Years, or King William's
Years—its effects were devastating, particularly in southwest Scotland. Those who could get out did. Most swarmed into Ulster. The
"last yeares want of Corne in Scotland," one report in the 1690s
claimed, has "brought over not lesse than 20.thousand poore, & not
less than 30.thousd before, since the Revolution."[62] However in-
flated this estimate sounds, it may not be far off. Patrick Fitzgerald
has recently determined that the long-held view "that 50,000 Scots
crossed to Ulster in the years between 1690 and 1698 sits fairly comfortably with the Scottish population figures." He suggests a conservative estimate of at least 41,000.[63] Even a portion of that number
would have seemed staggering to residents of Carrickfergus or Belfast, each with a population in Swift's day of around 2,000.[64] "[M]ul-
titudes" of Scots "go over every day," a writer reported in the 1690s,
and "the whole North of Ireland is inhabited by that Nation."[65] One
"index of this mass Scottish invasion of Ulster," writes historian
Thomas Devine, was the "expansion in the number of Presbyterian
ministers and congregations by about 50 per cent between 1689 and
1707."[66]

The new numbers frightened authorities, especially those in the
already *out*numbered episcopal Church of Ireland. Fears were
heightened by the presence of a Calvinist king who had doubled his
annual gift or *regium donum* to the Ulster Presbyterian clergy and
who had recently allowed the disestablishment of the Scottish Episcopal Church. These fears were also fueled by the growing strength
of the Synod of Ulster, which had come out as a visible and powerful
presence and by its close ties to coreligionists in Scotland. An Ulster
peer complained in 1691 that the northern Scots were in league
with their friends back home and that "theire great aim is to gett
presbitry established in this province."[67] A letter sent to Narcissus
Marsh, the Episcopal Archbishop of Armagh in the 1690s, advises

that "it is said of the Church of Scotland that it destroyed it self. . . . Episcopacy was ruined by it & Presbytery establisht. God grant that the Church of Ireland may not follow the same fate."[68] William Tisdall reported a plot in the 1690s "to *abolish Episcopacy in the North* of Ireland, *according to the Model* of Scotland" using as its chief argument "*that that Country was entirely* Scotch" already, "*at least of the Presbyterian Perswasion.*"[69] After the destruction of the Episcopal Church in Scotland, Ireland was next. In 1697, Bishop Tobias Pullein pointed to the "many thousand families . . . settling this Nation within these five years." The "dissenting ministers among" them, he claimed, "are all zealous for the Covenant, and tis not to be doubted but that the whole body of the people . . . are of the same persuasion with those teachers. And all of em being lately come from a Kingdom where episcopacy is abolished, and Presbytery established . . . and their aversion to our ecclesiastical polity being so deeply rooted in their natures, and their obligation to destroy it so strongly inforced upon their consciences, there is great reason to fear that when their power and numbers are increased, they will employ their utmost strength, and most vigorous endeavours to overturn . . . the established church."[70] The Presbyterian "religion of this country," said Bishop William King, is "rather a national faction . . . and I doubt where it will end."[71]

The flood of thousands of new Presbyterians into Ulster in the mid 1690s turned such fears "into near paranoia," as one historian notes, and brought "a new dimension to the dissenting question in Irish politics."[72] Another adds that the "fear that their numbers or their cohesion might allow Presbyterians eventually to achieve religious supremacy was slow to die completely."[73]

In Swift this fear never completely died. Jack is not a powerless figure whose story is in the past. After taking Scotland, he is alive and well and moving on Ireland. What happened in Scotland in the 1690s could easily happen there. This fear propels the representation of Jack, whom Swift takes to be a serious current threat to the Established Church. It also underlies Swift's later resistance to any attempt to lift the Test Clause in Ireland, which Lord Wharton and others tried to do. Sounding much like Bishop Pullein had in 1697, Swift would state that "how we reason here in *Ireland* upon this Matter" begins with the observation that "the *Scots,* in our *Northern* Parts," are

> extreamely devoted to their Religion, and full of an *undisturbed* Affection towards each other. Numbers of that *noble Nation,* invited by the Fertilities of the Soil, are glad to exchange their barren Hills of *Loughabar,* by a

Voyage of three Hours, for our fruitful Vales of *Down* and *Antrim*. . . . These People . . . soon grow into Wealth from the *smallest Beginnings,* never are rooted out where they once fix, and increase daily by new Supplies. Besides, when they are the superior Number in any Tract of Ground, they are not *over patient of Mixture;* but such, whom they cannot *assimilate,* soon find it in their Interest to remove. . . . Add to all this, that they bring along with them from *Scotland,* a most formidable Notion of our Church, which they look upon, at least, three Degrees worse than *Popery;* and it is natural it should be so, since they come over full fraught with that Spirit which taught them to abolish Episcopacy at home.

This comment clearly reflects Swift's own experience of Antrim in the 1690s during a time he was writing the religious sections of the *Tale.* Given their growing numbers, organization, and cohesion, the Presbyterians' power in Ireland was potentially far more lethal to the Established Church than the threat posed by the proportionately smaller numbers of Sir Humphrey Edwin's followers in England (though Swift did not like them either). Were the Test Clause to be suspended in Ireland, Swift states, Ireland will go the way of Scotland and "the Consequence will be an entire Alteration of Religion among us, in a no great Compass of Years."[74]

Long after writing *A Tale of a Tub,* Swift would continue to dwell on this threat. Even after the start of a huge exodus of Ulster Scots to North America in the second decade of the eighteenth century, Swift points to the alarming number of Presbyterians remaining "in the *Northern* Parts, where there may be three *Dissenters* to one *Churchman.*"[75] In *Queries Relating to the Sacramental Test,* written in 1732, he asks "whether many hundred thousand *Scotch* Presbyterians, are not full as virulent against the Episcopal Church, as they are against the *Papists,*" whether they are already throughout Ireland "equally numerous with the Churchmen," and whether steps should be taken "to prevent their further Increase?"[76] Writing in *The Presbyterian's Plea of Merit* (Dublin, 1733) Swift would argue that "a *Scottish* or Northern *Presbyterian* hates our Episcopal Established Church, more than *Popery* it self. And, the Reason for this Hatred is natural enough, because it is the Church alone, that stands in the Way between them, and Power; which *Popery* doth not." The Presbyterians in Ireland, he claims, "will and must endeavour by all Means, which they shall think lawful, to introduce and establish their own Scheme of Religion, as nearest approaching to the Word of GOD, by casting out all superstitious Ceremonies, Ecclesiastical Titles, Habits, Distinctions, and Superiorities, as Rags of *Popery;* in order to a *thorough Reformation;* and, as in Charity bound, to promote the Salvation of their Countrymen: Wishing with St. *Paul, That the whole Kingdom were as they are.*" Once they gain power, he goes on to say, the Presbyterians, like Jack, will refuse liberty of conscience to all those who refuse to rip off the "Rags of *Popery,*" to all those in other words who do not think as they do. In a note to this passage, Swift reminds the reader here to "see many hundred Quotations to prove this, in the Treatise called *Scotch Presbyterian Eloquence.*"[77]

Although ignored in critical discussions of *A Tale,* the crisis Presbyterianism created for the Established Church in Scotland *and* Ireland in the 1690s is a key to understanding Swift's religious satire. This crisis offers a specific historical occasion for that most occasional of satirists. Responding to *The Presbyterian's Plea of Merit,* an anonymous eighteenth-century writer would say that Swift "is resolv'd never to own that the Presbyterians did one good Thing" and that his "whole Design" is "to represent them as a turbulent *Faction.* . . . engaged for *one hundred and eighty Years* in one uninterrupted Course of Rebellion and Disloyalty."[78] This comment is correct. It would be true, too, of the *Tale's* satire on the "Rabble Reformation" and the resurgent threat posed to the established church by "*Knocking Jack of the North.*"

NOTES

1. Jonathan Swift, *A Tale of a Tub To which is added The Battle of the Books and the Mechanical Operation of the Spirit,* eds. A. C. Guthkelch and D. Nichol Smith, 2nd edition (Oxford: Clarendon Press, 1958), 204–5. All further references are to this edition.

2. Robert M. Adams, "The Mood of the Church And *A Tale of a Tub,*" in *England in the Restoration and Eighteenth Century: Essays on Culture and Society,* ed. H. T. Swedenberg, Jr. (Berkeley, Los Angeles: University of California Press, 1972), 71–99; esp. 74, 73, 99.

3. Samuel Butler, *Hudibras,* ed. John Wilders (Oxford: Clarendon Press, 1967), part I, canto iii, lines 1081–82, 91. I have explored Swift's interest in his grandfather's experience of the Civil Wars and the Harleys' involvement in the Herefordshire County Committee in "Getting Gotheridge: Notes on Swift's Grandfather and a New Letter from Thomas Swift," *Swift Studies* 20 (2005): 10–29. Swift's interpretation of the part played by Scots Presbyterians in England in the Civil Wars is discussed in Christopher Fox, "Swift's Scotophobia," *Bullán: An Irish Studies Journal* 6 (2002): 43–66; esp. 46. Some material from that essay appears here with permission of the publisher.

4. *A Tale of a Tub,* 70 and 70n.

5. *State-Cases Put to Jack Presbyter* (London, 1681).

6. See Tim Harris, *London Crowds in the Reign of Charles II* (Cambridge: Cambridge University Press, 1987), 170.

7. *A Tale of a Tub,* 141–42.

8. Ibid., 142n.

9. Ibid., 58, 58n.

10. Ibid., 154–55, 155n.

11. John Spurr, *The Restoration Church of England, 1646–1689* (New Haven, CT: Yale University Press, 1991), 382.

12. *A Tale of a Tub*, [2]. *A Modest Defence of the Proceedings of the Rabble* is, as promised, dutifully mentioned later in the *Tale*, preface, 54.

13. Louis Landa, *Swift and the Church of Ireland* (Oxford: Clarendon Press, 1954; rpt. 1965), 21. More generally, on Swift and the Church of Ireland, also see Christopher J. Fauske, *Jonathan Swift and the Church of Ireland 1710–1724* (Dublin and Portland: Irish Academic Press, 2002).

14. *A Tale of a Tub With Other Early Works 1696–1707* in *Prose Works*, ed. Herbert Davis (Oxford: Basil Blackwell, 1965), 1:xvi.

15. *An Enquiry Into the New Opinions (Chiefly) Propagated by the Presbyterians of Scotland* (London, 1696), 2.

16. An Account of the Persecution (London, 1690), [1].

17. *A Letter to a Friend, Giving an Account of all the Treatises that have been publish'd, with Relation to the Present Persecution Against the Church of Scotland* (London, 1692), 3–4. The author lists nineteen works published by that point to date in the 1690s.

18. *The History of Scotch-Presbytery: Being an Epitome of the Hind Let Loose By Mr Shields* (London, 1692), preface, [i]–[ii].

19. Craig Rose, *England in the 1690s: Revolution, Religion and War* (Oxford: Blackwell Publishers, 1999), 214.

20. Ibid., 210. For the rabblings and history surrounding them, also see Tim Harris, "Reluctant Revolutionaries? The Scots and the Revolution of 1688–89," in *Politics and the Political Imagination In Later Stuart Britain: Essays presented to Lois Green Schwoerer*, ed. Howard Nenner (Rochester: University of Rochester Press, 1997), 97–117; and T. N. Clarke, "The Scottish Episcopalians: 1688–1720," diss. University of Edinburgh, 1987, esp. 1–72.

21. Gibson Papers MS 929, folios 18, 20 [2 copies], Lambeth Palace Library.

22. Harris, "Reluctant Revolutionaries," in *Politics and the Political Imagination In Later Stuart Britain,* 107–8.

23. William Ferguson, *Scotland 1689 to the Present* (Edinburgh: Oliver and Boyd, 1968), 8, 13.

24. Gilbert Burnet, *History of His Own Time*, vol. 1 (London, 1724), 804–5.

25. Swift, *Miscellaneous And Autobiographical Pieces, Fragments And Marginalia*, in *Prose Works*, ed. Herbert Davis (Oxford: Basil Blackwell, 1969), 5:290.

26. Rose, *England in the 1690s*, 214.

27. Swift, *Miscellaneous And Autobiographical Pieces, Fragments And Marginalia*, in *Prose Works*, ed. Davis, 5:264.

28. Swift, *The Examiner*, no, 30 (March 1, 1710) in *The Examiner and Other Pieces Written in 1710–11*, in *Prose Works*, ed. Herbert Davis (Oxford: Basil Blackwell, 1966), Vol. 3:100–101.

29. Ferguson, *Scotland 1689 to the Present,* 14.

30. *The Case of the Present Afflicted Clergy In Scotland Truly Represented* (London, 1690), 5–6.

31. *An Account of the Persecution of the Church of Scotland in Several Letters* (London, 1690), 17.

32. Ibid.

33. *A Tale of a Tub*, 139, 138–39, 141, 200, 199.

34. Ibid., 139, 137, 138.

35. Phillip Harth, *Swift and Anglican Rationalism: The Religious Background of A Tale of a Tub* (Chicago: University of Chicago Press, 1961), 16.

36. *A Tale of a Tub,* 138n.

37. A. C. Elias, Jr., "Swift's Corrected Copy of *Contests and Dissensions,* with Other Pamphlets from his Library," *Philological Quarterly* 75 (1996): 167–95; esp. 169.

38. Ibid., 189. Since no date is mentioned in the manuscript table of contents, we do not know which edition of *The Scotch Presbyterian Eloquence* belonged to Swift.

39. See *The Scotch Presbyterian Eloquence; Or, The Foolishness of Their Teaching Discovered From Their Books, Sermons, and Prayers; And Some Remarks on Mr. Rule's Vindication of the Kirk,* 2nd edition (London, 1693). All further references are to this edition. For this chapter, I have examined the following editions of this work: 1692, 1693, 1694, 1718, 1719, and 1732. Further editions appeared in 1738, 1748, 1767, and 1786. One spin-off was *The English Presbyterian Eloquence: or, Dissenter's Sayings Ancient and Modern Collected from the Books and the Sermons of the Presbyterians* (London, 1720).

40. Elias, "Swift's Corrected Copy of *Contests* and *Dissensions,* with Other Pamphlets from his Library," 178–79. The only qualification to be made here is that the rabblings began before (rather than after) the legal actions to disestablish the Episcopal Church. There were complaints, of course, that the rabblings continued long after. See also the later debate over the outing and imprisonment in the Edinburgh Tolbooth of Episcopal minister James Greenshields, in *A Letter concerning the Affair of Mr. Greenshields* (n.p., 1711) and the response, *A Letter to a Gentleman in London from his Friend in Edinburgh, Occasion'd by the Calumnies and Groundless Aspersions thrown upon the Revolution, and the Church of Scotland, lately printed in Several Letters, Relating to the Case of Mr, Greenshields* (London, [1711]). Swift mentions this controversy and "Mr. *Greenshield's* Case, who hath been prosecuted and silenced for no other Reason beside reading the Divine Service, after the Manner of the Church of *England,*" in *The Examiner,* no. 30 for March 1, 1710, in *Prose Works,* ed. Davis, 3:100.

41. According to Maxwell, the Earl of Crawford was a rigid Presbyterian known for his "piety and fanaticism." See Thomas Maxwell, "*The Scotch Presbyterian Eloquence:* A Post-Revolution Pamphlet," *Scottish Church History Society* 8 (1944): 225–53; esp. 236. For the question of authorship of *The Scotch Presbyterian Eloquence,* see Maxwell, 229–30.

42. *The Scotch Presbyterian Eloquence,* A2–[A5,] 54, 9, 16. Also see 14: "With what Violence did they flee to Arms, and persecute all who were not of their Party, upon the occasion of the late Revolution!"

43. *The Scotch Presbyterian Eloquence,* 5–6, 17–18.

44. Ibid., 102.

45. *A Tale of a Tub,* 58, 156.

46. *The Scotch Presbyterian Eloquence,* 4th edition (London, 1732), plate opposite title page. I have not found this illustration in any of the earlier editions I have examined.

47. In parodying "the unorthodox rhetoric of enunciation common among enthusiastic writers," Clement Hawes astutely notes that the narrator of the *Tale* thus tends to collapse "language about madness into the language of madness." See *Mania and Literary Style: The Rhetoric of Enthusiasm From the Ranters to Christopher Smart* (Cambridge: Cambridge University Press, 1996), 101. On this, also see Robert Phiddian, *Swift's Parody* (Cambridge: Cambridge University Press, 1995), 20. In letting Jack speak for himself, *The Scotch Presbyterian Eloquence* collects the statements of the most extreme Presbyterians and represents them as the belief of *all* Presbyterians. On this, see Maxwell, "*The Scotch Presbyterian Eloquence:* A Post-Revolution Pamphlet," 239.

48. On Swift's copy of part 2 of the *Dissenters Sayings,* see Elias, "Swift's Corrected

Copy of *Contests* and *Dissensions*, with Other Pamphlets from his Library," 182–83; on the same work as a model for *The Scotch Presbyterian Eloquence*, see Maxwell, "*The Scotch Presbyterian Eloquence:* A Post-Revolution Pamphlet," 228.

49. *A Tale of a Tub*, 191, 194.

50. Ibid., 2.

51. Harth, *Swift and Anglican Rationalism*, 7.

52. Landa, *Swift and the Church of Ireland*, 8.

53. Irvin Ehrenpreis, *Swift: The Man, His Works, And The Age*, 3 vols. (Cambridge: Harvard University Press, 1962–1983), 1:159.

54. [William Tisdall,] The Conduct of the Dissenters Of Ireland With Respect Both to Church and State. . . . In a Second Letter to a Friend (Dublin, 1712), 22.

55. "The Duke of Schomberg to the King" on August 13, 1689, *Calendar of State Papers, Domestic, 1689–90*, 220.

56. Richard Dobbs, quoted in Ehrenpreis, *Swift*, 1:160.

57. According to Allen Ford, Brice was still at the time a member of the Established Church and presented to Kilroot in 1613 by William Edmonston, a Scots planter. See "The Origins of Irish Dissent," in *The Religion of Irish Dissent 1650–1800*, ed. Kevin Herlihy (Dublin: Four Courts Press, 1996), 9–30; esp. 15, 19.

58. On the Black Oath, see Phil Kilroy, *Protestant Dissent and Controversy in Ireland 1660- 1714* (Cork: Cork University Press, 1994), 7. On Glendinning and the Six Mile Water Revival, see Ford, "The Origins of Irish Dissent," in Herlihy, *The Religion of Irish Dissent*, 25–26 and M. J. Westerkamp, *The Triumph of the Laity: Scots-Irish Piety and the Great Awakening, 1625–1760* (Oxford: Oxford University Press, 1988), 23–26. Carrickfergus, as Raymond Gillespie notes, was also the site of "the first presbytery in Ireland" established in June, 1642 by Scottish clergy accompanying Sir Robert Munro's troops, sent in to quell the rising of 1641. See "The Presbyterian Revolution in Ulster, 1660–1690," in *The Churches, Ireland and The Irish*, eds. W. J. Shields and Diana Wood (Oxford: Basil Blackwell, for the Ecclesiastical History Society, 1989), 159–70; esp. 159.

59. According to Clarendon, the Earl of Stafford, Thomas Wentworth said "at his coming from Ireland" that "if he ever return'd to that Sword again, he would not leave a *Scot[t]ish*-man in that Kingdom." "And it was a good Resolution," wrote Swift next to this passage. See *Swift, Miscellaneous And Autobiographical Pieces, Fragments And Marginalia*, in *Prose Works*, 5:298.

60. R. J. Dickson, *Ulster Emigration to Colonial America 1718–1775* (Belfast: Ulster Historical Foundation, 1966; rev. ed, 1988), 2.

61. See Gillespie, "The Presbyterian Revolution" in *The Churches, Ireland and The Irish*, eds. Shields and Wood, 169; and T. C. Smout, "Famine and Famine-Relief in Scotland," in *Comparative Aspects of Scottish and Irish Economic and Social History*, eds. L. M. Cullen and T. C. Smout (Edinburgh: Donald, 1976), 21–31; esp. 23.

62. British Library, Sloane MS 2902, folio 218.

63. Patrick Fitzgerald, " 'Black '97': Reconsidering Scottish Migration to Ireland in the Seventeenth Century and the Scotch-Irish in America," in William Kelly and John R. Young, *Ulster and Scotland: History, Language and Identity* (Dublin: Four Courts Press, 2004), 79.

64. According to Philip Robinson, Carrickfergus had a population of 1,758 in 1707. See *Carrickfergus* (Dublin: Royal Irish Academy, 1986), Irish Historic Towns Atlas, no. 2, 9.

65. Francis Annesley, reported to be "a member of Bishop King's circle," quoted in Rose, *England in the 1690s*, 254.

66. T. M. Devine, *Scotland's Empire and the Shaping of the Americas 1600–1815* (Washington, DC: Smithsonian Books, 2003), 29.

67. Viscount Fitzharding, quoted in Rose, *England in the 1690s,* 228.

68. "Unsigned Letter to Narcissus Marsh," Lambeth Palace Library, MS 929, folio 96.

69. [Tisdall,] *Conduct of the Dissenters in Ireland,* 45.

70. Tobias Pullein, *A Defence of the Answer to a Paper entitled The Case of the Dissenting Protestants of Ireland* (Dublin, 1697), 8–9 as quoted in Fitzgerald, "Reconsidering Scottish Migration to Ireland in the Seventeenth Century," in *Ulster and Scotland,* eds. Kelly and Young, 80.

71. William King, as quoted in Gillespie, "The Presbyterian Revolution" in *The Churches, Ireland and The Irish,* eds. Shields and Wood, 164. On this point, also see Patrick Griffin, "Defining the Limits of Britishness: The 'New' British History and the Meaning of the Revolution Settlement in Ireland for Ulster's Presbyterians," *Journal of British Studies* 39 (2000): 263–87; esp. 275.

72. David Hayton, "Exclusion, Conformity, and Parliamentary Representation: The Impact of the Sacramental Test on Irish Dissenting Politics," in *The Politics of Irish Dissent 1650–1800,* ed. Kevin Herlihy (Dublin: Four Courts Press, 1997), 52–73, esp. 52–53.

73. S. J. Connolly, *Religion, Law and Power: The Making of Protestant Ireland* (Oxford: Clarendon Press, 1992), 168.

74. Swift, *A Letter from a Member of the House of Commons in Ireland to a Member of the House of Commons in England, concerning the Sacramental Test,* in *Bickerstaff Papers and Pamphlets on the Church,* ed. Herbert Davis, in *Prose Works* (Oxford: Basil Blackwell, 1966), 2:116.

75. Swift, *The Advantages proposed by Repealing the Sacramental Test Impartially Considered* in *Irish Tracts 1728–1733,* ed. Herbert Davis, in *Prose Works* (Oxford: Basil Blackwell. 1971), 12:249. In a *Modest Proposal* (1729), Swift ironically refers to the exodus from Ireland as "the Absence *of so many good Protestants,* who have chosen rather to leave their Country, than stay at home, and pay Tithes against their Conscience, to an idolatrous *Episcopal Curate.*" See Swift, *Prose Works,* 12:114.

76. Swift, *Queries Relating to the Sacramental Test,* in *Irish Tracts* 1728–1733, ed. Davis, *Prose Works,* 12:255–56.

77. Swift, *The Presbyterian's Plea of Merit,* in *Irish Tracts 1728–1733,* ed. Davis, *Prose Works,* 12:272, 276, 276n.

78. *A Vindication of the Protestant Dissenters From the Aspersions cast upon them In a Late Pamphlet, entitled, The Presbyterians Plea of Merit* (London, n.d.), 4, 19.

A *Tale of a Tub* and the Great Debate over *Substance,* with Regard to Sacrament, Church, and Nature

Anne B. Gardiner

AN IMPORTANT CONTEXT FOR SWIFT'S *A TALE OF A TUB* IS THE DEBATE OVER the word *substance* that engaged theologians, philosophers, poets, and satirists in the seventeenth century. This controversy intensified by midcentury after Descartes gave it as a self-evident principle at the heart of his philosophy that *substance* or *body* (the words were used interchangeably) equals extension.[1] This was the same principle Calvin had given in his *Institutes* when he attacked Transubstantiation.[2] Previously, the word *substance* had been defined as the "internal nature" of a body, something that exists prior to extension and is beyond the reach of the senses,[3] but now it was equated to some measurable quantity. The convergence of Calvinism and Cartesianism on this meaning of *substance* or *body* marks the genesis of eighteenth-century rationalism. Jonathan Israel observes that the revolution in ideas launched by Descartes continued to be venerated by the eighteenth-century philosophes "as marking the true beginning of 'modernity' and 'enlightenment.'"[4]

Swift sounds the alarm in *Tale of a Tub,* especially in the Digression on Madness where he drops his mask and declares that Calvinism and Cartesianism are closely related forms of "madness," because only madness can explain launching "new schemes in philosophy" and new "religions" from a material source. These "mighty revolutions" originate in identical "vapors" rising to brains from below, and the only thing left to investigate is "how this numerical difference in the brain can produce effects of so vast a difference from the same vapour, as to be the sole point of individuation between Alexander the great, Jack of Leyden, and Monsieur Des Cartes."[5] In this key passage of the *Tale,* Calvinist Jack and Descartes are distinguishable only in a *numerical* way: both lack an immaterial soul, but their material brains can be *individuated* by weighing or measuring them in an autopsy. Thus, Swift wittily adopts the key principle of his adversaries—substance equals extension—and turns it on them with a vengeance.

He drops his mask again when he explains that sanity means believing in invisible substances behind the phenomena. Without Calvin and Descartes, "the world would not only be deprived of those two great blessings, *conquests* and *systems,* but even all mankind would unhappily be reduced to the same belief in things invisible" (82). His phrase *things invisible* comes from the Nicene Creed—*visibilium et invisibilium*—where God is the creator of things invisible as well as visible. Without the new *systems* that reduce substance to extension, everyone would still believe in realities beyond the reach of our senses, such as the mysteries of Christianity, because sane people naturally follow the wisdom of their ancestors: "For the brain, in its natural position and state of serenity, disposeth its owner to pass his life in the common forms without any thoughts of subduing multitudes to his own *power,* his *reasons,* or his *visions*" (82). The words *subduing* and *conquests* point to the militancy of the new "prescribers," and *visions,* to the merely private light on which they base their grandiose schemes for changes in religion and philosophy.

Much of Swift's satire in the *Tale* is about the Church and whether its substance is visible or invisible. When he names the Church of England *Martin* (for Martin Luther) and distinguishes it sharply from *Jack* (for Calvin), he alludes to the 150-year debate over *substance* in the sacrament. The Lutherans affirmed that Christ was substantially, but temporarily present in the Lord's Supper alongside the unchanged substances of bread and wine. As High Church bishop Samuel Parker noted, Melanchthon asserted "the *Substantial* and *Corporeal Presence.*"[6] Since the Church of England had been mostly *Jack* from the reign of Edward VI, Swift is being subversive when he gives it the name *Martin* to hint that his Church, rightly understood, is closer to the Lutheran. In many ways, Swift takes the Laudian view of his Church's history.[7]

There had always been a small number of Martins in the Church of England. Peter Heylyn wrote that the "first reformers" in England looked with more respect on the Lutherans than Calvinists, because the first "approach't more near the Primitive Patterns" and did not "dig up a Foundation" just because "some superstructures of Straw and Stubble had been raised upon it."[8] The hallmark of these Martins was their using the phrase "sacrament of the altar." Thus, as Heylyn notes, Ridley affirmed that "in the Sacrament of the Altar is the natural Body and Blood of Christ."[9] A century later, Bishop Montagu had to steel himself to say that Christ's body and blood are "in the *Sacrament* (I dare call it so in despight of detraction) *of the Altar*," and he urged the term *transelementation* used by the ancient Fathers for a change in the elements after consecration.[10] In the Star Chamber, Archbishop Laud famously said of the altar: "*there* tis *Hoc est Corpus meum*, This is my Body. But in the *Pulpit*, tis at most, but; *Hoc est Verbum meum*, This is my Word. And a *greater Reverence* (no doubt) is *due* to the *Body*, then to the *Word* of our *Lord*."[11] And Henry Thorndike, though he denied the Lutheran presence, still called Melanchthon more "learned" and "Christian in spirit" than Calvin and affirmed that by "the un-interrupted custom and practice of the Church" the consecration changes the bread and wine into "the Body and Blood of Christ *Spiritually*, and *Mystically*." Nor did he mean something subjective by *spiritually*, for he called it an "Errour in the Foundation of Faith" to believe the real presence was caused by the receiver's faith, not by consecration.[12] All these churchmen rejected Transubstantiation, but they revered the Lord's Supper as the ancient and continuous center of the Church's visible worship.

In a marginal comment on the 1661 Savoy Convocation, Swift wrote, "I think they acted wrong."[13] He was referring to the bishops who reinserted the postcommunion rubric of Edward VI in the Common Prayer Book of 1662 and defended kneeling for communion against the charge of idolatry on the ground that Christ's body was *not there*, but in heaven. Commenting on that rubric, Abraham Woodhead said it appeared to abet an "absolute non-presence of Christ's Body in the Eucharist,"[14] and Dryden lamented that the bishops in 1661 had changed not just the *substance* of their sacrament—"For *real*, as you now the word expound, / From solid substance dwindles to a sound."—but also the *substance* of their Church—"Your churches substance thus you change at will, / And yet retain your former figure still."[15] Samuel Parker, Bishop of Oxford, recalled that after 1660 his Church no longer mentioned the "*real Presence*," but resolved the matter into a "meer Sacramental Figure," though the former [Laudian] Church, while denying Transubstantiation, had asserted both "the *Certainty* of the real *Presence*, and the *Uncertainty* of the *Manner* of it."[16] Also, he said that when Stillingfleet (a spokesman for the new rationalist clergy) called "the Learned Men of the Church of *Rome*" mere "*Sots* and *Ideots*" for revering the sacrament of the altar, he was targeting high-church divines as well.[17] One could say the same thing about *Tale of a Tub*: Swift pretends to answer Calvinists outside his Church, but he is in fact aiming at those who were, after 1690, in high places within it.

In the *Tale*, Swift gives a sly Laudian defense of kneeling when he presents Calvinist Jack as making it "a part of his religion never to say grace to his meat." (93–94) Those inclined to Calvinism in the Church of England defended kneeling as avoiding "disorder" and signifying a "grateful acknowledgement" of benefits, but Swift goes much further. He speaks of saying "grace" before communion, which is a prayer, and then uses the word *meat* to hint at an objective real presence. Yet the new "*Rubrick,*" as Stillingfleet was happy to insist, accused of "*Idolatry*" any receiver who knelt to a "corporal presence of Christs natural Flesh and Blood."[18] Thus, the rubric glanced at Laudians who knelt to an objective bodily presence, however "mystical." In 1662, after the insertion of the rubric, Thorndike made a strong defense of adoration of the Eucharist against the new charge of idolatry in the Book of Common Prayer.[19] Like the name *Martin* for his Church, then, Swift's words *meat* and *grace* can be read as a cryptic confession of Laudian High-Church belief. Later, in Dublin, he would do just as Thorndike recommended[20]—follow "the primitive practice" of giving the sacrament "every Lord's day," and "he constantly attended that Holy Office: consecrated and administred the Sacrament, in person."[21] Even so, he regarded Transubstantiation as one of the "material points" of difference between the Anglican and the Roman Catholic Church.[22]

That *A Tale of a Tub* may be read as a satire from the High-Church viewpoint is suggested by the lavish praise it received from Francis Atterbury. This spokesman for the High-Church—one of only three churchmen whom Swift, in 1713, considered *orthodox,*[23] and one who made his reputation in the 1680s defending Luther against Abraham Woodhead[24]—wrote a letter to Bishop Trelawney on June 15, 1704, in which he called Swift's *Tale* "a book to be valued, being an original of its kind, full of wit, humour, good sense, and learning."[25] Note the word *learning.* To understand the *Tale,* it is evidently necessary to study it in the context of the learned debates of the late seventeenth century, the time when it was composed. Atterbury did not see read the *Tale* as the author's profane jest on church history. Rightly so, for Swift's loyalty to his Church, as one critic puts it, "appears at every stage of his ecclesiastical activity."[26]

The speaker in the *Tale* comes straight out of Atterbury's famous sermon, *The Scorner Incapable of True Wisdom* (1694), where the Scorner thinks he is alone "in the Right" and attacks sacred mysteries with a "Bold Jest," trampling on "those Truths, which the rest of the World reverence." Since he "imagines" everything is a "cheat and imposture," he ends up deceiving himself "for very fear of being deceiv'd by Others."[27] This is where Swift's speaker ends, too, embracing "the sublime and refined point of felicity, called *the possession of being well deceived*" (84).

In the *Tale*, Swift depicts the Primitive Church as three coats bequeathed by a dying father—visible coats, rather than the naked word (as in Bishop Croft's *Naked Truth*).[28] The brothers also receive at the same time a "Will" or "testament" containing "very exact" rules about wearing their coats. Just as Christ prayed that his disciples might "be one" (Jn 17), and promised that the gates of Hell would not prevail against them (Mt 16:18), so the father tells his sons to "live together in one House" and promises that their "coats" will remain "fresh and sound" as long as they live (34). The brothers have no names until they part, which occurs only in section 6, the second millennium. For a thousand years, they live together and agree on all kinds of ridiculous additions to their coats—a process of degeneration that starts early. For after just seven years of heroic wandering, the brothers come to town and are immediately seduced by a pagan "system" of idolatry, according to which "the soul was the outward and the body the inward clothing." Thus, the Primitive Church goes astray by agreeing with pagan philosophers that *substance*("soul") equals extension ("clothing"). Some professors of the materialist philosophy prove "by scripture" that "clothing" is divine, the *"all in all"* and the substance in which *"we live, and move, and have our being"* (37).

The brothers see that, to impress the world, they need to make changes to their coats. By way of a "Distinction" that is "immediately approved by all," the "Book-learned brother" twists his father's Will into allowing shoulder-knots. Without such an accessory to their coats, the brothers fear the world will think they have "no soul" (38). This passage echoes low-church Bishop Croft, who blames the "Primitive" Fathers because they "were very unwilling to abandon quite these their long studied and dearly beloved sciences, (falsly so called) and therefore translated them into Christianity, applying their School terms, distinctions, syllogismes, etc to Divine matters; intending perchance, through indiscreet zeal, to illustrate and imbellish Christian knowledge with such artificial forms and figures, but rather defaced and spoyled it." [29] Croft's phrase *artificial forms and figures* captures well the shoulder-knots, yards of gold lace, silver fringe, embroidered images, and tagged points that soon cover up the brothers' "very plain" coats. For Croft, *nakedness*—i.e., the bare biblical word—is the *substance* spoiled by any added articles of faith. He wants to return to the bare substance of the Church: "is not the body more than the rayment, substance more then Ceremony?"[30]

But Swift depicts the original Church as a *coat* because from the start it was vested with creed and sacrament.

Later Swift uses the word *substance* tellingly—first when he depicts Martin reforming his coat with care because he is resolved "in no case whatsoever that the substance of the stuff should suffer injury" (66); and second when Jack rips his coat to shreds: "What little was left of the main substance of the coat, he rubbed every day for two hours against a rough-cast wall in order to grind away the remnants of *lace* and *embroidery*, but at the same time went on with so much violence that he proceeded a *heathen philosopher*" (98). By getting rid of the *substance* of his coat, i.e., replacing the Lord's Supper with sermons, the Aeolist worship of "wind," Jack ends up with no worship, only a pagan philosophy.

Bishop Croft's 1675 attack on the early Fathers, echoed in the *Tale,* was answered by Francis Turner, later Bishop of Ely, who denied that the "Primitive Doctors and Fathers" were "*defacers* or *spoilers* of *Christianity*" by their "school-divinity and human learning." Without their "*Rational Deductions, an Human* (or Heathen) *way of argumenting* (as he [Croft] words it)," this high churchman insisted, those fathers could not have stopped the Arians from robbing the Church of Christ's divinity.[31] Thus the councils saved, rather than marred, the substance of the Church. Swift shares this respect for the ancient Church's decisions.

Andrew Marvell, who declared his admiration for Croft's *Naked Truth,* published in 1676 a similar attack on the early Church's councils. Only, Marvell's tone was different: he jeered at those councils, as when he called First Nicene (325) "the greatest Ècumenical blow that by Christians was given to Christianity," and when he treated the Nicene Fathers as Yahoos, "Bawling, and Scratching one another, as far as their Nails (which were yet more tender, but afterwards grew like Tallons) would give them leave." By imposing the Nicene Creed, he said, these Fathers had violated "our Saviour's Institution of a Church, not Subject to any Addition in matters of Faith" and undermined "the fabrick of Christianity."[32] His phrase *not subject to any addition* sums up the attitude of the *Tale*'s speaker toward any article added to the coats.

In a key passage, Marvell throws light on section 2 of Swift's *Tale.* He complains that the "great business" of First Nicene was "but one Single Letter of the Alphabet, about the inserting or omitting of an *Iota*" in a word.[33] This debate was in fact about substance, for the Nicene Fathers argued about the iota in the Arians' *homoi-oúsion,* and finally rejected it in favor of *homo-oúsion toi patrí,* meaning, of the same substance with the Father, for they wanted to assert that according to apostolic tradition, the Son is consubstantial with the first Person of the Trinity, not just of like substance. In the *Tale*, the great business of the three brothers is about the single letter "k" in *knot*. Just as the word *knot* and especially the letter *k* cannot be found in the Will, so *homo-oúsion* was not found in Scripture. The story of the shoulder-knots is a way of mocking the addition of an unscriptural word to the Creed. As Anthony Milton points out, Calvinists charged that "Rome's additions touched upon fundamental points" and led to "idolatry" and "apostasy," but the Laudians countered that Rome's errors were "only additions to the foundation." Laud was accused at his trial of having "identified no point of popery which overthrew the foundation."[34] Swift is close to Laud, for while he did not regard ancient councils as infallible, he still saw them and the Church of antiquity until the eighth century as "fundamental," insisting that they should not be publicly opposed.[35] He would have agreed with the high-churchman Hammond, who found it "piously credible" that God would not let "a Council truly General and Free" err in fundamentals.[36]

That the brothers keep adding new trappings to their coats without ever removing any of the old reflects how general councils were cumulative: the Church Fathers would repeat the Nicene Creed, confirm the decrees of former councils, and then add their own articles to settle a current crisis. After the shoulder-knots, the brothers add fifty yards of gold lace. Marvell offers a clue when he protests that nine creeds were made not long after First Nicene, because creeds were now in fashion and "whatsoever Creed they light upon, that was the 'catholic faith, without believing of which no man can be saved.'" The windings of lace make the brothers look as if "closed up in Bars," which again glances at Marvell, who laments that "every Creed was grown up to a Test"[37] (a measure of orthodoxy), while Swift defends the sacramental test as a way of keeping militant dissenters in check. Marvell's history of the first councils has a touch of sour grapes, for, as Charles Leslie observes, Calvinists knew that antiquity was not on their side, so they would "run down Fathers, Councils, and Ecclesiastical Histories, all in a lump." [38]

When the brothers want to add a flame-colored lining to their coat, they look for a "positive precept" in the Will, because a lining is "held by orthodox writers to be of the essence of the coat" (41). But the father's Will is of no use in this case, so the learned brother annexes a "Codicil" written by their grandfather's dog-keeper, which the brothers approve, and the old scroll is given "equal authority" with the Will. This passage seems to glance at the *Tome* of Pope Leo I, a letter sent to Flavian that was received with loud acclamations at the Council of Chalcedon in 451 as expressing the faith of the apostles. The Council treated it as a codicil to Peter's confession of Christ's divinity in Matthew 16:16, and the formulary of faith it issued—that Christ is "consubstantial with the Father according to divinity, and consubstantial with us according to human nature," and that these two natures are united "in one person and substance"[39]—was based on Leo's *Tome*. Again, the debate was about substance.

As the *Tale*'s church history unfolds, the brothers revive "an old Fashion, long antiquated, of *Embroidery* with *Indian figures* of Men, Women and Children." They have trouble adding these "*figures*" to their coats (i.e., putting images in their churches) because their father expressed "utter Detestation" of them in his Will (Exodus 20:4). So they agree on another distinction—"that these Figures were not at all the *same* with those that were formerly worn, and were meant in the Will" (42). The brothers' distinction parallels that of the Church Fathers at the Second Nicene Council (787), when they declared that images forbidden by Mosaic law were not the same as those of Christ and his saints; that only an honorary worship was given to icons (*honorariam adorationem*, or *dulia*), not *latria*. Once again, the debate was about things invisible and the unseen substance behind the phenomena, for Article VII of the Council cited St. Basil, "For the honor of the image passes to the original" and commented: "he who shows reverence to the image, shows reverence to the substance of Him depicted in it," and that "reverence to the image" is reverence to the substance of Him depicted in it."[40]

The High Church view was that Christians were not tied by the second commandment: Thorndike strongly defended images as "lawful," pointing to the Lutheran use of them as memorials.[41] Swift also defended images for historical reasons. But in one of many attacks on Christian art printed in the Restoration, Daniel Whitby sounds a lot like Swift's speaker when he says, "*Image-worship* looks so ill, it seems so manifestly repugnant to the Command, forbidding us to *worship any similitude of any thing in Heaven or Earth*."[42] Stating that he disagrees with Thorndike, Whitby blames the Fathers of Second Nicene for making false "Distinctions" between heathen and Christian imagery and between honorary worship and divine adoration.[43] Whitby represents the greater part of the Restoration clergy, who saw this council as the point where tradition replaced scripture as the rule of faith.

Tellingly, after they add those figures to their coats, the brothers lock the Will away in a strongbox. Here we reach the second millennium: for Stillingfleet charged that Pope Gregory VII was the first to restrain the reading of Scripture in the vernacular, on the ground it was "obscure, and apt to be misunderstood and despised," and after him Innocent III prohibited the laity from reading the Bible except for the psalms, and these not in the "*vulgar*" tongue.[44] In the *Tale* the result of locking up the Will is that the brothers add an infinite number of tagged silver points to their coats, i.e., rules about faith and discipline tagged with penalties, called decretals.

Taking up the history of church councils again in section 4, the speaker treats of the Fourth Lateran Council (1215), which defined Transubstantiation. Almost every treatise attacking Transubstantiation in the 1680s referred to this council. In the *Tale*, the council is depicted not as adding another accoutrement to the coats, but as causing the brothers' separation. Here again the topic of *substance* is of crucial importance. "Lord Peter," who receives a name for the first time, suddenly calls himself the eldest, sets up a "*Whispering-Office*," and orders his brothers to kick out their wives (51, 55). These actions refer to Pope Innocent III making confession a yearly obligation in 1215 and Gregory VII ordering married priests to put away their wives in 1076. The rest of section 4 is a scoffing account of how Lord Peter imposed Transubstantiation on his reluctant brothers. The speaker says, "I have chosen to relate this worthy matter in all its circumstances, because it gave a principal occasion to that great and famous *rupture* which happened about the same time among these brethren, and was never afterwards made up" (57). The phrase *about the same time* implies that the brothers began to split after 1215, and a *principal occasion*, that Transubstantiation was a main reason for the split. William Wake was typical when he said that Transubstantiation had been imposed by the "arbitrary" and "sole Authority" of Innocent III in 1215 and that it was the remote cause "of the Great *Reformation*"[45] In the *Tale*, Lord Peter swears: "G—— confound you both eternally if you offer to believe otherwise," an echo of the "anathema" appended to a definition of doctrine.

Section 4 is mostly a burlesque of the Catholic Mass, as supposedly instituted in 1215: Peter serves a loaf to his brothers with "all the formality of a city feast" and invites them to "fall to, and spare not; here is excellent good mutton" (56). This invitation echoes the consecration, "Take and eat, this is my Body," while the word *mutton* glances at the Agnus Dei, the invocation of the Lamb of God before Communion. Such ridicule of Holy Communion impugns the faith of high churchmen like Andrewes, Forbes, Montagu, and Thorndike, for they believed that the bread was changed supernaturally by consecration to another "use." In his scoffing tone, the speaker mimics John Tillotson, Archbishop of Canterbury, who asserted no other real presence when he ridiculed the Mass as a juggling trick, saying that the magician's *hocus pocus* derived from *Hoc est Corpus meum,* Christ's words at the Last Supper (Mt 26, Mk 15, Lk 22).[46] The *Oxford English Dictionary* still cites him for this etymology. The Catholic responder John Gother said that Tillotson had juggled with "our Saviour's own Words" and laughed at his "Institution,"[47] that he was an apostate, "another *Lucian* renouncing the Christian . . . to ridicule the most sacred Mystery of our Religion," to asperse the Gospels—as when, in his *Rule of Faith,* he called it uncertain if "any Book (for example S. Matthew or any other of the Evangelists), is so Ancient as it pretends to be, or that it was Written by him whose Name it bears."[48]

At that time, historical criticism of the Gospels was associated with atheism, so no wonder the high churchman Alexander Monroe wrote that "all the Atheistical Wits of *England*" were hailing Tillotson "as their true Primate and Apostle."[49] Swift himself writes that Tillotson is "the person whom all English freethinkers own as their head" and that he denies both original sin and the eternity of hell.[50] That the speaker in section 4 sounds like Tillotson makes it likely that this raillery is that of an ironic persona, i.e., the Scorner.

The High Church clergy did not use theological argument to defend their belief in real presence, but they expressed great devotion to the Eucharist and were far from the derision for mystery found in Tillotson. For example, Richard Fiddes, a clergyman who was once Swift's protegé, writes about the Lord's Supper in striking language, saying, we have here "a fresh and lively Scene" of Christ's dying agonies "open'd to the Eye of Sense. His Blood is again shed, and his Body broken before us; and the blessed Symbols of his Love are put into our Hands, in order to our feasting upon them." He calls it a "holy Mystery," where we "feast upon the Sacrifice of his very Body and Blood" and Christ "is still pleas'd to descend again as it were in Person from Heaven, among us." He defends kneeling because this "sacred Feast" requires "profound Reverence of Body, as well as inward Veneration of Mind." Yet his theology goes no further than that "in this holy Sacrament there is a Virtual Presence of the blessed Body and Blood of my Redeemer, and a real Presence as to all the Spiritual Benefits and Intents of them."[51] *Virtual presence,* as William Jane and Symon Patrick explained in 1686, is how "the Sun is *Really* in the Bowels of the Earth," and the way "*Christ* was *Really* in the Hem of his Garment (Mt 9:20, 14:36).[52]

In section 4, Peter's brothers have no inkling of even a virtual presence when they partake the "feast" of the lamb. They complain that it contradicts their senses to affirm they are eating mutton when they are eating bread. One of them protests, with an oath, "By G——, my lord, . . . I can only say that to my eyes, and fingers, and teeth, and nose, it seems to be nothing but a crust of bread" (56). This passage mimics Tillotson's raillery, as when he asserts that our senses must determine that "what we see and handle and taste to be *Bread* is *Bread,* and not the *Body of a man.*[53] John Gother complained that Tillotson "idolized" with the senses.[54] In the Elizabethan church of the 1560s, Alexander Nowel asks this key question in his official catechism: "What is the Heavenly, or Spiritual part of the Lord's Supper, which no sense is able to discover?"[55] His phrase *no sense is able to discover* is opposite to Tillotson's contempt for the mystery.

John Gother—a convert from Presbyterian to Catholic—noted that Tillotson had attacked "the Doctrine of the English Church concerning the Real Presence," and he challenged the "Genuine Sons of the English Church" to answer him and show they followed Andrewes on the "True Presence of Christs Body in the Sacrament."[56] Another convert, Joshua Basset, asked how it could be that a real presence had been held in the reign of James I, but now the sacrament was "merely figurative" without "one single Church of *England* Man (at least that I have heard of)" writing "one word in Vindication of their ancient Church: Nor one small Pamphlet to oppose the Innovation of these usurping Sacramentaries?"[57] The term *sacramentaries* referred to those who saw the sacrament as a bare symbol, like Zwingli. Yet another convert Edward Sclater charged that between the Reformation and the Restoration, the real presence had fallen into a real absence: "from that unhappily fruitful Womb of Separation, which gave leave to every one to coin his own Faith, sprang the Denyal of Christs real and substantial Presence, and the making the Elements bare signs and figures: From these a generation worse than them, that make them meer Cyphers."[58] This zero-presence is found in section 4, Tillotson, Wake, and Tenison.

Bishop Parker in the 1680s tried to explain that even for Catholics the real presence was not local and carnal, but "*sacramental,* after an *ineffable manner.*"[59] In 1544, Luther had made the same point in defending his followers from the accusation of being Capernaites,[60] "mad, senseless, raving people who held that Christ was locally in the sacrament and was eaten up piecemeal as a wolf devours a sheep." Luther's word *sheep* parallels *mutton* in section 4. Luther added: "even the papists have never taught such things, as they [the "fanatics"] clearly knew."[61] In fact, Wake admitted that Catholics and Protestants both taught that Christ's body was in the sacrament

"Spiritually" and differed only in what they meant by *spiritually*—Catholics meant that the body was "present after the manner of a Spirit," and Protestants, that it was "present to our *Spirit only*."[62] Yet though Wake said *after the manner of a spirit* in one place, elsewhere in the same pamphlet he mocked Catholics for failing to realize that "what all the World *Sees*, and *Feels*, and *Smells*, and *Tasts*, to be *Bread* and *Wine*, is not changed into the very natural *Flesh* and *Blood* of a Body before existent."[63] His words *smells*, *tastes* and *sees* imply that sense perception at the moment of communion is the test of real presence. So the presence would have to be local and carnal.

The issue of what the senses perceived at reception was a major point of debate. Against Jane and Patrick, Bonaventure Giffard, in a conference before the king in 1686, quoted Cyril of Jerusalem saying, "Judge not the thing by the *Taste*, but rather hold it by *Faith* for most certain, so as not to doubt in the least, that his Body and Blood is given to thee.[64] Gother collected many such passages, such as Gregory Nyssa saying that what appears to the senses has been trans-elemented into the "Body" of Christ, and John Chrysostom saying that Christ's words "cannot deceive, but our Sense may be easily mistaken."[65]

Joshua Basset calls William Wake a "Disciple of *Zuinglius*," and Wake himself confirms it by declaring that Zwingli (with whom Luther refused to shake hands in 1529, because of their great difference on the Eucharist) held the same view of the real presence as the Church of England.[66] Basset is indignant and exclaims that Bishop Forbes would spit in Wake's face and that Wake is not "worthy to have carried Mr. Thorndykes Papers after him."[67] He reveals a great chasm between the Martins and the Jacks within the Church of England at the end of the seventeenth century. The Jacks believed the substance of the Church was the naked word, not the coat.

Besides ridiculing the Fourth Lateran Council, section 4 attacks the Council of Constance (1415), where communion in one kind was instituted, on the ground of "concomitance," that the body and blood of Christ are both present under each of the elements. This council is depicted by Peter's giving his brothers "another large dry crust, bidding them drink it off" (57). Not long before, Whitby had published a lengthy attack on this council, accusing it of having debarred the laity of the cup.[68]

The story of the coats resumes in section 6, which tells of the Reformation. Martin and Jack acquire names as soon as they quarrel about the way to "reduce" their coats to "to their father's model." Calvinist Jack tears "the *main body* of his *coat* from top to bottom" out of hatred for Peter and even throws pieces of it into the gutter.

Martin begs him "not to damage his coat by any means; for he never would get such another," and reminds him that even though their Father's "testament" was "very exact" about how to wear their coats, it "was no less penal, and strict, in prescribing agreement and friendship and affection between them" (64–67). Martin's irenic view of the Roman Church is like Laud's, who said at his trial: "I have ever wished, and heartily Prayed for, the Unity of the whole Church of *Christ,* and the Peace and Reconciliation of torn and divided Christendom," but only such as would "preserve all the Foundations of Religion entire."[69] This view was shared by Swift, who approved of Charles Leslie's scheme to reunite the Gallican and Anglican churches.[70]

At this point in the *Tale,* the controverted term *substance* is applied explicitly to the Church of England as Swift, letting down his mask, tells how Martin "narrowly missed" doing irreparable damage to his coat at the Reformation when he pulled off the silver "points" (decretals) added in the Middle Ages. After that, he used more "dexterity and application" in removing "the embroidered" images of "men, women, and children" forbidden by his "father's testament," and he even let some embroidery remain whenever it was "worked so close" that removing it could damage "the body of the coat." Martin resolved "in no case whatsoever that the substance of the stuff should suffer injury" (65–66). What Swift means here by the *body of the coat* and the *substance of the stuff* goes right to the heart of the *Tale.* For the term *body* evokes St. Paul's name for the church, "Body of Christ" (Rom 12:5). Swift declares that Martin best resembles the apostolic Church because his coat is "well reduced into the state of innocence," but by leaving behind some embroidery, i.e., allowing Christian images and other liturgies that developed in antiquity, Martin keeps continuity with the visible Church of all ages.

A "mortal breach" ensues between Martin and Jack during the Reformation when the first will not follow the second and "strip, tear, pull, rend, flay off all" (67–68), the word *flay* implying that the Church is to be lacerated in her very body. The high churchman Turner had used the same word *flay* in his reply to Croft's attack on the first councils: "this is stripping the Church bare to the very skin, nay, skin and all must go, an Article of a Creed if need be. . . . Methinks he should have call'd his Pamphlet the Truth Fley'd, for Naked Truth is too short. . . ."[71] For Turner, an article of the Creed added by First Nicene is the very *body* of the Church.

Meanwhile, Jack founds a sect of Aeolists, worshipers of invisible wind who discover new forms of Eucharist—they *ingest* the "sacred belches" coming from their preachers' mouths, a communion derived from Delphi, and they take the "very skin of parchment" of the Will to be "meat" and "drink"—i.e., the literal text of the Bible supplants the Lord's Supper (93). Thus, Jack reduces Christianity to "*naked truth*," to the material Will without the ageless coat.

Swift's attitude toward the Scorner, who is his mask in the *Tale*, is well expressed by someone he greatly admired, Archbishop Sancroft,[72] who complained that the "*Reformers* of the *World* . . . Men but *of Yesterday*" think themselves "*better than all the Fathers*" and serve "all *Antiquity*" as "*Procrustes* did his Guests." Sancroft put the highest value on the ancient councils and traditions of the church, as when he defended the consecration of bishops as the "*Universal Practice* of the *Antient Church*," part of the constitutions handed to posterity by "*Tradition,* and *conformity* of *Practice;* and by Degrees inserted into the *Canons* of the old *Councils,* as occasion was offered, and into the *Ordinals* of several *Churches*."[73] For him—unlike the *Tale*'s speaker—the ancient councils were certainly not steps in the church's degeneration.

In the Digression on Madness, Swift does not say right away whether the identical, subterranean "vapours" that rise to the brains of Calvin and Descartes come from a physical or a metaphysical *below*. But he soon announces that "these active spirits" from below are like "those that haunt other waste and empty dwellings," alluding to Mt 12:44 (84). In other words, to reduce Christian mysteries to physical substance and measurable extension amounts to behaving like someone possessed. Swift sees the powers of hell at work in the materialism and irreligion of his day, but not in the ecclesiastical history of the Church, because as a Laudian, he cherishes an unbroken succession of bishops from the apostles to his day. This is why he shows Peter as absurd, not wicked, and implies that his coat is intact under all the additions.

Now Swift was writing the *Tale* at a time when the notion of *substance* as extension was being hotly debated. Even in Mary Astell's 1705 book on the *Christian Religion* we find her disagreeing with Locke on *substance* and glancing at the question, "whether Extension be the Essence of Body."[74] John Howe blames Aubert de Versé, who pretended to confute the impiety of Spinoza, for giving "*self-originate, independent Matter*" alone the attributes of both "*Extension* and *Thought*."[75] And Charles Gildon reflects that he has "no Idea of Substance distinct from that of Body," so his memory, wit, and judgment may derive from "the Mechanism of the Brain."[76] This is close to Swift's "vapour" rising to the brains of Calvin and Descartes to create an unheard-of philosophy and religion.

There was a larger European context for this debate about *sub-*

stance. In 1680, a Jesuit named Louis de Valois published *Sentimens de M. Des Cartes,* dedicated to the archbishops and bishops of France, in which he argued that Descartes' great principle related to *substance* was identical to Calvin's and that the convergence of the two was dangerous to the Eucharist: "il ne s'agit de rien moins que de conserver ou de perdre le plus saint & le plus auguste de nos Sacremens," i.e., nothing less is at stake here than preserving or losing the most holy and august of our Sacraments. The ideas of Descartes no longer have the charm of novelty, for they were held by Calvin, and now they holding up and offering a new support to a tottering Calvinism — "le Calvinisme ébranlé, & prest tomber, s'il ne trouve un nouvel appuy."[77]

In the last part of his book Valois gives a detailed comparison between Cartesian and Calvinist writings about *substance* in relation to the Eucharist. Although he was not the first theologian to remark that Descartes' idea of *substance* gave support to Calvinism, he was the first to devote a whole book to that topic. He focused on the definition of *body* or *substance* as extension ("l'étenduë"), which Calvin had given in his *Institutes* when he attacked Transubstantiation. Calvinists kept arguing from this definition that it was "impossible" for Christ to be substantially present in the sacrament without his being there in his full size and three dimensions. In reply, Valois brings in Jerome saying that Christ's body is present in the sacrament in the manner of a spirit, i.e., without extension. When the Calvinist principle became the key principle of Cartesian philosophy, the convergence of these two types of modernism on one meaning of *body* gave a huge impetus to the Enlightenment and its rationalist debunking of Christian mysteries—almost all of which had to do with *substance*.

Thomas Tenison, one of the bishops Swift despised (he called him "the most good for nothing Prelate I ever knew"),[78] published an attack on Transubstantiation in which he echoed Calvin and Descartes by equating *substance* with quantity and size, along with other exterior properties: "to talk of a Substance distinct from the Colour, Tast, Smell, and from the very Quantity and Dimensions also, is but a piece of Scholastick Nonsense." Tenison's drollery reminds us of Swift's speaker, when he says that if a man showed him a "little black dog" and told him it was no dog, but the whole city of Rome crowded in one place, even if that man raised twenty-five persons from the dead to prove it, he (Tenison) would reply that his "Sense and Reason" gave him "greater evidence that this is a Dog still."[79] In a pamphlet Tenison translated from the French, we find the same convergence of Calvinism and Cartesianism: in it the Calvinist La

Placette argues that it contradicts Descartes to say that a body is present "after the manner of *Spirits*," since in that case, the idea of a body can no longer be affirmed.[80] Moreover, Tenison puts a Cartesian emphasis on *certainty* when he contends that Transubstantiation "overthrows the certainty of our Reason," and "destroys the certainty of Demonstration." This emphasis on certainty is found in Tillotson, too, as in this passage where he harps on the word *certain:* "if this [Transubstantiation] be true and certain, then nothing else can be so; for if we be not certain of what we see, we can be certain of nothing."[81]

Atterbury was believed to have attacked Tillotson in his sermon, *A Scorner Incapable of True Wisdom* (1694),[82] published near the time Swift was writing his *Tale*. The Scorner will not believe any truth of faith, Atterbury observes, unless he has a Cartesian-style certainty of it: "He desires to be excused from entertaining any proposition as true which he doth not perfectly comprehend. If he cannot give himself a certain plain account in what manner, and to what end, God did a thing, he wisely resolves, that therefore he did it not at all. If he hath not as clear an idea of every term in an article of faith, as he hath of those in a mathematical proposition, it is presently unphilosophical, absurd, and foolish: invented by those whose interest it is to puzzle men's understandings."[83] Mary Astell also thought that Tillotson had no tolerance for religious mystery, and she quotes him disapprovingly for saying, "*Reverence due to Mysteries and Miracles in Religion, is only where they are certain and necessary in the Nature and Reason of the thing.*"[84] Swift was close to Atterbury in his reverence for mysteries, as in his "Ode to Sancroft," where he defends the mysteries in the manner of Pascal, not with rational argument but emotional resolve.

Descartes not only gave the same definition of *substance* as Calvin, but he also made it one of his clear, certain, self-evident principles on which his new philosophy was based. He advanced this definition in the strongest terms, answered objections to it (like those of Antoine Arnauld), and made it "one of the first principles of human knowledge." As more and more universities embraced Cartesianism—at Louvain, Valois alleged, fourteen out of sixteen professors were Cartesian—the new definition of *substance* as extension gave the deathblow to metaphysics. Pierre Bayle noted in 1684 that Cartesianism was attractive to the rising generation: "the young have a hundred times more pleasure in the new philosophy than in the old."[85] As Valois pointed out, they were now supposed to conceive of extension without thinking of it as the extension of anything that existed, because for Cartesians, *substance, space, extension, body,* and *matter* were all equivalent terms.

Before Valois, another Catholic theologian named Du Hamel had objected to Descartes' definition of *substance* and warned that philosophers must be careful "not to take up principles" that do not "seem to accord well with our faith, especially if these principles are based only on the prejudices of our senses."[86] His point, that Descartes' principle is grounded on *the prejudices of our senses,* is the same as Swift's when he lets down his mask in the Digression on Madness and shows Descartes inspired by a material vapor rising to his material brain.

Valois remarks that in the 1670s, when he is writing his book, French Calvinists are openly embracing Cartesianism. He says they "receive everywhere the philosophy of Descartes with great applause and send their children to study under known Cartesians, even when these are Catholics and priests, without any of their former anxiety. They see Cartesianism as a new support and give it vogue to confirm several points of their religion. In particular, they use Descartes to establish their heresy against transubstantiation."[87] Swift did not have to read Valois to learn about the new convergence of Calvinists and Cartesians on the principle of *substance* and how it was perceived in France as a danger to the sacrament. The news had made its way to England thirty years earlier, in 1665, when Oldenburg wrote to Robert Boyle and told him that Cartesianism is "distasteful to theology because it seems to favor the atheist and the heretics," and that the new philosophy shows "there can be no conversion of bread and wine in the Eucharist into the body and blood of Christ."[88] In 1671, Louis XIV condemned Cartesianism, but this did not stop its progress in the universities.[89]

Pierre Bayle, an author who interested Swift, compiled a little book on the topic in reply to Valois. According to Bayle, *Sentimens de M. Des Cartes* had greatly alarmed the Cartesians in France: they feared they would have to subscribe to a formulary or be excommunicated. Although they answered Valois, their works had a small circulation, so Bayle decided to publish some of these in 1684 in the *Recueil de quelques pieces curieuses.* Swift may have read this *Recueil,* for in the *Tale* he seems to borrow a joke from Bayle's essay entitled "Remarques." Bayle writes that men have an unruly *(déreglé)* desire to know, which is natural to them and the source of all their straying and misery. To stop them from being curious in excess, they should be allowed a harmless plaything like philosophy, as an exercise for their curiosity, to keep them from attacking religion. Swift adapts this joke to the English scene by having his speaker urge that religion could serve as a harmless plaything or "tub" that will amuse the freethinking Leviathan and keep him from endangering the English government.[90]

Bayle was only joking, because in the "Avis au lecteur," he says something quite different: there he presents the Cartesian philosophy as no harmless plaything but an instrument designed to end the 150-year controversy over the real presence. He concedes that Louis de Valois is correct about the "Doctrine" of Descartes being "absolument incompatible" with the Council of Trent's declaration on Transubstantiation. He confides that this is the very reason he has published his *Recueil*—to resolve once and for all the "celebre controverse de la Réalité" (i.e., this famous controversy over the Reality [i.e., of Christ's body in the Lord's Supper]). There will be peace in Europe only when Catholics accept that Transubstantiation is "impossible" and find another mode of real presence with which Calvinists can agree. Thus, Bayle hopes to reconcile *all* Christians under the aegis of Descartes. In fact, he thinks the strife is virtually over. No need to "torment" ourselves any more about interpreting *This is my Body*, he exclaims. "Let the Catholic Church pile volume on volume to prove the literal sense," and just "two pages will suffice us to confound her, in which we will prove to her geometrically that just as it is impossible that there should be an equality between one and nothing, so it is impossible that a body be in some place with the penetration of parts." The phrase *penetration of parts* means without extension. Bayle's proof against Transubstantiation, note well, will be *geometrical.* A religious controversy is now to be resolved by science! When he speaks of piling volume upon volume, Bayle refers to the huge tomes of *La Grande Perpetuité,* a work by Pierre Nicole (but then attributed to Arnauld) in defense of the Eucharist, remarkable for the fact that in this enterprise Jesuits and Jansenists were collaborators.

The Digression on Madness in the *Tale* represents what happens to those who embrace the idea that *substance* is merely extension. They no longer see a *soul* or an interior *substance* in other human beings, but only layer upon layer of raw matter that only gets uglier and uglier the farther they probe beneath the skin. The speaker complains: "Last week I saw a woman *flayed,* and you will hardly believe how much it altered her person for the worse," and when the carcass of a beau was stripped and opened for dissection in his presence, the "defects" only increased in "number and bulk." In revulsion at a world that is only material through and through, the speaker resolves to be happy with Epicurus, content "with the *films* and *images*" that fly off "the *superficies* of things," never again to probe the depths (84). The word *superficies,* about which Descartes had written, meant two dimensions, like the surface of a playing card.

When he lets down his mask, Swift ridicules the dogmatism of Calvin and Descartes and wonders what "faculty of the soul" can make someone advance "new systems" in matters "agreed on all hands impossible to be known." The phrase *impossible to be known* glances at interior realities and religious mysteries. Each mad prescriber in religion and philosophy thinks he has the "power to reduce the notions of all mankind exactly to the same length, and breadth, and height of his own" (80). And he finds "implicit disciples" without fail because their brains, too, are only material strings wound to the "right key" and so they strike in "necessary sympathy" at the same time" (93). Thus, the very thoughts of Jack and Descartes have length, breadth, and height and a predictable, deterministic effect. They are just quantity and extension through and through. Swift might be thinking here of Bayle's claim that he could give a *geometrical* confutation of the real presence, and of Spinoza's boast that his system in the *Ethic* was "geometrical." Again, Swift describes Descartes' thought as a material vortex in danger of sucking other vortices into his own: "Cartesius reckoned to see, before he died, the sentiments of all philosophers, like so many lesser stars in his *romantic* system, wrapped and drawn within his own *vortex*" (80). Surely, in such passages Swift is turning the tables on Calvin and Descartes and making the chief principle of his adversaries the very basis of his satire against them.

The point Swift makes about modernist thought having "length, breadth, and height" is important. He is saying that Cartesian and Calvinist dualism, where thought is the second "substance," is unstable and quickly collapses into materialism, where the products of the brain are added to substance as extension. Valois pointed out that the definition of *body* or *substance* as extension came from geometry, where *body* was defined as a quantity called *depth,* as distinguished from *line* and *surface.* So Cartesians simply took the geometers' definition of *body* and applied to *bodies* in the natural world. The Cartesian Pierre Cally argued that Descartes was not the first philosopher to define *body* as extension and cited as proof the ancient philosopher Ammonius. But Valois replied that in the passage Cally quoted, Ammonius spoke as a *geometer.* When writing as a philosopher, Ammonius always used *body* to mean a being or subject that was extended, but when writing about geometry, he used *body* to mean a quantity called *depth,* distinguished from *line* and *surface.* And then, in reply to Cally's claim that Augustine had also defined *body* as extension, Valois said that in that quoted passage Augustine had spoken as a geometer, not a philosopher, and had explained elsewhere that when he used the term *body* to mean the quantity called *depth*, he was not speaking of a natural body or "substance," but of *body* as distinguished from *line* and *surface*.[91] Thus, the Cartesians were doing something unheard-of in antiquity—transferring the definition of *body* as *extension* from geometry to natural philosophy, blurring the line between mathematics and reality, and relegating religious mystery to the sphere of the irrational.

In the seventeenth century, mathematics replaced religion and metaphysics as the key to ultimate reality. Suddenly, *substance* in the real world meant only extension. No longer were a multitude of underlying realities or invisible subjects thought to lie behind the phenomena. As the Cartesian Malebranche put it, matter was to be thought of henceforth as one sole being and substance in which extension diversely figured and agitated created all that is seen in the material world.[92] At one stroke, a whole vast universe of individual substances was swept away, leaving behind a single substance—pure matter diversely modified. Swift, like Pascal, is a quixotic figure fighting a lonely rearguard battle against the loss of mystery. *A Tale of a Tub* is an early version of the satire on irreligion that informs *Gulliver's Travels.*

NOTES

1. R. S. Woolhouse, *Descartes, Spinoza, Leibniz: the Concept of Substance in Seventeenth-Century Metaphysics* (London: Routledge, 1993).

2. "On the Reality of Christ's Body," book 4, chapter 17, section 29, in the *Institutes of the Christian Religion,* 2 volumes, edited by John T. McNeill, translated by Ford Lewis Battles (Philadelphia: Westminster Press, 1960), 2:1400. Calvin says, "But it is the true nature of a body to be contained in space, to have its own dimensions and its own shape. Away, then, with this stupid fiction which fastens both men's minds and Christ to bread!"

3. John Gother, *An Answer to a Discourse against Transubstantiation* (London: Brabazon Aylmer and William Rogers, 1687), 5.

4. Jonathan I. Israel, *Radical Enlightenment: Philosophy and the Making of Modernity 1650–1750* (Oxford: Oxford University Press, 2001), 24.

5. *A Tale of a Tub and Other Works,* edited by Angus Ross and David Woolley (Oxford: Oxford University Press, 1986), 82.

6. [Samuel Parker, Bishop of Oxford], *Reasons for Abrogating the Test Imposed upon all Members of Parliament Anno 1678* (London, 1688), 31. Parker mentions Luther's condemnation in 1545 of those who made the real presence figurative.

7. Nicholas Tyacke, "Archbishop Laud," in *The Early Stuart Church, 1603–1642,* edited by Kenneth Fincham (Stanford, CA: Stanford University Press, 1993), 57.

8. Peter Heylyn, *Cyprianus Anglicus: or, the History of the Life and Death of the Most*

Reverend and Renowned Prelate William [Laud], by Divine Providence, Lord Archbishop of Canterbury (Dublin: John Hyde and Robert Owen, 1719), 3.

9. Ibid., 14–15.

10. Richard Montagu, *Appello Caesarem: A Just Appeale from Two Unjust Informers* (London: Matthew Lownes, 1625), 294–96.

11. William Laud, *A Speech concerning Innovations in the Church* (London, 1637). Facsimile reprint (Amsterdam: Da Capo Press, Theatrum Orbis Terrarum Ltd., 1971), 47.

12. Herbert Thorndike, *Just Weights and Measures; that is, the Present state of Religion Weighed in the Balance, and Measured by the Standard of the Sanctuary* (London: J. Martyn, 1680), 215, 95. The remark on Melanchthon is on 251, where he adds that the Church of England differs from both the Lutheran and the Calvinist, so why follow either except "as it agrees with the Catholick [i.e., Primitive] Church?"

13. Jonathan Swift, *Miscellaneous and Autobiographical Pieces Fragments and Marginalia,* edited by Herbert Davis (Oxford: Basil Blackwell, 1969). Note on Gilbert Burnet, *History of His Own Times,* 270.

14. [Abraham Woodhead], *Animadversions upon the Alterations of the Rubrick in the Communion Service in the Common-Prayer-Book of the Church of England,* the first of *Two Discourses concerning the Adoration of our Saviour in the Eucharist.* (Oxford: Obadiah Walker, 1687), 32. One the chief spokesmen for Catholics in the Restoration, Woodhead (a fellow of University College, Oxford) had been High Church before he converted to Catholicism in the 1650s.

15. *The Hind and the Panther* (1687), 2:46–51, in *Poems 1685–1692,* edited Earl Miner and Vinton A. Dearing, in *The Works of John Dryden,* ed. H. T. Swedenberg, Jr., et al., 20 vols. (Berkeley: University of California Press, 1956), 3:141.

16. Parker, 47, 66.

17. Ibid., 70.

18. Edward Stillingfleet, *A Discourse Concerning the Idolatry Practised in the Church of Rome, and the hazard of Salvation in the Communion of it.* 2nd edition (London: Henry Mortlock, 1672), 103, 93.

19. Thorndike, *Just Weights,* 5, 125–26. He even says regarding kneeling, "Were worshipping the Host Idolatry; Christianity using the gesture of kneeling to signifie the worship of Christ, were enough to sanctifie it to Gods service."

20. Ibid., 154: "the pretense of Reformation is not made good, till . . . the Eucharist be celebrated all Sundays and Festivals, in all Churches and Chappels." Also, 96, 161.

21. Patrick Delany, *Observations upon Lord Orrery's Remarks on the Life and Writings of Dr Jonathan Swift* (London, 1754), 46–47.

22. *A Preface to the B–p of S-r-m's Introduction to the Third Volume of the History of the Reformation of the Church of England,* by Gregory Misosarum [Swift], 2nd edition (1713), in *Writings on Religion and the Church, The Prose Works of Jonathan Swift,* edited by Temple Scott, 2nd edition (London: George Bell and Sons, 1909), 4:153.

23. Ibid., 4:173, 187.

24. He answered Woodhead's *Concerning the Spirit of Martin Luther,* the first of *Two Discourses* (Oxford: Obadiah Walker, 1687).

25. *Memoirs and Correspondence of Francis Atterbury, D. D., Bishop of Rochester,* ed. Folkestone Williams, 2 vols. (London: W. H. Allen, 1869), 1:99.

26. J. C. Beckett, "Swift as an Ecclesiastical Statesman," in *Fair Liberty Was All His Cry,* edited, A. Norman Jeffares (London: Macmillan and St. Martin's, 1967), 162.

27. Francis Atterbury, *The Scorner Incapable of True Wisdom: a Sermon before the Queen at White-Hall, October 28. 1694* (London: Thomas Bennet, 1694), 6, 10.

28. [Herbert Croft], *The Naked Truth. Or, the True State of the Primitive Church. By an Humble Moderator.* (n. pl. 1675), 18.

29. Ibid., 5

30. Ibid., 17.

31. [Francis Turner], *Animadversions upon a Late Pamphlet Entituled the Naked Truth; or the True State of the Primitive Church* (London: Benjamin Tooke, 1676), 6, 9–10.

32. Andrew Marvell, *A Short Historical Essay touching General Councils, Creeds, and other Impositions in Matters of Religion.* (London, 1680), 19, 29.

33. Ibid., 20.

34. Anthony Milton, *Catholic and Reformed: the Roman and Protestant Churches in English Protestant Thought 1600–1640* (Cambridge: Cambridge University Press, 1995), 180–84.

35. See my essay "Swift and the Idea of the Primitive Church," in *Sustaining Literature,* edited by Greg Clingham, forthcoming.

36. Turner, 21. He cites Hammond's *Paraenesis.*

37. Marvell, 25, 30.

38. *A Dissertation concerning the Use and Authority of Ecclesiastical History. In a Letter to Mr. Samuel Parker on his Abridgment of Josephus* (1703), in *The Theological Works of the Reverend Mr. Charles Leslie,* 2 volumes (London: W. Bowyer, 1721), 1:730.

39. "Council of Chalcedon," in Henry Denzinger's *Enchiridion Symbolorum,* translated under the title, *The Sources of Catholic Dogma,* by Roy J. Deferrari (Fitzwilliam, NH: Loreto, 1955), 60.

40. "Council of Nicea II," 787, in Denzinger, 302.

41. Thornkike, *Just Weights,* 167–68, 200–201. See also 127.

42. [Daniel Whitby], *The Fallibility of the Roman Church, Demonstrated from the manifest Error of the 2d Nicene and Trent Councils, which assert, that the Veneration and Honorary Worship of Images, is a Tradition Primitive and Apostolical* (London: Randal Taylor, 1687), 38.

43. Ibid., 44–45, 50–51.

44. [Edward Stillingfleet], *The Council of Trent Examin'd and Disprov'd by Catholick Tradition* (London: Henry Mortlock, 1688), 57–58.

45. William Wake, *A Discourse of the Holy Eucharist, in the Two Great Points of the Real Presence and the Adoration of the Host in Answer to the Two Discourses [by Abraham Woodhead] lately Printed at Oxford on this Subject.* 2nd edition (London: Richard Chiswell, 1688), vii–viii, 31.

46. [John Tillotson], *A Discourse against Transubstantiation* (London: Brabazon Aylmer and William Rogers, 1684), 34. This key work was reprinted in 1685, 1722, and 1728.

47. John Gother, *An Answer to a Discourse against Transubstantiation* (London: Henry Hills, 1687), 74–75, 80. Gother, a secular priest, had been a Presbyterian and had converted to Catholicism.

48. John Gother, *Transubstantiation Defended . . . against a Discourse against Transubstantiation* (London: Henry Hills, 1687), 7, 3.

49. Alexander Monroe, *The Charge of Socinianism against Dr Tillotson Consider'd,* 13, cited in [Sir Robert Howard], *A Twofold Vindication of the late Arch-Bishop of Canterbury* (London, 1696), 29.

50. *Mr. C——ns's Discourse of Freethinking Put into Plain English* (1713), in Swift, *Prose Works* 3:191, 177.

51. R[ichard] Fiddes, *A Preparative to the Lord's Supper. Or, a Discourse, wherein the Nature of this Holy Sacrament, the Ends for which it was instituted, the Duties pre-requir'd,*

in order to a more worthy Receiving of it, are consider'd . . . To which is added, An Appendix, with Meditations and Prayers . . . with Devotions proper before, and at the Time of receiving this Holy Sacrament, and after it. 2nd edition (London: Bernard Lintott, 1718), 35, 93–95, 135–36, 104–5.

52. [Bonaventure Giffard], *A Relation of a Conference before his Majesty, and the Earl of Rochester . . . concerning the Real Presence and Transubstantiation, Nov. 30, 1686. Now publish'd to Obviate the false Account given thereof, by Laurence Echard A. M. in his History of England* (N. p. 1722), 4.

53. Tillotson, *Discourse*, 2.

54. Gother, *An Answer to a Discourse [Tillotson's] against Transubstantiation.* (London: Henry Hills, 1687), 9, 36, 80.

55. Heylyn, *Cyprianus Anglicus*, 16.

56. Gother, *Transubstantiation Defended*, Preface, A2.

57. Joshua Basset, *Reason and Authority . . . together with Remarks upon some late Discourses against Transubstantiation* (London: Henry Hills, 1687), 64.

58. *Consensus Veterum: or, the Reasons of Edward Sclater Minister of Putney, for his Conversion to the Catholic Faith and Communion* (London: Henry Hills, 1686), 97.

59. Parker, 21, 26.

60. The word *Capernaites* refers to those who abandoned Christ in John 6, imagining that he meant cannibalism when he said his flesh was "food indeed."

61. *Brief Confession concerning the Holy Sacrament* (1544), translated by Martin E. Lehmann, in *Luther's Works*, 55 volumes, edited by Jaroslav Pelikan and Helmut T. Lehmann (Philadelphia: Fortress Press, 1971), 38:292–93.

62. Wake, 61–66.

63. Ibid., 11.

64. Giffard, 13, citing Cyril's *Catechetical Discourses*. In reply, Jane and Patrick question whether Cyril wrote this, and Giffard replies, these works were attributed to Cyril by Jerome and others until Rivetus, a Calvinist, raised doubts "by his frivolous conjectures."

65. Gother, *Nubes Testium* (London: Henry Hills, 1686), 118, 121. This was a major work that provoked a volley of pamphlets in rejoinder.

66. Wake, 83.

67. Basset, 71. 82–83.

68. Daniel Whitby, *A Demonstration that the Church of Rome, and her Councils have Erred* (London: Randal Taylor, 1688), 21–28, 33, 41, 52–55, 65.

69. [Henry Wharton], *The History of the Troubles and Tryal of . . . William Laud* (London: Richard Chiswell, 1695),159. In one of the fourteen articles of impeachment, Laud was charged with having "trayterously and wickedly endeavoured to reconcile England and Rome."

70. *The True Notion of the Catholick Church, in a Letter to the late Bishop of Meaux, written by the Reverend Mr. Charles Lesley [26 September 1703].* (London: Richard Sare, 1705), 313. Swift approves of this scheme in *A Preface to the B-p, Prose Works.* 4:79–80.

71. Turner, "To the Reader."

72. See his "Ode to Sancroft," written around the same period as the *Tale*.

73. *Occasional Sermons Preached by . . . Sancroft* (London: Thomas Bassett, 1694), 26.

74. Astell, 251.

75. John Howe, *The Living Temple* (London: R. Clavell, J. Robinson, and A & J Churchill, 1702), part 2, 1, 57.

76. Charles Gildon, *The Oracles of Reason* (London, 1693), 186–88.

77. "Epistre, a Messeigneurs les Archevesques et Evesques de France," in Louis

de la Ville [pseudonym], *Sentimens de M Des Cartes touchant l'essence & les proprietez du corps, opposez a la doctrine de l'Eglise, et conformes aux erreurs de Calvin, sur le suject de l'Eucharistie* (Paris: Estienne Michallet, 1680), [unpaginated] *a v.*

78. Swift, *Miscellaneous,* 260.

79. [Thomas Tenison], *Of Transubstantiation: or, a Reply to a Late Paper, call'd, a Full Answer to Dr. Tenison's Conferences concerning the Eucharist* (London: Richard Chiswell, 1688), 1–2.

80. M. De la Placette, *Six Conferences concerning the Eucharist,* translated by Thomas Tenison (London: Richard Chiswell, 1687), 32, 39–40, 72–73, 76.

81. Tillotson, *Discourse,* 3.

82. Sir Robert Howard, *A Twofold Vindication of the late Arch-bishop of Canterbury, and of the Author of the History of Religion* (London, 1696).

83. Atterbury, *Scorner,* 7.

84. [Mary Astell], *The Christian Religion as Profess'd by a Daughter of the Church of England*
[London: R. Wilkin, 1705], 412.

85. [Pierre Bayle], "Avis au lecteur" [unpaginated], in *Recueil de quelques pieces curieuses concernant la Philosophie de Monsieur Descartes* (Amsterdam: Henry Desbordes, 1684).

86. Louis de Valois, *Sentimens,* 55–60. Du Hamel had made an abridgement of Descartes' philosophy.

87. Ibid., 299.

88. Tad M. Schmaltz, *Radical Cartesianism: The French Reception of Descartes* (Cambridge: Cambridge University Press, 2002), 31.

89. Ibid., 4.

90. "Remarques sur le Concordat d'entre les Jesuites et les Peres de l'Oratoire," in *Recueil,* 44: "Enfin les hommes sont naturellement curieux, et pour les empecher de l'etre avec excés, il est bon de laisser dans la Philosophie un exercice innocent leur curiosité." He cites an ancient Father (Gregory Nazianzen) as saying that error in philosophy is not so dangerous.

91. Valois, *Sentimens,*173, 178.

92. Ibid., 145.

Pastures and Masters: Swift the Pastor and the Politics of Pastoral

James Ward

"To submit myself to all my governors, teachers, spiritual pastors and masters": so the Anglican catechism defines neighborly duty. While "teacher," "governor" and "master" might describe other aspects of Swift's career and ambitions, the authority figure who embodies the connection between Swift's roles as priest and satirist is the *pastor*. The term has no official status in the Church of Ireland and when it is used, whether by Swift, his contemporaries, or his critics, it tends not just to act as a synonym for "clergyman" but also to imply a symbolic relation between Swift's literary and clerical careers. This implication often works in tandem with a second set of meanings, invoked by the fact that "pastor" can also refer to a figure in pastoral poetry. The canonical and most widely imitated pastoral poem is Virgil's first Eclogue, a dialogue between two shepherds (*pastores*), Meliboeus and Tityrus. When they meet on a country road, Meliboeus is vacating the lands that have been confiscated from him by the government in Rome, while Tityrus returns to take possession of lands to which he has been restored through the intercession of a patron in the capital. Raising issues of patronage, exile, material deprivation, and inequality, Virgilian pastoral imbues the term "pastor" with a further symbolic resonance germane both to major themes in Swift's life and work, and to the wider political context of eighteenth-century Ireland.

Whether it means a priest or a Virgilian shepherd, the word "pastor" connects Swift the priest's social mission to Swift the political writer's sense of ideological commitment. Because it stresses a local, sectarian and paternalistic context for his politics rather than a national, pluralistic, and egalitarian one, the term also helps fend off temptations to accommodate Swift's satire to modern notions of social justice or nationalist political sentiment. Instead, by grounding the politics of Swift the poet and the priest in the ownership and control of land, my essay develops a materialist reading of the trope

147

of the pastor and the pastoral genre. I will begin with a look at how some earlier critics have depicted Swift in this dual "pastoral" role.

"Dean Swift was a very wonderful pastor," concludes a 1939 study by Robert Wyse Jackson entitled *Jonathan Swift: Dean and Pastor.* Now seldom read, the book has some claim to a mention in the present volume as the first modern critical interpretation of Swift's work as a clergyman, one that adds a symbolic aspect to this role by calling Swift a "pastor." However, the terms used by the book to portray Swift's relationship with his Dublin parishioners suggest an unsettling lack of critical distance from the mindset of Gulliver among the Yahoos. "Swift loved his flock, even though he could not help being angry at their stupidity and bestiality," says Jackson; "[h]e burned to see his simple people treated with justice, yet he could not help loathing their sordid fecklessness with anger and disgust."[1] Lacking Jackson's willingness to identify Swift's "flock" as sordid, stupid, feckless, bestial, and disgusting, Louis Landa deploys a more measured use of the "pastor" trope in the conclusion to his classic book *Swift and the Church of Ireland.* Landa offers an image of consolation that owes something to pastoral poetry as well as to the Christian figure of the pastor. Much as Tityrus comforts Meliboeus at the end of Virgil's first Eclogue, Swift, in Landa's vision, extends a consoling embrace to the dispossessed Irish people. Swift's "conception of pastoral care," Landa writes, "widened out to embrace the nation. If Ireland irritated and displeased him in many respects, it also gratefully received his warm commiseration, as of a pastor to his flock."[2]

The warmth and width of Swift the pastor's embrace have since been questioned. Although they remain indebted to his scholarship, studies since Landa have refused overly inclusive conceptions of the Irish "nation," emphasizing Swift's own partisan belief "that it was essential for the [Anglican] church and nation to be one," in D. George Boyce's words.[3] In contrast to earlier depictions of Swift as a despairing observer, they have adverted to his role as an agenda-driven participant in Irish domestic politics. Swift may have addressed himself to "the whole people of Ireland" but, as Joseph McMinn says, this aspiration to a national audience was "largely rhetorical," and his appeal was in practice confined to "the Church of Ireland 'middle rank,' those with enough property to come within his stern definition of responsible citizenship."[4] Christopher Fauske echoes this view. He shows how Swift's work up to the year 1724 must be understood in the context of a continuing effort to defend the interests of the Church of Ireland in a changing society, a conflict that can be expressed in its most basic economic form as a "struggle for the control of rents."[5] Under George I and a London Whig ministry perceived as openly hostile to the Anglican clergy, the Church's constitutional and financial position looked increasingly precarious—an instability not helped by such developments as the expiry of Irish land leases granted as part of the Williamite settlement. In a new political dispensation and with the land itself up for grabs, it became imperative to enlist support to the Church's cause. Boyce, again dealing with Swift's career to 1724, emphasizes the pragmatic nature of this mission by describing it as "a question of holding ground, maintaining numbers, calculating religious and political arithmetic."[6] Such visions of Swift as an astute politician making strategic appeals to "national" interests in order to safeguard vested ones are a far cry from earlier images of a cantankerous but kindly shepherd ministering to the needs of his flock. But as I will argue here, such images conceal a history of dissension and dispute that, ironically enough, was articulated using the "pastoral" language that twentieth-century critics later borrowed to portray Swift kindly ministering to his flock. To uncover this history, this essay will discuss the trope of the pastor and its relation to the genre of pastoral, dealing particularly with the period after 1724, when Swift achieved national fame as the author of the Drapier's Letters. My reason for concentrating on this period is to argue that even after he had become a unifying figurehead in Ireland, Swift continued to intervene in political disputes that were the source of bitter internal divisions, sometimes between the Anglican clergy and other political interests, sometimes even within his own Church.

To trace these divisions I will discuss some meanings of the term "pastor" and the conflicting roles that it encompassed, citing firstly a politicized representation that depicts Swift the clergyman as a Virgilian shepherd and secondly Swift's own portrayal of his superior in the Church of Ireland, Archbishop William King of Dublin. The purpose of this section is to establish the context of Swift's personal and ecclesiastical politics and the place of the pastor figure and pastoral imagery within it. I will then go on to discuss some of the connections between the Christian conceit of the pastor as shepherd and the symbolic vocabulary of pastoral poetry in the Virgilian tradition, showing how Swift adopts the persona of St. Patrick to fuse these two versions of "pastoral" but also to reveal the tensions between them. This will lead us on to a dispute in which Swift participated, and which was conducted and read allegorically using pastoral poetic conventions. The "tithe agistment controversy," which peaked in 1736, could itself be called "pastoral" to the extent that it concerned the management of flocks and grazing lands, and

I will discuss Swift and his contemporaries' use of these conventions to intervene in the dispute. Looking finally at a verbal and topographical legacy that could be said to represent Swift's final satiric comment on this controversy, I will assert that this matter of pastors, pastures, and their masters was far removed from the easy rural contentment that the term "pastoral" has come, regrettably, to imply. Instead, the image of the pastor shifts from that of kindly consoler to become an uncertain, threatened, and threatening figure, one whose desire for vengeance brings the pastoral genre into proximity with those modes of satire and invective that have come to be regarded as more typically Swiftian.

In the sense being developed here, the term "pastor" is a pun or concept-metaphor through which the social mission of the Anglican clergyman meshes with the political themes of pastoral poetry. As many commentators on the subject have indicated, the pastoral genre is closely intertwined with ideas of social justice, and the secular literary tradition of pastoral is rooted in material unhappiness. In Virgil's first Eclogue a joyful shepherd sings the praises of his patron while the strains of his dispossessed friend provide a troubling counterpoint. The Eclogue stages what Annabel Patterson calls a "dialectic of opposed fortunes,"[7] where Tityrus praises an unnamed benefactor (usually assumed to be the Roman triumvir Octavian) for restoring him to his confiscated lands, while Meliboeus laments that he has been turned off his farm and forced to leave for the city. The fates of the two pastores are grounded in historical political upheavals. The Eclogue alludes to Octavian's attempt in 41 BCE to settle veterans of the recent civil war on lands from which political opponents had been forcibly removed, a conflict that establishes the politics of possession and dispossession as a muted but persistent theme of the genre.[8] With its central motif of the unequal justice meted out to the two pastores, the pastoral mode constructs a space in which material political concerns are always a complicating presence.

Such pastoral subtexts of expropriation and territorial dispute as long-term consequences of war have a notable relevance to Ireland in the first half of the eighteenth century. They surface within the specific context of the conflict between the Church of Ireland and the landed interest, with Swift in a starring role, in a 1739 adaptation of the first Eclogue by Edward Lonergan entitled *The Dean and the Country Parson*. This parallel translation, which places Virgil's Latin text alongside its own updated version, is founded on the pun whereby "pastor" means both a Virgilian shepherd and a clergy-

man. It features Swift as Tityrus. Protected by his patron, the Earl of
Oxford, the Dean's fortunes are contrasted to those of the country
parson whom he meets on the road. As in Virgil's original, the fortu-
nate pastor offers his dispossessed friend food and lodging, but their
coming together represents only a temporary suspension of the conflict in which they are both caught up. The dean may accommodate
the country parson for one night and even allow him to preach in
place of his absent curate the next day, but as morning draws near
(and "Beaux to Dress them for a Castle rise / And Barber's-boys,
with Powder blind our Eyes") so does the reality of the country parson's predicament, which he contrasts with the dean's situation:

> I envy not the Blessings you possess,
> But wonder *Malice* cannot make Them less;
> How in such ticklish Times you'r suffer'd Ink,
> And let to speak ev'n part of what you Think;
> While we with fruitless Efforts, strive to claim
> Raiment for Pow'r and Food instead of Fame:
> Our Flock, alas! on Grounds unfit to Till,
> Best part were ravag'd by the Herbage Bill;
> Our Corn the surly Fanaticks refuse,
> Taught by that Bench, which grumbles at our DUES;
> Blest as we are to catch a dropping Crown,
> To pay for Pipes or mend a tater'd Gown [. . .][9]

While Swift lives comfortably off the proceeds of his writing, the
minor clergy struggle to make ends meet. Deprived of income by
parliamentary edict in the form of the Herbage Bill (which disadvantaged the Church of Ireland by promoting the grazing of cattle over
the growing of tithable crops), they are further impoverished by a
conspiracy in the courts between dissenters ("Fanaticks") and mag-
istrates (the "Bench," drawn from the landed gentry) to deprive
them of the tithes that are their rightful "DUES." The depth of resentment against the payment of tithes is shown in a guide adver-
tised for sale in 1726, which claimed to be "most useful for the
Country Inhabitants of this kingdom Generally oppress'd by the
Lawless Insolence of Tythers."[10] Complaints against the clergy and
tithers, the agents who collected tithes on their behalf, became increasingly vocal. By 1729 they were being expressed in a memorial
of dissenting ministers, a petition to the Lord Chief Justice William
Conolly,[11] and in a letter to Swift, who responded with an uncompromising assertion that the clergy and not the rural community
were the sufferers in this dispute: "I defy the wickedest and most
powerfull Clergy-men in the kingdom to oppress the meanest

Farmer in the Parish; and I likewise defy the same Clergy-man to prevent himself from being cheated by the same Farmer, whenever that Farmer shall be disposed to be knavish or peevish." (*PW*, 12:78). As this response suggests, it was clear from the outset whose side Swift took in the battle of the clergy to obtain the dues they saw as rightfully theirs. Drawing on such statements of allegiance, *The Dean and the Country Parson* casts Swift in the role of one who has escaped the privations to which the minor clergy are subject, but who nonetheless speaks out on behalf of his oppressed brethren—so forcefully as to cause wonder that he is allowed to "speak ev'n part of what you Think."

In his own writing on the Church of Ireland and its role in the war over land and tithes, Swift retains the capacity to speak his mind, but loses his privileged status as the beneficiary of a patron. He becomes instead a figure more like Meliboeus, dispossessed and disillusioned by those who should afford him protection. This contrast emerges via "An Excellent New Song upon His Grace Our Good Lord Archbishop of Dublin," published at the height of the Drapier's fame in 1724. The poem, narrated "By Honest Jo, One of His Grace's Farmers in Fingal," depicts a politicized rural idyll. In a tableau that anticipates the earnest swains of Goldsmith's *The Deserted Village* (1770), workers lay down their plough to attend to Swift's words:

> To every farmer twice a week all round about the yoke,
> Our parsons read the Drapier's books, and make us honest folk.
> (*Poems*, 279–80, ll. 39–40)

Swift's picture of rural bliss is rendered dramatically ironic by his subsequent challenge to the "knavish" and "peevish" farmers of Ireland. It is also undermined by the author's fractious real-life relations with the title figure. In private the dean's dealings with Archbishop King were often bad tempered. "[Y]our Grace hath thought fit to take every opportunity of giving me all sorts of uneasiness, without ever giving me, in my whole life, one single mark of your favour beyond common civilities," he once complained. "And, if it were not below a man of spirit to make complaints," he continued somewhat disingenuously, "I could date them from six and twenty years past." This quarter century of unease may have helped earn King the designation *u.* (for ungrateful) when, looking back on his life and career, Swift compiled a graded list of friends and colleagues. As I shall discuss at the end of this essay, such gestures of silent retribution became an important adjunct to Swift's conception and execution of his pastoral role.[12]

The fact that in his published writing Swift had only praise for King's record of public service makes his private assessment all the more damning. The poem depicts the archbishop as an exemplary steward of the land as well as the people in his cure. Jo maintains that only through the archbishop's benevolence is he able to maintain his status as an undertenant. The speaker explains that he subrents "a little piece of ground" from King, who holds a lease on land that is owned by a "squire" of the local gentry. He adds that the secular landlord's demands on his finances are such that only the cleric's generosity enables him to survive. Jo says of his squire that "the land I from him hold is so stretched on the rack / That only for the Bishop's lease 'twould quickly break my back" (ll. 45–6). The speaker becomes a jubilant Tityrus, while Swift's private complaints against his archbishop relegate the author to the status of a disadvantaged and disgruntled Meliboeus. Lauded in public as the protector of the powerless, but privately unwilling to bestow "one single mark of [. . .] favour," King combines the conflicting roles of beneficent patron and callous agent of dispossession. Together, these representations show how the pastoral genre and the figure of the pastor within it form a dialectic in which the roles of patron and exploiter, victim and beneficiary, alternate in a widening spiral of praise, blame, and recrimination.

This dialectic continues in Swift's "Verses Occasioned by the Sudden Drying Up of St Patrick's Well near Trinity College Dublin." The title refers to an event of 1729, which was widely reported at the time, although the poem was not printed until 1763, in the eleventh volume of George Faulkner's ever-expanding edition of Swift's works, complete with scholarly notes by Faulkner, which draw attention to the poet's use of "Scripture Figure" or typological readings.[13] This apocalyptic mode is actually one of two symbolic registers deployed in the poem, which treats the well's drying up as the last in a series of omens and types sent to warn Irish "swains." As this last term signals, the poem employs several markers of the pastoral genre, such as when St. Patrick asserts in the poem that he banished the snakes from Ireland so that "[t]he shepherd in his bower might sleep or sing, / Nor dread the adder's tooth nor scorpion's sting" (*Poems*, 376, ll. 41–2). Obeying the poem's instruction to heed "types" (44) and "Emblems" (55), we might read the "shepherd in his bower" as a version of the pastor figure that brings the two discourses of the poem together by putting the literary genre of pastoral in contact with Anglican iconography. Indeed, the conceptual pun of the pastor figure is built into the poem's subject matter, as St. Patrick (unlike Swift) attained the office of bishop and bran-

dishes one of its symbols, the rod known as the pastoral staff, modeled on the shepherd's crook. With "this crozier in my hand," the
saint asserts, "I drove the venomed serpent from thy land" (39–40).
But not all Patrick's successors exercise their powers benevolently.
Some, indeed, take on the status of the noxious pests that the saint
had formerly expelled:

> With omens oft I strove to warn thy swains,
> Omens, the types of thy impending chains.
> I sent the magpie from the British soil,
> With restless beak thy blooming fruit to spoil,
> To din thine ears with unharmonious clack,
> And haunt thy holy walls in white and black.
> What else are those thou seest in bishop's gear
> Who crop the nurseries of learning here?
> Aspiring greedy, full of senseless prate,
> Devour the church, and chatter to the state.
>
> (44–52)

Along with other species such as frogs and rats, which were believed
not to be indigenous but to have established themselves in Ireland
over the course of the seventeenth century,[14] the magpie is poeti-
cally styled as an invader from Britain. Deriving from the resemblance between the bird's plumage and episcopal vestments,
"magpie" was also a nickname for Anglican bishops, a fact that Swift
exploits to cite the bird's taste for "spoil" and its "unharmonious
clack" as further shared attributes.[15] The reference here is to En-
glish-born clergy appointed to Church of Ireland bishoprics over the
heads of locals, a practice by which the Church of England threatens
to "devour" its Irish counterpart, nominally a separate institution.
Although no names are given, it is likely that Swift's poem has actual
individuals in mind here. When he was translated from the see of
Carlisle to become bishop of Derry, for example, William Nicolson
cropped the local "nurseries of learning" to produce a survey of the
country's manuscript collections.[16] Another notable "magpie"
might have been Archbishop Hugh Boulter of Armagh, an appoin-
tee of Walpole's whom Swift regarded as little more than a high-
placed informer posted to Ireland to "chatter to the state." Neither
Boulter nor Nicolson had much sympathy with political opposition
in Ireland to the policies of the Walpole administration. In the campaign against the Declaratory Act of 1720, Nicolson saw a seditious
spirit that was "daily animating the populace to assert their Irish liberties, exempt from the dominion of (what they call) foreigners,"
while Boulter described the opposition to Wood's halfpence as hav-

ing "a very unhappy influence on the state of this nation."[17] By contrast, native-born clergy like Swift or Archbishop King regarded these campaigns as crucial to the survival of the Church of Ireland and the country as a whole.

Swift's portrayal of fellow clergy as English "magpies" sent to plague the Irish is thus informed by an antagonistic complex of church, national, and party politics. Anodyne overtones of pastors and flocks give way to bitter undertones; St. Patrick wields his shepherd's crook as a rod of retribution to indict Britain and "the pastors of thy ravenous breed, / Who come to fleece the flocks, and not to feed." Here we find Swift using the term "pastor" in the dual sense that I identified earlier. The word means a literal clergyman such as those who had been appointed to the sees of Derry and Armagh, but it also refers to a wider history in which Britain asserted, and abused, authority over the neighboring island. This encompasses, in a broader historical sweep, colonial depredations carried out under the pretext of religious reform, whereby self-proclaimed civilizers merely "fleece" the natives. Swift's poem uses the pastoral metaphor to appropriate a sense of grievance from these larger historical antagonisms. The Church of Ireland, elsewhere an unfortunate bystander to "the long wars between the Invaders and the Natives," here assumes the abject state of a "native" institution beset and despoiled by "invaders" from Britain.

I will discuss a similar but more personalized appropriation of victim status in the final part of this essay. For now I wish to cite this poem's use of types and antitypes as typical of the brand of politicized pastoral under discussion here. Swift wrote within a reading culture well versed in the genre's ability to carry a relatively transparent allegorical subtext, enabling political comment that is coded but not so subtle as to lose its polemical impact. This strategy is further evident in an anonymous poem, dedicated and addressed to Swift, which also mixes rural themes with apocalyptic schemes. A riddling narrative, *The Old Woman and her Goose* [. . .] *Inscrib'd to the Revd. Jonathan Swift* (1736), deals with the widespread conversion of cultivated land to pasturage, encouraged by successive pieces of legislation, that angered Swift and his fellow Anglican clergy. In the course of a fable, it presents the move as a concerted policy worked out between tenants and landlords. Looking for a way to maximize his profits, the landlord of a particular farm calls together all his tenants, plies them with food and wine, and persuades them to turn the entire estate over to the growth of asparagus. Only one tenant dissents. By drawing attention to the absence of the local parson from the feast, this tenant figures the sidelining of the church in national affairs and the usurpation by landowners of its mentorial role:

> [. . .] if I right aread the Matter,
> You know not what about you Chatter.
> Landlord, Sorry I am to say
> Our Parson is not here to Day
> For he a good Man is, and Wise,
> And might afford right Advice[.][18]

The suggestion here is that rural mismanagement is essentially a matter of misreading in the senses implied by the word "aread"—a failure to take advice, to interpret omens correctly, and to speak out. As if to underline this failure, the poet challenges Swift to interpret his moral correctly: "Now tell me, ken you Master Dean / What 'tis thy Meagre Bard doth mean?"[19]

The probable answer to the question is found in a petition brought before a committee of the Irish House of Commons in 1736. Pro-clerical polemics, such as the two poems inscribed to Swift, alleged a conspiracy between landlord and tenant to deprive the clergy of tithes by converting arable land to pasture. The petition, however, made a counteraccusation, asserting that the Church of Ireland clergy had abused their temporal powers by attempting to exact tithes on cattle, to which they had no legal right. The petitioners complained that "many of the Clergy in the several Parts of this Kingdom" had begun to contest their legal right to "a new Kind of Tythe, under the Name of Agistment for dry and Barren Cattle." They alleged that "Suits in Equity for such Tythes multiply very fast" as a result of "the Clergy taking Example from one another." The gentlemen landholders' petition closes with the apprehension that the clergy's demands will "greatly impoverish the Petitioners, and many others of his Majesty's faithful Subjects, and impair the Protestant Interest and Strength of this Kingdom."[20] Faced with such testimony, the committee concluded that the clergy's demands were indeed likely to "prejudice and endanger the Protestant Religion, Interest, and Strength of this Kingdom." They also found in favor of the allegation that the clergy's demand was without suitable precedent. Upon "the strictest Inquiry," it emerged that the first attempt to establish the church's legal right to this tithe had been made as recently as 1722.[21] The tone of the report does not quite do justice to the temper of the proceedings in the Commons. According to one account these were "Conducted and carryed on with great Heat;" the "most virulent Resolutions" were proposed and the Judges of the Exchequer were "abused in almost every Speech."[22]

Swift reacted to the landowners' victory with equal heat in *A Char-acter, Panegyric and Description of the Legion Club* (1736). He was, as we have seen, more than capable of adapting pastoral language to sa-tiric ends in order to attack his fellow clergy. But the *Legion Club* saw him close ranks to present the Church as united against the gen-try—or at least united by its powerlessness before a landed elite, which Swift embodies as yet another marauding animal. The poem singles out MP Sir Thomas Prendergast as a leading figure in the gentry's assault against the church:

> Let Sir Tom, that rampant ass,
> Stuff his guts with flax and grass;
> But before the priest he fleeces
> Tear the Bible all to pieces.
>
> (*Poems*, 552, ll.63–66)

Revisiting a pun from the verses on St. Patrick's Well, Swift mixes metaphors to depict a natural order gone even more seriously awry than in the earlier poem. Where once their flocks were at risk, pas-tors themselves are now in danger of being "fleeced" by a rampant ass who, reflecting the gentry's encroachment on the Church's au-thority, seems to have leapt the fence from a neighboring field. At the clergy's expense, asses like Prendergast now grow fat on flax for linen and grass for grazing, two crops on which the claim to levy tithes was disputed, and which were favored respectively by Dissent-ing Protestants in the North of Ireland and those whom Swift would call the "abominable race of graziers." As in the imitation of Virgil and the fable of the asparagus growers, Swift suggests that dissenters have formed a conspiracy with the gentry to shut out the clergy from their rightful income. Bathetic as Swift and his contemporaries' rep-resentations of this controversy now seem, it should not be allowed to occlude the fact that Ireland's green pastures were the site of an unholy struggle between and secular and ecclesiastical claims to profit from the land. With the outcome of this conflict never really in doubt, the losing pro-clerical side might have taken solace in the literary sophistication of their interventions. And while *The Legion Club* represents Swift's attempt to have the last word on the matter, he later managed with typical stubbornness to insert a final last word elsewhere.

So far I have cited the pastor figure and the pastoral genre as ele-ments within allegorical and typological codes employed by Swift and contemporaries to represent divisions within the Church of Ireland, and between the Church and its opponents. As I have pointed out, their references were relatively transparent and depended on being easily interpretable for their impact. However, Swift's last use of these codes involves a much more involved process of textual and political reading. This begins in a field in Dublin. The final clause of Swift's will deals with "the Lease of a Field [. . .], commonly called the *Vineyard*," and leaves instructions for its future care: "My Will is, that the Ground inclosed by the great Wall, may be sold for the Remainder of the Lease, at the highest Price my Executors can get for it, in Belief and Hopes, that the said Price will exceed Three Hundred Pounds at the lowest Value: For which my Successor in the Deanry shall have the first Refusal: and it is my earnest Desire, that the succeeding Deans and Chapters may preserve the said *Vineyard* [. . .] so as to be always in the Hands of the succeeding Deans during their Office (*PW* 13, 156–157).

This complicated set of instructions is noteworthy because of a shift in its language. As the clause progresses, it slips from dispensing demands in accordance with Swift's "Will" and begins instead to express his "Belief and Hopes" and his "earnest Desire." Swift is not adamant that the piece of land is as valuable as he thinks it is, nor does he insist that his successors must continue to preserve decanal jurisdiction over this ground: he merely wishes that these things should happen. The uncertainty may reflect an attachment that was as much emotional as financial. Swift certainly went to considerable lengths to make the vineyard a place of his own. As well as securing it with a wall, which he forced the laborers to rebuild several times when their initial efforts were not satisfactory, he seems to have devoted some effort to bringing the piece of land within the jurisdiction of the deanery. He obtained it in 1721 from the neighboring estate in exchange for some land at the west side of the Deanery garden.[23] Given the degree of investment during his lifetime, Swift's provisions for what happened to the vineyard after his death were suitably elaborate but also strangely precarious.

At the time of Swift's death, as the will states, the lease of the field was being held "in Trust" for him (*PW*, 13:156). Presumably, then, if Swift wanted the field to remain decanal property as earnestly as he claims to have done, he could simply have bequeathed the lease to his successor. Rather than making such a bequest, the will stipulates that the lease on the vineyard be sold for the "highest Price." If Swift's "earnest Desire" is fulfilled, the tract will indeed pass into the "Hands of the succeeding Deans during their Office," but only by a circuitous method. The arrangement depends on the next dean

after Swift buying back the land from the estate of his dead prede-
cessor, not cheaply but at the "highest Price my Executors can get,"
and on the further condition that this next holder of the office initi-
ate a procedure for passing on the field to subsequent incumbents.
If this arrangement were taken up, then every time the office is va-
cated, the land would be sold on to the new holder, with the added
proviso that "each Dean lessen One Fourth of the Purchase Money
to each succeeding Dean, and for no more than the present Rent,"
thus obtaining a negative return on his investment. Bearing these
obstacles in mind, it is certainly a technical possibility that the vineyard would have been preserved for the use of each succeeding
dean, but also a remote one. The feasibility of the scheme depends
on the willingness of Swift's successors to enter into a perversely
complicated and unprofitable arrangement, a contract that offers
ample scope to be broken from the outset by offering "first Refusal." There are surely easier and more efficient ways of fulfilling
one's "earnest Desire."

Swift may have professed to "hate the tribe of Lawyers," but he
seems to have been competently versed in the procedures of be-
queathing land and leases to ensure that they would remain in the
desired hands.[24] Unfamiliarity with due process does not explain the
eccentricity of the provisions made concerning the vineyard. Instead, by relying on the goodwill of his successors to fulfill his "earnest Desire," Swift seems to be emphasizing the precious and
personal character of an inherited trust and even defying his successors to break that trust at a time when "there is hardly any remainder left of Dean and chapter lands in Ireland" (*PW*, 12:185–186).
Somewhere along the line of Swift's posterity, the chain of succession was indeed broken. The plot remained in the hands of Swift's
successors for a few years: a plan of the vineyard dating from 1749
describes it as "belonging to the Dean and Chapter of St. Patrick's
Dublin' and being 'in lease to Mr. John Rose.'"[25] By the end of the
century, however, the site had been acquired for the Meath Hospital.
Unlike the hospital he founded, Swift's vineyard was not incorpo-
rated into the Dublin cityscape as a permanent token of his guard-
ianship. During the time he maintained it, the garden retained a
personal character. It was for him a private retreat, a "secure 'island,'" in Michael DePorte's words, where the dean and his horses
could exercise.[26] As his death approached, Swift consigned the vineyard to posterity in such a way that, although it could potentially remain unchanged, its purpose and ownership would most probably
change with time. In one sense the continued survival of this pastoral retreat was jeopardized even by its connection with a more public

place of asylum, St. Patrick's Hospital, the "house for fools and mad" that was also instituted in Swift's will and that is today "still flourishing as one of the leading psychiatric institutions in the British Isles."[27] By instructing his executors to sell the lease on the garden for at least three hundred pounds, Swift may have hoped to raise extra funds for the projected institution. The "satiric touch" achieved in the construction of this building was also perhaps a step toward obliterating the personal touch through which Swift made this corner of Dublin his own.

One further incongruity sets this transient and quirky memorial apart from Swift's more enduring legacies. Although the will states that it was "commonly called the *Vineyard*," this field was not used for the cultivation of vines. The climate would probably not have permitted the growth of grapes, even though the south-facing wall had been faced with bricks to trap the sun's heat.[28] It did produce "excellent crops of peaches, nectarines, pears and paradise apples,"[29] but "Vineyard" was plainly a poetical rather than a descriptive title, and also an incomplete one. Although the will insists upon a more anonymous designation, the garden's full name, as used by Swift in his correspondence and on the plan of 1749, was "Naboth's Vineyard." In the first Book of Kings, Naboth is asked by Ahab to exchange his vineyard either for money or for a better one. When an echo of the same request was put to one of Swift's successors, it was obviously accepted. Naboth, however, refuses because God has forbidden him to part from the inheritance of his fathers. Ahab's wife, Jezebel, then conspires to cheat Naboth out of his inheritance. With the help of two corrupt witnesses, Naboth is found guilty of blaspheming and of cursing the king and is stoned to death for his alleged crimes. Ahab takes possession of his vineyard, whereupon he is cursed by the prophet Elijah, who swears that Ahab will suffer a more ignominious death than his humble victim.[30]

Various commentators have unraveled the allegorical resonance of Swift's act of naming, and have applied the meaning of the biblical tale in diverse ways. Michael DePorte reads Swift's choice of name as an oblique comment on the greed and thoughtlessness of kings, and connects it to a more general antimonarchical tendency in his work.[31] Joseph McMinn argues that the spirit of Naboth helped Swift to "dramatize his own sense of trusteeship" in the time of a "new colonial settlement dedicated to the 'improvement' of confiscated territories." McMinn also contends that Swift was attracted to the tale of Naboth because of the victim's refusal "to negotiate or compromise with tyranny."[32] Carole Fabricant provides an alternative reading, taking a cue from Swift's own account of how he obtained the land. Laetitia Pilkington, in her *Memoirs* (1748–19), recalls how Swift took her into his vineyard, which he described to her as "a Garden—I cheated one of my Neighbours out of."[33] The comment would imply that Swift is portraying himself as the usurper rather than the victim. As Fabricant comments, it is "*Ahab's* role (though often combined with Naboth's) which Swift is symbolically acting out."[34] A further comment on the significance of Naboth's story comes from Renato Poggioli, who does not mention Swift's use of the tale. Poggioli does, however, argue that the story exemplifies certain underlying themes of pastoral, such as justice, ownership, and expropriation, that have been central in my own discussion of the genre. Poggioli comments that the tale of Naboth reads like "a scriptural variant of [Virgil's] First Eclogue. The gist of both tales is that the wicked and the mighty covet the property of the meek and that by fair means or foul succeed in satisfying their evil greed."[35] This observation enables the inference that as well as combining the roles of Ahab and Naboth, Swift was also presenting his garden as a site where two further versions of himself encounter each other. In Naboth's vineyard, a jubilant Tityrus encounters a despondent and dispossessed Meliboeus. And though the vineyard is now so well trodden as to have given the title to a book,[36] there is still something to be said about Naboth's status as a martyr.

Swift's appropriation of the figure of Naboth represents an attempt to restore the missing term to a dialectic that sets the fortunes of the Church against the "evil greed" of the gentry. The vineyard sat outside the jurisdiction of the cathedral until Swift annexed it in 1721, when it became an island of ecclesiastical authority enclosed by the neighboring estate. Since Swift claims to have cheated "one of [his] Neighbours," presumably the owner of the estate or his agents, out of the piece of land in question, there is a potential to read the expropriation in terms of the antagonism between the church and the landed interest, which erupted so poisonously in the tithe agistment controversy. In the shrunken arena of Swift's garden, the battle is replayed. The Anglican establishment takes on the role of the dispossessed victim, and Swift becomes a suitably bathetic and belated Elijah, speaking up for Naboth after his death. He performs an unconvincing and unconvinced exorcism of the church's historical possession by the spirit of the dispossessed Meliboeus; a tentative reversal of traditional roles in the competition between the ecclesiastical and secular establishments for dominion over the land. As I have tried to show in this essay, that struggle was both written and read through the figure of the pastor and the conventions of pastoral. And as I have further argued, this was a mode that took on not merely the topical import of satire but also its capacity to express a festering resentment far removed from the images of contentment or consolation with which the genre is often associated. But one respect in which such political pastoral differs from satire is that it does not bring catharsis or closure. Swift the satirist may claim in his epitaph to rest "where savage indignation can no longer lacerate his breast," but Swift the pastor went to his grave nursing an inconsolable grudge, and issuing instructions for its posthumous prolongation.

NOTES

I am grateful to David Fairer, Eric Langley, and Shaun Regan for their advice.

1. Robert Wyse Jackson, *Jonathan Swift: Dean and Pastor* (London: Society for Promoting Christian Knowledge, 1939), 167, 174–75.

2. Louis Landa, *Swift and the Church of Ireland* (Oxford: Clarendon Press, 1954), 195.

3. D. George Boyce, "The Road to Wood's Halfpence and Beyond: William King, Jonathan Swift and the Defence of the National Church, 1689–1724," in *Political Discourse in Seventeenth- and Eighteenth-Century Ireland,* ed. Robert Boyce Eccleshall and Vincent Geoghegan (Basingstoke: Palgrave, 2001), 81–109, 82–83.

4. Joseph McMinn, ed., *Swift's Irish Pamphlets: An Introductory Selection* (Gerrards Cross: Colin Smythe, 1991), 17.

5. Christopher J. Fauske, *Jonathan Swift and the Church of Ireland 1710–1724: An Accidental Patriot* (Dublin: Irish Academic Press, 2002), xx.

6. Boyce, "The Road to Wood's Halfpence," 82–83.

7. Annabel Patterson, *Pastoral and Ideology: Virgil to Valéry* (Oxford: Clarendon Press, 1988), 216.

8. L. P. Wilkinson, "Virgil and the Evictions," *Hermes* 94 (1966): 320–24, 320; Patterson, *Pastoral,* 2–3.

9. Edward Lonergan, *The Dean and the Country Parson. An Imitation of the First Eclogue of Virgil* (Dublin: E. Waters, 1739), 3.

10. *Dublin Intelligence,* August 16, 1726.

11. Archbishop Boulter to the Duke of Newcastle, March 13, 1729. In *Letters written by His Excellency Hugh Boulter, D. D.,* 2 vols. (Dublin: George Faulkner and James Williams, 1770), I:231, 232, cited by Landa, *Swift and the Church of Ireland,* 155; Petition addressed to Lord Justice Conolly, January 6, 1729.

12. Swift to Archbishop King, May 18, 1727, *Correspondence,* ed. Woolley, 3:87; *Correspondence,* ed. Williams, 5: Appendix 30, 270.

13. Quoted in *Poems,* 792n.

14. *Poems,* 793n., citing Faulkner's note.

15. *OED,* s.v. "Magpie."

16. William Nicolson, *The Irish Historical Library. Pointing at most of the Authors and Records in Print or Manuscript, which may be serviceable to the Compilers of a General History of Ireland* (Dublin: Aaron Rhames, 1724).

17. Nicolson to Archbishop Wake, September 1, 1719. Quoted by Isolde Victory, "The Making of the Declaratory Act of 1720," in *Parliament, Politics and People: Es-

says in Eighteenth-Century Irish History, edited by Gerard O'Brien (Blackrock: Irish Academic Press, 1989), 9–29, 21; Boulter, *Letters,* I:7.

18. *The Old Woman and her Goose. A Tale Devised on Account of a Certain Late Project* (Dublin: 1736), 6.

19. Ibid., 8.

20. *Journals of the House of Commons of Ireland,* 19 vols. (Dublin: George Grierson, James King and Abraham Bradley King: 1797–1800), Appendix to vol. 4, lxv. Published separately as *Report from the Committee appointed to take into Consideration the Petition of Samuel Low, and others* (Dublin: Samuel Fairbrother, 1736).

21. *Journals of the House of Commons of Ireland,* lxv, lxvi; Landa, *Swift and the Church of Ireland,* 136.

22. "Some Considerations upon the Late Proceedings in Ireland, in opposition to the Clergy's Demand of Tythe, Herbage, or Agistment for the Pasture of Dry and barren Cattle," BL Add. MS 21,132, Papers Relating to Ecclesiastical Affairs in Ireland, fols 49^r–53^r; repeated on fols 54^r–58^r and 60^r–63^v.

23. J. H. Bernard, *The Cathedral Church of St. Patrick: A History & Description of the Building, with a Short Account of the Deans* (London: George Bell and Sons, 1903), 28.

24. Swift to Alexander Pope, September 29, 1725, *Correspondence,* ed. Woolley, 2:606.

25. Edward Malins and The Knight of Glin, *Lost Demesnes: Irish Landscape Gardening, 1660–1845* (London: Barrie & Jenkins, 1976), 35.

26. Michael DePorte, "Avenging Naboth: Swift and Monarchy," *Philological Quarterly* 69 (1990): 419–33; 427.

27. <http://www.stpatrickscathedral.ie/St_Pats_Hospital.htm> (accessed July 20, 2006).

28. *Memoirs of Mrs. Laetitia Pilkington,* 2 vols. (Dublin: repr. London: R. Griffiths and G. Woodfall, 1748–49), I:77.

29. Malins and The Knight of Glin, 33.

30. I Kings 21. vv. 1–16.

31. DePorte. "Avenging Naboth," 422.

32. Joseph McMinn, "The Gardener in the Deanery," in *Swift, The Enigmatic Dean: Festschrift for Hermann Josef Real,* edited by Rudolf Freiburg, Arno Löffler, and Wolfgang Zach, with the assistance of Jan Schnitker (Tübingen: Stauffenburg, 1998), 127–35, 129; "Pastoral Properties: Swift and Gardens," *British Journal for Eighteenth-Century Studies* 22 (1999): 15–34, 22.

33. Pilkington, *Memoirs,* 1:77; see Carole Fabricant, *Swift's Landscape* (Baltimore: Johns Hopkins University Press, 1982), 71; "The Garden as City: Swift's Landscape of Alienation," *ELH* 42 (1975): 531–555, 533.

34. "Garden as City," 533. Emphasis in original.

35. Renato Poggioli, "Naboth's Vineyard; or, The Pastoral View of the Social Order," *Journal of the History of Ideas* 24 (1963): 3–24, 7.

36. Fox and Tooley, *Walking Naboth's Vineyard: New Studies of Swift,* edited by Christopher Fox (Notre Dame, IN: University of Notre Dame Press), 1995.

Swift's Idea of Christian Community
Daniel Lupton

WHEN CONFRONTING THE PROBLEM THAT IS THE COMPLEX RELATION-
ship between Gulliver, the Houyhnhnms and the Yahoos in book 4
of *Gulliver's Travels,* critics have framed the questions proposed by
the text in some very particular, and particularly restrictive, ways.
Especially during the first three-quarters of the twentieth century,
critics seemed determined to read book 4 allegorically, miring themselves in seemingly irresolvable debates about what, exactly, the
Houyhnhnms and Yahoos are meant to represent. Are they, respectively, man's reasonable and passionate natures?[1] Man as essentially
benevolent and man as essentially corrupt?[2] Man's mind versus
man's body?[3] Locke's and Hobbes's contrasting states of nature?[4]
Looking at the debate as a whole, it seems impossible to determine
which aspects of humanity are represented by the Houyhnhnms and
the Yahoos or, indeed, whether either of the two groups (or any
combination of them) can be said to represent humanity at all. Instead of entering into this long-running debate, I would like to avoid
these allegorical readings of book 4, recentering my discussion of
the Houyhnhnms and Yahoos around how they appear from Gulliver's perspective and paying particular attention to Gulliver's decision to join the Houyhnhnms' community rather than the Yahoos'.
On the surface, Gulliver's decision seems correct; after all, who
would want to enter into a society as violent and despicable as the
Yahoos'? However, even if we sympathize with Gulliver's decision to
align himself with the Houyhnhnms, we might still wonder if that
decision is *right,* especially when examined with Christian principles
in mind.[5] When read in light of the avowed faith in revealed religion
Swift professed repeatedly throughout his ecclesiastical writings,
Gulliver's decision seems remarkably un-Christian, since he chooses
the Houyhnhnms' atheistic utopia (in which Swift's particular version of Christianity could never gain a foothold) over the Yahoos'
degenerate society in which Christianity could, in theory at least,
thrive. Further, reading book 4 in this manner gives us a portrait of

Swift that is largely consistent with biographical evidence of how Swift situated his own identity within the groups with which he aligned himself (most famously the High Church and the Tory party[6]) and also lessens the tension, at least somewhat, between Swift's seemingly contrary roles as clergyman and satirist.

Before I turn to book 4, though, I want to identify a trend in Swift's own group affiliations. As many scholars have noted, Swift's relationships with groups (whether social, political, professional, or religious) were extremely complicated. Swift purportedly hated *all* groups,[7] yet he publicly aligned himself with several of them. Even the group in which Swift seemed most invested—the Anglican Church—frowned upon much of his behavior, particularly his passions for satire, irony, and politics. Despite the fact that Swift is often pithily described as a "High Church Tory," neither Swift's affiliation with the Church nor his affiliation with the Tory Party are adequate to explain the depth or breadth of his thought on matters of church or state. Indeed, one would hardly expect Swift to profess an unqualified allegiance to any group, but if Swift was so steadfastly individual in his own thought then why did he align himself with these groups? I want to argue that Swift maintained these affiliations because he was fascinated with the ways in which groups grow, change, and interact with their own members as well as within the larger society against which they define themselves. Further, Swift personally valued the type of reformist impulse that leads one to reshape and redefine a group's identity (rather than, for instance, simply abandoning the group). Christopher Fauske has described Swift as "an embattled Anglican conservative waging an often lonely fight."[8] This description not only conveys the violence with which Swift often expressed his opinions, but it also conveys Swift's position relative to the groups with which he aligned himself: nominally a member, but never going so far as to confuse his own identity with that of the group.

The way that Swift maintained his own individual identity against the collective identities of these groups was by adopting the rhetorical ethos of the underdog. In other words, Swift seemed reflexively to define his own position as the minority interest against a more powerful, potentially hegemonic background. While this is not true of all of Swift's work, it is true of a broad swath of Swift's writing, from straightforward, seemingly earnest sermons such as "On Brotherly Love" to highly ironic essays such as "An Argument against Abolishing Christianity." Swift's writings against the Wood's halfpence (1723–25) also serve as an example of this trend. Throughout the Drapier's first letter Swift refers to Ireland and the

Irish with diminutive terms such as "poor"[9] and "dear" (*PW*, 10:3) while the English interest is personified by "great lawyers" (*PW*, 10:8) and "his Majesty's broad seal" (*PW*, 10:4). The Irish are so poor, in fact, that the comparatively well-to-do M. B. Drapier has reminded them that "one copy of this paper may serve a dozen of you, which will be less than a farthing apiece" (*PW*, 10:3). Swift's evocation of sympathy for the Irish is so powerful that it is difficult to imagine the Drapier's Letters having been written any other way, but we must remember that Swift could easily have adopted a very different rhetorical stance. Swift could have presented himself as a representative of a potentially powerful majority interest within Ireland or played up his own connections to England's political elite. He also might have gone the route often taken by politically minded sentimental writers (the textbook example being Harriet Beecher Stowe), establishing himself as a member of a morally and economically superior upper class who takes pity on the "downtrodden," but instead Swift included himself (rhetorically, at least) among a poor, voiceless group being oppressed by a wealthy colonial power. Further, even within that minority group (i.e., the Irish), the voice through which Swift speaks is that of a comparatively well-to-do shopkeeper who actually has some amount of silver at his disposal; in other words, M. B. Drapier is a minority interest among the minority interest.

Swift's activist streak is also apparent in his relationships to the two dominant political parties of his day. Swift's defection from the Whigs in 1710 is well documented and certainly betrays his unwillingness to blindly maintain party allegiances, but more pertinent to the picture I would like to paint are Swift's relationships to the Whigs and Tories while he was actively involved in each party, relationships that were always contentious and sometimes antagonistic. As Ian Higgins argues in his well-researched study *Swift's Politics*,[10] scholars are hard pressed to categorize Swift's political thought since even qualified descriptions such as "Old Whig" or "Non-Jacobite Tory" pose problems. Indeed, as Higgins explains, Swift's very first political pamphlet for the Whigs, "A Discourse of the Contests and Dissensions . . . ," was criticized for being essentially un-Whiggish,[11] and after Swift defected from that party William King wondered how Swift had managed to pass for a Whig at all.[12] However, this was not simply a case of Swift's ideas failing to gel with the Whig party platform, since Swift's tendency to define himself as the minority interest within his own party continued during his tenure as a Tory propagandist. In his *Examiner* essay dated February 15, 1711, Swift writes of the difficulty of maintaining a moderate political stance: "I am worried on one side by the *Whigs* for being too *severe,* and by the *Tories* on t'other for being too *gentle*" (*PW,* 3:88). As evidence of his status as a political outsider, Swift prints one letter each from a Whig and a Tory, each of whom views him as an extremist (*PW,* 3:88–90). While one might expect this type of rhetorical device from a paper that purported to be apolitical or moderate, we must remember that the *Examiner* was, in no uncertain terms, a Tory paper. This makes Swift's decision to distance himself rhetorically from certain segments of his own party an interesting move though, I argue, one consistent with the general patterns of Swift's interaction with groups.

While Swift never underwent a change in religious affiliation as dramatic as his change in political affiliation, one also finds Swift negotiating his place in the church in similar ways. Scholars are apt to describe Swift simply as a "High Churchman," which downplays the aggression with which Swift asserted his own influence within the church establishment, even when his degree of influence would seem to be extremely limited. Take, for instance, Swift's move in 1711 to petition Queen Anne for remission of the Crown Rents. As Christopher Fauske describes, "it was an audacious idea, particularly in that such a request had been sanctioned neither by the Irish bishops nor by a convocation of the Church of Ireland."[13] Swift, despite the wariness of his superiors, viewed this scheme as essential to the welfare of the church and thus used what leverage he had to gain his superiors' permission and put the plan into execution.[14] Swift also gained the disapproval of prominent figures in the church establishment with his violent opposition to the proposed repeal of the Test Act in 1708, which Swift realized would have far greater political ramifications in Ireland, where the conforming population did not dwarf the dissenting population as it did in England.[15] Swift's penchant for aggressive political maneuvering strained his relationship with Church authorities such as Archbishop William King, who viewed theological doctrine as the Church's chief public relations tool.[16] However, Swift's injection of political concerns into the Church's collective consciousness served much the same purpose as his vocal advocacy of Church interests within the Tory Party, forcing the Church to engage with the outside world rather than being swallowed up in the whirlpool of self-referential rhetoric that characterized theological debate.

Just as he wanted his literary work to "vex" the public,[17] Swift's presence often served to disrupt the momentum of the groups with which he was involved, preventing the inertia of group activity from hurling the party's rhetoric into absurdity. While a number of schol-

ars (most notably Edward Said[18]) have noted this "anarchic" spirit
in Swift's rhetoric, I contend that this impulse—whether we refer to
it as "anarchic," "activist," "reformist" or by some other term—also
manifested itself in many other aspects of Swift's behavior, particularly in his capacity as a member of groups such as the church establishment and the two major political parties. Relatedly, the problem
with characters such as *A Tale of a Tub*'s Grub-Street hack and the
unambitious scholar who writes "A Tritical Essay Concerning the
Faculties of the Mind" is not simply that these writers have con-
sumed, digested, regurgitated and reconsumed their own rhetoric
until meaning has been eradicated; the clumsy rhetoric employed
by these authors is also meant to satirize other more deeply rooted
character traits such as laziness and an overzealous desire to please.
Judging by his own behavior and the kinds of behavior he tended
to satirize, we can confidently characterize Swift's ideal for group
interaction as, at the very least, a mean between the Puritans' utter
rejection of mainstream society[19] and the hack writer's parroting of
the rhetoric associated with his fellow Grub-Street scribblers. However, we can also tentatively argue that Swift's ideal for group interaction included a willingness to enter the fray and assert one's own
perspective within the larger group, particularly when that perspective is in danger of being annihilated by the momentum of group
consciousness. As I will argue in the next section, Gulliver's behavior
in Houyhnhnmland is nothing like Swift's ideal for group interaction, and when we criticize Gulliver's behavior on these grounds a
very interesting Christian reading of book 4 emerges.

As many scholars have noted, criticism of book 4 of *Gulliver's Travels* tends to divide, more or less neatly, into so-called "hard" and
"soft" readings. The "hard" readings take the Houyhnhnms as an
ideal and generally culminate in the argument that Swift was a misanthrope while "soft" readings argue that real human nature is a
mean between the Houyhnhnms' and the Yahoos' two extremes
(though, as I mentioned above, scholars hardly agree upon the nature of those extremes). I want to begin by arguing that the "hard"
reading is correct, at least insofar as it insists that the Houyhnhnms
are to be taken as a kind of ideal. Indeed, we can find antecedents
for most of the Houyhnhnms' social institutions—most obviously
the eugenics-based system that governs marriage and reproduc-
tion—in fictional utopias such as Plato's Kallipolis and More's Utopia, though Lycurgus's Sparta appears to have been Swift's primary
source.[20] However, more important than the resemblance of any particular features of Houyhnhnmland to features of these other real
and imagined polities are the assumptions on which this sort of uto-

pian thought is based. All four of these civil societies (Sparta, Kallipolis, Utopia, and Houyhnhnmland) take it as one of their guiding
premises that the desires of the individual are best served by eradi-
cating the desire for personal pleasure, particularly the sensual pleasures associated with food and sex. While any society reckons with
the problem of balancing the interests of the individual with the interests of the populace as a whole, the utopian collapses the distinction between these two perspectives, in effect making civic virtue
and individual virtue the same thing.[21] These ideal societies are not
ideal because of their political or social institutions; rather, they are
ideal because their citizens are ideally constituted to live in civil society.[22] The efficiency of the Houyhnhnms' social institutions clearly
indicates that they are such ideal citizens, and Gulliver is right to
admire the Houyhnhnms as models of civic virtue.

Perhaps understandably, most political philosophers (including
Hobbes and Locke) oppose the utopian project of subjugating individual desire to the interests of the state, either on moral or on practical grounds. Indeed, some proponents of the "soft" reading would
put Swift in this camp, reading Swift's portrayal of the Houyhnhnms
as purely satirical.[23] However, I argue that Houyhnhnm society is
Swift's rather straightforward attempt to imagine how classical concepts of virtue (particularly civic virtue) might play out within a population of ideal citizens.[24] Of course this reading bears some
explaining, particularly in light of Swift's ecclesiastical writings. Like
Pope,[25] Swift insisted upon the superiority of Christian wisdom to
any sort of heathen thought—see, for instance, "A Sermon Upon
the Excellence of Christianity," in which Swift argues that "the wisdom and virtue of all unrevealed philosophy in general, fell short,
and was very imperfect" (PW, 9:243).[26] However, Swift's interest in
the work of classical thinkers seemed as strong as—if not stronger
than—his interest in Christian thought, particularly during the years
that Swift spent at Sir William Temple's estate at Moor Park. Without
arguing about the extent to which Swift admired either classical or
Christian wisdom more than the other, it seems obvious that any
reading of book 4 that wholly sacrifices one of these sets of values to
the other would seem wanting. Hence my argument that Houyhnhnm society was Swift's earnest attempt to imagine a utopian society
founded on classical ideals. If we take Swift's comments about the
superiority of Christian wisdom at face value—and assume, further,
that the intent behind book 4 was consistent with that belief—we
can see the rhetorical value in an even-handed illustration of the
benefits of classical virtue. One can see a similar rhetorical strategy
at work in (of all places) Descartes' attitude toward skepticism in his

Meditations. Descartes realized that the only way to refute the skeptic was to see the world through his eyes, to concede to him in every dispute and to build only upon the common ground he could establish with the skeptic, no matter how slight that ground appeared to be. Of course, it did not hurt that Descartes himself was clearly intrigued by skeptical thinking, even if his ultimate mission was to disprove the skeptics' arguments. Similarly, Swift concedes every point to the classicist in his depiction of the many advantages of Houyhnhnm society (such as peace, stability, and freedom from psychological pain), so much so that it is quite easy for a reader to be seduced by the beauty and order in the Houyhnhnms' society.[27] Indeed, Swift valued classical thought a great deal, which would have only made it easier for him to slip into the voice of a writer who values classical concepts of virtue above all other wisdom.

Still, as advocates of the "soft" reading would insist, there are many clues in book 4 that point toward apparent shortcomings in Houyhnhnm society, the first and most obvious of which is the mere fact that the Houyhnhnms are horses. Swift states in "A Sermon upon the Excellence of Christianity" that heathen wisdom "is earthly, sensual, [and] devilish" (*PW*, 9:247); these first two adjectives might be applied quite easily to horses, but Swift might have applied the last to the Houyhnhnms as well. Indeed, depicting this utopia as a group of horses implies that there is something (both literally and figuratively) inhuman about the Houyhnhnms and their political and social institutions, but this depiction also gives book 4 a distinct air of ridiculousness. The idea of a horse merely *talking* made audiences laugh for six seasons and countless reruns of the television show *Mr. Ed,* but the Houyhnhnms' actions are far more ridiculous. Picture, for instance, the scene in which Master Houyhnhnm "put his fore-hoof to his mouth [. . .] and made other signs, to know what [Gulliver] would eat" (*PW*, 11:214) or the tasks that the Houyhnhnms manage to perform with their hooves and pasterns. In addition to possessing the ability to thread a needle, the Houyhnhnms "milk their cows, reap their oats, and do all the work which requires hands" (*PW*, 11:258) using this bizarre and comical method. Even the staunchest "hard" reader must crack a smile at the image of a horse milking a cow, and such a patently silly image calls into question any unqualified admiration of the Houyhnhnms. However, while many readers are apt to gloss over the more ridiculous aspects of Houyhnhnmland, most readers do note that the most pleasurable emotion that the Houyhnhnms seem capable of is contentment; they do not seem to possess the capacity for happiness, much less joy, ecstasy, or exhilaration. In turning their well-honed rational faculties toward the "earthly" and the "sensual," the Hou-yhnhnms have freed their species from life's difficulties, but they have also explained away most of life's pleasures as well.

We should also be suspicious of Gulliver's enthusiasm for the Houyhnhnms, especially when taken alongside the Houyhnhnms' inhumanity. In "The Excellence of Christianity," Swift argues that classical talk of virtue was "but vain babbling, and a mere sound of words [. . .] because they [classical authors] were not agreed what this virtue was, or wherein it did consist" (*PW*, 9:244). We can find just this sort of inconsistency in Gulliver's conception of virtue. For instance, Gulliver reports that "friendship and benevolence are the two principal virtues among the Houyhnhnms" (*PW*, 11:252). How-ever, the Houyhnhnms do not relate to one another in any way that one might reasonably call friendship; indeed, that the Houyhnhnms do not have individual names for one another seems to preclude the type of individuation that friendship requires (would a person ever say she is friends with someone whose name she does not know?). Further, the very ideas of friendship and benevolence seem to be in tension, the former describing a deep relationship among close associates while the latter refers to an impartial distribution of kind-ness and generosity among a larger population.[28] This confusion seems to parallel the conflation of individual and civic virtue in the work of utopian writers, but we cannot pin Gulliver's conflation of friendship and benevolence solely on his clear preference for the classical values that Houyhnhnm society upholds, since classical au-thors drew a distinction between the two concepts as well. In Cice-ro's *De Amicitia* (without question the most comprehensive and authoritative classical treatise on friendship), Laelius argues that "this thing called friendship has been so narrowed that the bonds of affection always unite two persons only, or, at most, a few."[29] Out-lining the ways in which Cicero's conception of friendship is incom-patible with general benevolence could be the subject of an entire essay, but it seems important to note that the occasion of Laelius's lecture on friendship in *De Amicitia* is the death of Scipio. Fannius and Scaevola ask Laelius how he bears the death of his friend since he appears to retain such composure. Laelius begins his reply by noting that he is "indeed moved by the loss of a friend such, I be-lieve, as I shall never have again, and—as I can assert on positive knowledge—a friend such as no other man ever was to me."[30] Not only does Laelius note the grief he feels, but he also repeatedly as-serts the unique nature of his friendship with Scipio. The Houyhnh-nms, by contrast, are able to bear one another's deaths without even the slightest pang of sadness, a clear indication of the species' deep-seeded incompatibility with the notion of friendship. That Gulliver, despite this glaring contradiction, still identifies friendship as the Houyhnhnms' chief virtue seems to call into question his entire rationale for idolizing the Houyhnhnms.

Thus, even if we still have difficulty imagining a good reason why Gulliver would want to join the Yahoos, we now see that it is possible to criticize the reasoning behind Gulliver's decision to join the Houyhnhnms' society.[31] In the second half of this essay I would like to further that argument by speculating about why Gulliver does not so much as mention Christianity during his stay in Houyhnhnmland. When we combine the rhetorical emphasis on minority interests outlined earlier in this essay with the anti-theoretical vision of Christianity that Swift proposes in his surviving sermons as well as the character and epistemology of the Houyhnhnms and Yahoos, we find that Christianity's absence from book 4—which we ultimately must blame on Gulliver—is even more conspicuous than we originally might have thought. However, before I make this argument I would like to explore what made Swift's take on Christianity unique and why this is important to our reading of book 4.

Perhaps the most important tenet of Swift's religion is his conscious decision to avoid complicated, controversial matters of abstract theology. A quick glance at the titles of Swift's surviving sermons—"On Brotherly Love," "On False Witness," "Doing Good," etc.—confirms Swift's emphasis on Christianity's more practical ethical aims; the only sermons whose titles allude to the age's most virulent theological controversies are "On the Trinity" and "On the Testimony of Conscience."[32] Indeed, in Louis Landa's introduction to Swift's sermons he emphasizes Swift's "conservative adherence to simple and indisputable orthodoxy as he conceived it" (*PW*, 9:101). When Swift does engage with theological controversy, as he does in "On the Trinity," it is only to dismiss it as unimportant. As he argues in that sermon, it is useless to expend so much effort in squabbling about an issue that is, at best, only marginally relevant to Christianity's more important ethical mission: "they [i.e. those who argue against the logic of the Trinity] presently conclude, that the Truth of the whole Gospel must sink along with that one Article; which is just as wise, as if a Man should say, because he dislikes one Law of his Country, he will therefore observe no Law at all" (*PW*, 9:159). Not only will Christianity not be toppled by these obscure theological debates but also Christianity has little, if anything, to gain from these disputes. Swift's analogy with criminal law further implies that a primary aim of Christianity, like criminal law, is to regulate and change social behavior, rather than simply to provide a philosophically coherent justification for one's established beliefs and practices.

While Swift is uninterested in articulating the specific tenets of his practical Christian ethics (likely because he believes they are obvious), we can see that the antihegemonic attitude described in the first section of this essay is one of his key moral assumptions. As Swift states in the sermon "On Brotherly Love," "there is no Duty more incumbent upon those who profess the Gospel, than that of Brotherly Love; which whoever could restore, in any Degree, among Men, would be an instrument of more Good to human society, than ever was, or will be done, by all the Statesmen and Politicians in the World" (*PW*, 9:171). While this statement aims to draw a distinction between Christianity and politics, it is perhaps more interesting to think about the ways in which Swift compares the two. Both Christianity and politics are forces that, ideally, make a positive difference in the world, but political party and the Church are also similar in that they are both institutions composed of individuals with differing aims, perspectives and opinions, yet each is most effective when it latches onto a coherent collective identity. In "On Brotherly Love," Swift envisions Christians, with their unifying motive of brotherly love, working collectively against a larger current of indifference and arrogance within society as a whole.[33] While he never confirms this explicitly, throughout his sermons Swift seems to have an ethical requirement that the good Christian's actions not only be consistent with orthodoxy but contrary to the current of mainstream society as well. In other words, for Swift the good Christian will always be an activist, a term that, as I will explain more fully below, could hardly be applied to the Gulliver of book 4.

The primary focus of Swift's sermons is on matters of practical ethics, but his theoretical justification for this approach reveals one of Swift's most important theological assumptions: a belief in what Swift called "revealed religion." For Swift, this term signified his opposition to the deistic proposition that clear rational understanding is a necessary condition for (not just religious, but any type of) belief. This tenet posed a threat to the very epistemological foundation of Christianity since, as a corollary to this proposition, many deists argued that belief in core Christian concepts such as the Trinity and Christ's miracles (and perhaps even God himself) was not possible because these concepts could not be grasped and explained by man's rational faculties. Swift, in opposition, insisted that reason was not involved in—or, at the very least, not an essential component of—the process of accepting the tenets of Christianity. Swift's example, as one might expect, is the mysterious metaphysical status of the

Trinity: "So, if I were directly told in Scripture, that *Three* are *One,* and *One* is *Three,* I could not conceive or believe it in the natural common Sense of that Expression, but must suppose that something dark or mystical was meant, which it pleased God to conceal from me and from all the World" (*PW,* 9:161). Swift insisted that there were certain truths that, for reasons known only to God, cannot be explained by human reason. Further, the ability to take these matters on faith is one of the essential characteristics of the true Christian.

That the Houyhnhnms would be unreceptive to Swift's conception of revealed religion seems obvious. Not only would the Houyhnhnms have no use for Christianity since they live in an environment that has all the features of an unfallen Golden Age[34] but also their language would, presumably, lack the terminology necessary to explain the purpose of Christianity (for instance, the Houyhnhnms appear to have no words for particular sins or the concept of sin in general). While most readers are apt to take these aspects of Houyhnhnmland as positive traits, one must concede that it is also possible to view the Houyhnhnms' perfect reasonableness as harmful insofar as it renders the Houyhnhnms constitutionally immune to revealed wisdom. According to Houyhnhnm etymology, the word they use to refer to their species means, literally, "the Perfection of Nature" (*PW,* 11:219). We also know from the Master Houyhnhnm that "nature and reason [are] sufficient guides for a reasonable animal" (*PW,* 11:232), though he later simplifies his statement, lecturing to Gulliver that "reason alone is sufficient to govern a rational creature" (*PW,* 11:243). Judging by these statements, it seems as if the Houyhnhnms' faith in their own perfection lies in their assumption that reason is fully capable of explaining nature, an assumption they share with deists. The Houyhnhnms believe that they exist in a Baconian world of clear, observable facts and, because of this assumption, Christianity simply could not be revealed to them. Further, the Houyhnhnms do not exhibit any psychological phenomenon that resembles the kind of faith that Swift's Christian must possess.

Like the Houyhnhnms he idolizes, in book 4 Gulliver seems incapable of accepting Christianity's revealed wisdom. Gulliver fails to live up to Swift's definition of Christianity in either his theological assumptions or in his practical ethics, facts that are apparent whenever Gulliver writes about the Yahoos. First, Gulliver's sympathy with the deistic notion of belief is evidenced in his disgust with the Yahoos for being "unteachable," an assessment he repeats several times (*PW,* 11:219, 250). However, just as Gulliver's identification of the Houyhnhnms' chief virtues (i.e., friendship and benevolence) seemed self-contradictory, Gulliver also contradicts his statement of one of the Yahoos' chief shortcomings. Despite his insistence that the Yahoos are unteachable, Gulliver notes that the Houyhnhnms have trained the Yahoos to do simple tasks of manual labor such as pulling sledges (interestingly, a task that horses perform in European society). While this seems like a contradiction, we might give Gulliver the benefit of the doubt, refining our notion of "teachable" to include not only the ability to perform a task reliably and on demand, but also self-consciousness of how and why one does the task. The Yahoos clearly lack the latter capability, which is the shortcoming that Gulliver seems to refer to when he labels them "unteachable." However, this more complex definition of "teachability" introduces a new wrinkle into our evaluation of Gulliver's disgust with the Yahoos. According to Swift, the self-consciousness that Gulliver's definition of "teachability" seems to depend upon is not necessary for Christianity.[35] Indeed, the overuse of that faculty (as in the case of the Deists and, probably, the Houyhnhnms) is more likely to lead one *away* from true Christianity. Thus, we see that Gulliver's assumptions about the nature of belief would have prevented him from accepting Swift's particular take on Christian theology.

Perhaps more important, though, is Gulliver's inability to live up to Swift's vision of the Christian as activist. Gulliver's actions in book 4 could not be more unlike the ideal for social interaction I described in this essay's first section. As I have already mentioned, Gulliver's relationship with the Houyhnhnms smacks of the same type of uncritical enthusiasm that Swift satirizes in characters such as *A Tale of a Tub*'s Grub-Street Hack and the writer of "A Tritical Essay Concerning the Faculties of the Mind." Gulliver displays no apparent desire to criticize or even question the Houyhnhnms' actions; he idolizes and imitates the animals in every respect, from insignificant characteristics such as their gait to their most serious moral precepts, such as their emphasis on "friendship and benevolence." That Gulliver's admiration for the Houyhnhnms' institutions is not based on rational principles is evidenced by yet another apparent contradiction. When Gulliver tells the Master Houyhnhnm about the medical profession in England, Gulliver criticizes one of the profession's primary treatments as follows: "For Nature (as the Physicians alledge [*sic*]) having intended the superior anterior Orifice only for the *Intromission* of Solids and Liquids, and the inferior Posterior for Ejection; these Artists ingeniously considering that in all Diseases Nature is forced out of her Seat; therefore to replace her in it,

the Body must be treated in a Manner directly contrary, by inter-
changing the Use of each Orifice; forcing Solids and Liquids in the
Anus, and making Evacuations at the Mouth" (*PW,* 11:254). Gulliver
treats this theory with derision, but just a few pages later he notes
the ingeniousness of the Houyhnhnms' cure for a Yahoo disease
called *Hnea Yahoo:* "the Cure prescribed is a Mixture of *their own
Dung* and *Urine,* forcibly put down the *Yahoo*'s throat." Gulliver even
enthusiastically recommends this course of treatment to his fellow
Englishmen (*PW,* 11:262). While the implementation of the Houyhnhnms' cure is slightly different from English doctors', the theory
behind disrupting the normal flow of the digestive system in order
to shock the body into health is suspiciously similar. Thus, we see
that Gulliver's idolization of the Houyhnhnms has resulted in a
value system in which anything associated with the Houyhnhnms is
good and anything associated with the Yahoos is bad. While Gulliver
can be critical of a medical theory when it is associated with the Yahoos, his propensity to think for himself vanishes when the same
theory is supported by Houyhnhnm thought.

However, Gulliver's deference to the Houyhnhnms is only one
manifestation of his antiactivist bent. Gulliver's behavior toward the
Yahoos resembles the other extreme of group interaction, in which
the individual has no investment at all in the collective identity of
the group. Gulliver repeats his suspicion that he is, in fact, a Yahoo
several times throughout book 4 (*PW,* 11:213–14, 219, 224, 242 and
[most to the point] 251, to cite but a few references), yet he never
considers the Yahoos as anything but an utterly lost and hopeless
race. Since the Houyhnhnms themselves repeatedly acknowledge
Gulliver's physical similarities to the Yahoos, Gulliver is unable to
deny completely his resemblance to the "unteachable brutes." However, Gulliver takes great care to distance himself rhetorically from
the creatures, even as he lumps the rest of the human race in with
Houyhnhnmland's Yahoos. Not only does Gulliver express indignation whenever he is mentioned in the same breath as Yahoos, but
also he takes care to attach to himself terms that are antithetical to
terms he applies to the Yahoos, such as when the Master Houyhnhnm compliments Gulliver for his "Teachableness, Civility and
Cleanliness" (*PW,* 11:234). This pattern continues even as Gulliver
gradually becomes convinced that human beings and Yahoos really
are the same species. Gulliver develops a habit of casually referring
to human beings as Yahoos (such as when he notes the "fifty *Yahoos*"
under his command when he was a captain (*PW,* 11:243) or when
he speculates that "about a Million of *Yahoos*" have been killed in
England's current war with France (*PW,* 11:245)) even as he care-

fully qualifies any identification of himself with the Yahoos (such as when he inserts the parenthetical "as he called them" after the Master Houyhnhnm refers to the Yahoos as Gulliver's "brethren" (*PW*, 11:259]). Just as Swift believed the Puritans had done to the Established Church in his own country, Gulliver has absolved himself of any responsibility toward the Yahoos by refusing to identify with the group.

After the general assembly of Houyhnhnms "exhorts" the Master Houyhnhnm to cease keeping Gulliver "in his family more like a Houyhnhnm than a brute animal" (*PW*, 11:263), Gulliver understands the decision facing him as composed of two binary options: become a Yahoo and live with the uncivilized Yahoos or reject this identification with the Yahoos and leave the island. However, as a Christian, a third option should have been visible to Gulliver: change Yahoo nature.[36] Thus, our main criticism of Gulliver is not for his pride,[37] but for his shortsightedness, cowardice, and selfishness. Gulliver is unwilling to enter into a community that, with a significant amount of work and self-sacrifice (not to mention near-constant practice of the Christian virtues), he could improve immeasurably.

However, is the reader justified in expecting Gulliver to be an evangelist? One might remember that in *Robinson Crusoe* Gulliver's chief literary foil not only deepens his own religious conviction during his exile but manages to convert the savage Friday as well. Gulliver, by contrast, never mentions his religion while he is in Houyhnhnmland, even when explaining the notion of religious war to the Master Houyhnhnm (Gulliver notes that conflicts have begun over "whether *Flesh* be *Bread,* or *Bread* be *Flesh:* Whether the juice of a certain *Berry* be *Blood* or *Wine*" (*PW*, XI:246), condescendingly recasting these theological debates as semantic controversies). While it is impossible to predict how a writer as imaginative and as innovative as Swift would have solved the problem of injecting Christianity into book 4 of *Gulliver's Travels,* it seems clear that making Gulliver into a Christian evangelist would have disabled the type of satire that Swift attempts in book 4. Throughout book 4, Swift guards against any attempts the reader might make to identify with Gulliver's detestation of the Yahoos. While Gulliver's aversion to the species is perhaps understandable given his rude introduction to the Yahoos (a group of them defecate on his head), he tends to take his lack of concern for the Yahoos' welfare too far. In particular, his decision to make clothes and shoes out of Yahoo hides strikes us as barbaric, and his cool, uninterested account of the Houyhnhnms' debate about whether to "exterminate" (*PW*, 11:271) the Yahoos strikes us as inhuman. By refusing to let the reader identify with his protagonist, Swift prevents the simple attitude of dismissive scorn that readers often take toward the objects of satire. Swift also undercuts this type of simple dismissal when the Master Houyhnhnm observes that "the *Yahoos* were known to hate one another more than they did any different Species of Animals" (*PW,* 11:260). Swift implies that it is not enough simply to hate vice because to hate vice is to hate human nature, as Gulliver does at the end of book 4. The sophisticated Christian reader, unlike Gulliver, will not simply dismiss and ignore vice, but will be prompted to examine the causes of vice and attempt to change them.

The affinities between the activist impulse so desirable in the Christian and the moral outrage that defines the satirist should be obvious. Just as the satirist cannot let vice amble forward without criticism, so should the Christian be unable to tolerate the entropic slide toward nonsense and vice as the perspective of the individual is subsumed into the identity of the group. Further, the ideal Christian should not simply abandon a group heading in the wrong direction; he should work actively to effect positive changes in the larger group identity. Were Swift in Gulliver's place, one could easily imagine him diving headfirst into the world of the Yahoos, just as he dove into Britain's seedy, immoral underbelly in many of his other works of poetry and prose. However, Gulliver does not possess this impulse; he is unwilling or unable to imagine the ways in which Yahoo society (or Houyhnhnm society for that matter) could be better. For Swift, Christianity is embedded in a world that operates, by and large, contrary to its values. However, rather than rejecting this world, it is the responsibility of Christians (both as a group and as individuals) to assert their perspective, to change the world's momentum. Such an attitude is necessary if Christianity is expected to thrive. That Gulliver does not possess such an attitude is perhaps his chief shortcoming.

NOTES

1. Samuel Holt Monk, "The Pride of Lemuel Gulliver," *The Sewanee Review* 63 (1955): 48–71.

2. Roland Mushat Frye, "Swift's Yahoo and the Christian Symbols for Sin," *Journal of the History of Ideas* 15 (1954): 201–17.

3. This interpretation has a long tradition that continues today, but one might start with this textbook example that includes copious references: Mary Nichols, "Rationality and Community: Swift's Criticism of the Houyhnhnms," *The Journal of Politics* 43 (1981): 1153–69.

4. T. O. Wedel, "On the Philosophical Background of *Gulliver's Travels.*" *Studies in Philology* 23 (1926): 434–50.

5. It is hardly a unique proposition to discuss Gulliver 4 in terms of Swift's ecclesiastical writings. However, where those studies tend to build an allegorical reading of book 4 based on Swift's views on human nature, I would like to concentrate on how Swift imagined Christianity should have informed Gulliver's decision about which group to join when he lands on the shore of Houyhnhnmland.

6. One must note that Swift's allegiance to the Tory Party was complicated and never explicitly expressed. However, Swift wrote political propaganda exclusively for the Tory Party after 1710, and for the purposes of this paper I will accept this as an indication of party affiliation.

7. David Woolley, ed., *The Correspondence of Jonathan Swift, D.D* (Frankfurt am Main: Peter Lang, 1999), 2:606–7.

8. Christopher Fauske, *Jonathan Swift and the Church of Ireland, 1710–1724* (Dublin: Irish Academic Press, 2002), 23.

9. Jonathan Swift, *The Prose Writings of Jonathan Swift*, ed. Herbert Davis (Oxford: Basil Blackwell, 1939–74), 10:4. All subsequent references to Swift's prose works will refer to the Davis edition and will be cited parenthetically with the prefix *PW.*

10. Ian Higgins. *Swift's Politics: A Study in Disaffection* (Cambridge: Cambridge University Press), 1994.

11. Ibid., 4. Higgins also directs us to F. P. Lock, *Swift's Tory Politics* (London: Duckworth, 1983), 146–61.

12. Fauske, *Ireland,* 33.

13. Ibid., 30–32.

14. Ibid.

15. Ibid.

16. For a detailed look at Swift and King's complicated relationship, see Fauske, *Ireland,* 36–45.

17. Woolley, *Correspondence,* 2:606.

18. Edward Said, "Swift's Tory Anarchy." *Eighteenth-Century Studies* 3 (1969): 48–66.

19. For details about Swift's thoughts on Puritanism, see chapter 3, "Fanaticism and Freedom" in Patrick Reilly, *Jonathan Swift: The Brave Desponder.* Carbondale: Southern Illinois University Press, 1982; and Thomas L. Canavan, "Robert Burton, Jonathan Swift and the Tradition of Anti-Puritan Invective." *Journal of the History of Ideas* 34 (1973): 227–42.

20. For a longer discussion of the influence of Sparta on *Gulliver's Travels* see: Higgins, Ian. "'Gulliver's Travels' and Sparta." *Modern Language Review* 78 (1983): 513–31.

21. This collapse of individual and civic virtue often manifests itself rhetorically in the form of the man-as-microcosm metaphor, a device that plays an extremely prominent role in Plato's and More's texts.

22. Plato is very clear about his intentions in the *Republic;* his mission is not to imagine a set of political institutions that will elevate his current society to the level of an ideal society but to imagine what political institutions would look like under a set of ideal circumstances.

23. For example: Boris, Ford. "The Limitations of the Houyhnhnms," in *Readings on Gulliver's Travels,* edited by Gary Wiener (San Diego: Greenhaven, 2000), 147–55.

24. The terms "classical" and "Christian" are used rather loosely throughout this essay. I define Swift's utopian project as "classical" since it is based on premises

established by classical authors and does not engage with Christian thinking, at least on a literal level.

25. See, for instance, the prose argument for "Messiah:" Alexander Pope. *The Poems of Alexander Pope: A Reduced Version of the Twickenham Text* (New Haven: Yale University Press, 1963), 189.

26. According to Louis Landa's introduction to Swift's sermons in volume 9 of the Davis edition, it is impossible to give even a rough estimation of when this sermon was composed, as it was not published until after Swift's death. However, due to the nature of Swift's sermons, that this was a position he would have held was very obvious to any good Christian, since he rarely addressed controversial or difficult concepts in his sermons.

27. Another attractive aspect of this reading is that it frees advocates of the "hard" reading from the rather insulting accusation, often repeated by "soft" readers, that they confuse Swift's attitudes with those of his creation. Instead, I would argue that these critics are simply seduced by the same philosophy that seduces Gulliver (and, Swift would argue, seduces most anyone not open to Christianity).

28. The *Oxford English Dictionary* does admit a definition of benevolence as "goodwill (towards a particular person or on a particular occasion)" that was in use during the eighteenth century (though it is now obsolete). However, it is almost certain that Swift used the word according to its much more common meaning of "charitable feeling (as a general state or disposition towards mankind at large)."

29. Virgil, *Eclogues, De Senectute, De Amicitia, De Divinatione,* Loeb Classical Library (1923), 129.

30. Ibid., 119.

31. Of course Swift does not present Gulliver's desire to join the Houyhnhnms as a consciously deliberated choice. While I do write of Gulliver's "choice" to join the Houyhnhnms throughout this essay, I do this only as a means of shorthand for referring to the complex set of assumptions, desires, and predispositions that leads Gulliver to join the Houyhnhnms. In fact, I argue below that it is quite telling that Gulliver never seriously considers joining the Yahoos (despite his physical affinities with that species) as it signals just how deeply antithetical to Christian values Gulliver's world view really is.

32. That Swift's sermons provided the best articulation of his own theology and ethics is, of course, debatable. However, looking to these documents is convenient since one does not have to peel back the layers of irony that characterize Swift's writing in other genres. I have attempted to be conservative in my analysis of Swift's sermons, reserving my judgments to conclusions that could be corroborated (or, at the very least, not easily refuted) by his more well-known writing.

33. One might also note that within the sermon Swift's own persona is defined against a similarly undesirable trend within the church itself, adding a further layer to his underdog persona. See, in particular, the passage on "the Man truly Moderate" (*PW,* 9:177–8).

34. Houyhnhnmland resembles traditional representations of the Golden Age in a number of respects, the most obvious of these being the easy availability of honey in hollow trees (*PW,* 11:260).

35. Of course a version of Christianity that relied solely on this sort of revealed wisdom would be decidedly bare bones. However, these matters that the Christian must take on faith are what separate Christianity from other systems of moral philosophy, including the classical systems that the Houyhnhnms' society seems to be based upon. In that sense, at least, this leap of faith is what defines Christianity and is its essential component.

36. Interestingly, this option is actually proposed by the Master Houyhnhnm at the general assembly. Based on the evidence of Gulliver's reason, the Master Houyhnhnm proposes educating the Yahoos, raising their status in society, and employing asses to perform the manual labor the Yahoos currently perform. However, the assembly rejects the Master Houyhnhnm's proposal.

37. Pride figures prominently in much criticism of Gulliver's character. See, for instance, Samuel Holt Monk, "The Pride of Lemuel Gulliver," *The Sewanee Review* 63 (1955): 48–71; and Kathleen Williams, "Gulliver's Voyage to the Houyhnhnms." *ELH* 18 (1951): 275–86.

Swift and Religion: Notes Toward a Psychoanalytic Interpretation

Louise K. Barnett

THE CHARGE THAT SWIFT WAS NOT ENTIRELY RELIGIOUS HAS HAD A LONG history, plaguing him for much of his life and continuing down into the present. Like certain other professions, notably medicine, religion is generally regarded as a calling as well as a living: we are uncomfortable when the latter seems to eclipse the former, or when the practitioner's best energies go elsewhere. The particulars of Swift's biography suggest both of these possibilities.

Swift would have preferred a career in the world of politics rather than the church, and it is equally true that the church, then as now, was a political as well as a religious institution: churchmen might be expected to be as concerned with their advancement as careerists in other professions. Being a priest was Swift's job, not his chief enthusiasm, and the generally unmemorable and uninspired nature of his pronouncements on religion contrasts sharply with what is memorable and inspired in his writing—his satiric observations on the human condition and his polemics. Swift was "not the gravest of divines," as he styled himself in "Stella's Birthday" (1727).[1] On the contrary, outside the pages of his fictions, when religion is the subject he is invariably grave, often to the point of dullness. Louis Landa's comments on the few sermons that have been preserved are apt. He writes: "Swift's attitude toward his sermons, so far as it has been recorded, was one of casual interest or of indifference, if not outright depreciation. There is nothing to suggest that he desired their publication; and his letters are almost devoid of comment upon his preaching." Swift indignantly rejected the advice of Archbishop King that he advance himself by writing theological treatises.[2] Although the indignation was directed more at the archbishop than the treatises, theology as a subject held small interest for him. It comprised little of his library and less of his conversation. Yet, in his long life as an active priest, Swift served his church wholeheartedly and ably. In an essay published fourteen years after his book, *Swift*

and the Church of Ireland (1954), Louis Landa accords Swift a secure
place as "defender of the Establishment."[3] But in spite of Swift's excellent record as a conscientious churchman, even a scholar as informed as Landa has some hesitation. As for "defender of the
faith," he writes, "that is another matter, in which he qualifies less
well".[4] I am not certain what Landa intends by this since Swift recognized no difference between the religious establishment, the
Church of England, and the faith. When he uses the words religion
and Christianity, both typically refer to the faith purveyed by the
Church of England.

That Swift was scrupulous in observing the rituals of his Church,
both in his role as dean of St. Patrick's and in the privacy of his own
house, is indisputable, but when he cloistered himself for personal
devotions, was he perhaps actually engaged in some other pursuit?
We can only say that his observed behavior does not encourage such
suspicions. If suspicions have nevertheless persisted down through
the centuries, they can be accounted for in two primary ways. The
first and most pervasive cause is the sense of incongruity between a
perceived lack of decorum in some of Swift's writings and a religious
vocation, buttressed by the lurid picture of Swift composed of distortions, misinformation, and some genuine mysteries about his character and life. A Swift such as Thackeray imagines, for instance,
could hardly be sincerely religious, but we know today that this Swift
is a fiction, and we are more willing to accept that other negative
assessments are compounded of narrowly conceived standards of
proper or improper behavior. Today, we can more easily dismiss this
first area of suspicion about Swift.

The second cause is more problematic since it relates to the difficulty of constructing a valid relationship between the invisible realm
of intention/motive/belief and the visible world. Making a simplis-
tic connection between one such sign, *A Tale of a Tub,* and the beliefs
of the man, Queen Anne refused to give Swift an English pulpit.
Scholars of our time may be more sophisticated readers than that,
yet their questioning of Swift's sincerity in spite of the record of his
actions is both a visceral and an intellectual response to the lack of
passion in his religious utterances, the formulaic and perfunctory
qualities that caused Camille Looten to complain that Swift lacked
"the inner feeling of God."[5] How can Swift's "inner feelings" be
determined? Only by outward indications whose relationship to the
inner we must interpret. Swift spoke to this problem when he observed on a key issue of his time, that of compelling religious conformity, that "you may force men by interest or punishment to say
or swear they believe, and to act as if they believed: you can go no

further" (*PW,* 9:261). This is the difficulty facing such an investigation. Swift's own speech and actions, the outward indications, presume the inner belief, and while we might speculate on the applicability of interest or punishment to his own situation—that is, he needed to demonstrate belief in order to make his living—we can go no further in determining the existence of "the inner feeling of God" in Swift (or, for that matter, in anyone). Nevertheless, we will look at some of the indications.

Swift's role as part of a religious institution is well documented and has been addressed in detail by Landa, Irvin Ehrenpreis, and Andrew Carpenter, among others. My interest here is in what William James defined as religion: "the feelings, acts, and experiences of individual men in their solitude, so far as they apprehend themselves to stand in relation to whatever they may consider the divine."[6] James described two kinds of temperament, "men who seem to have started in life with a bottle or two of champagne inscribed to their credit" and "others [who] seem to have been born close to the pain-threshold, which the slightest irritants fatally send them over."[7] Does it not appear, he asks rhetorically, that "one who lived more habitually on one side of the pain-threshold might need a different sort of religion from one who habitually lived on the other?"[8] Or, as W. W. Meissner asserts, "In psychological terms each man creates his own image of God, even though that individualized image is in contact with a shared set of communal beliefs. . . ."[9] All Christians believe in the concept of God the Father, for example, but the way in which this abstraction is translated into an image will differ from one individual to another as well as from one community of believers to another. The believer who feels secure grounds that security in a caring God; the believer who feels guilty and insecure imagines a wrathful and punitive God who reinforces this self-image; the believer who feels estranged mirrors this condition in a distant deity, or—conversely—compensates with a warm and loving God.[10]

I propose to bring a psychoanalytic approach to bear upon the kind of belief Swift articulates, the kind of God image his utterances suggest, on the premise that "the sense of self is in fact in dialectical interaction with a God representation that has become essential to the maintenance of the sense of being oneself."[11] Everyone of necessity forms some internal God representation, which is developed and transformed as the individual goes through the life cycle and adds new experiences to the inner representational world. Thus, something of Swift's sense of self might be inferred from his remarks on God. Swift's biography is in fact congruent with the kind of God figure that his references to God suggest.

Freud wrote that "a little boy is bound to love and admire his father, who seems to him the most powerful, the kindest and the wisest creature in the world. God himself is after all only an exaltation of this picture of the father as he is represented in the mind of early childhood."[12] A real father might well be less than ideally powerful, kind, and wise, but Swift never knew his father because of his posthumous birth, a deprivation that freed him to imagine the paternal figure as he pleased. Where the ordinary child experiences parental security, Swift as a child faced a void, a condition that might be expected to have multiple and far-reaching effects. As Freud wrote: "The individual's emotional attitudes to other people are already established at an unexpectedly early age . . . All of his later choices of friendship and love follow upon the basis of the memory-traces left behind by these prototypes."[13] Swift himself acknowledged such a principle at work in his life when he wrote to Bolingbroke and Pope about a forming experience of his childhood: "I remember when I was a little boy, I felt a great fish at the end of my line which I drew up almost on the ground, but it dropt in, and the disappointment vexeth me to this very day, and I believe it was the type of all my future disappontments."[14] Whether or not Swift remained incorrigibly disappointed over the lost fish, he wanted to present himself in this light to a close friend; he had an investment in this self-constructed portrait of primal and repeated disappointment. If it is not the literal truth, it is nevertheless significant as a consciously contrived self-image that Swift wanted to present to an intimate.

Swift's image of self also suffered from an early lack of parental response, an experience he was doomed to reenact.[15] Throughout his life he would remain vulnerable to the need for an idealized father figure or mentor to replace the absent father. Of one of those figures, Archbishop King, Swift wrote: "In thy great Care we place our Trust, / Because thour't GREAT and GOOD and JUST."[16] Another poem addressed to King observes, "Without your Breast all Wisdom lyes."[17] This is the ideally sagacious father Swift had not had and accordingly could not find in the archbishop.

As for the kindness that a father would ordinarily exemplify for a child, here, too, a flesh and blood father would have had opportunities of the sort that Swift could not have experienced but understandably always hungered for at the hands of father substitutes. Ehrenpreis observes that Swift "had looked to a paternal figure for blessings which his grace had reserved for compliant proteges and blood kin."[18] Persisting in the early pattern of discouragement on account of the "Ill Treatment of his nearest Relations" (*PW*, 5:192),

Swift at sixty wrote a bitter reproach to the archbishop, complaining that "your Grace hath thought fit to take every opportunity of giving me all sorts of uneasiness, without ever giving me, in my whole life, one single mark of your favour beyond common civilities" (*Corres.*, 3:87). The tone is that of the frequently chastized son who never wins the father's approval, whereas he described his politician employer, Robert Harley, as an indulgent father, "a Person . . . who hath always treated me with the Tenderness of a Parent and never refused me any Favour I asked for a Friend" (*Corres.*, 1:338).

Like his relations with father figures, Swift's image of God was affected by his early experience of deprivation: the Heavenly Father is neither approachable nor comforting, not kind and loving so much as strong. Usually Swift refers to God's power rather than to any other attribute. Thus, he writes: "May God work a miracle, by changing the hearts of an abandoned people" (*Corres.*, 4:107). He describes his life as a burden "that I must heartily beg God Almighty to enable me to bear" (*Corres.*, 2:660). In both instances Swift is a suppliant before the power of God, but characteristically these expressions have a perfunctory, formulaic quality.

An enraptured, celebratory description of God, such as these lines from Gerard Manley Hopkins, is unthinkable in Swift:

> Oh, morning, at the brown brink eastward, springs—
> Because the Holy Ghost over the bent
> World broods with warm breast and with ah! bright wings.
>
> (12–14)[19]

The particularization of God as a warm, brooding, nurturing—even feminine—presence does not correspond to Swift's temperament or his image of God. A seventeenth-century poet whose rigorous sense of human sinfulness and Anglican faith make him a more appropriate figure of comparison with Swift wrote as follows:

> But as I raved and grew more fierce and wild
> At every word,
> Methought I heard one calling, *Child!*
> And I replied, *My Lord.*
>
> (33–36)[20]

Herbert, too, is far removed from Swift in his vivid sense of relationship and dialogue with God. Swift makes formulaic calls upon God's mercy without conveying any sense of individual relationship or real speech. On the contrary, God remains distant and impersonal—

unapproachable. Swift exclaims in *Thoughts on Religion:* "Miserable Mortals! can we contribute to the Honour and Glory of God? I could wish that expression were struck out of our prayer-books" (*PW,* 9:263). This is one of the few Swiftian utterances on religion that displays strong feeling about a purely theological matter rather than the practical consequences of religious doctrine.

Swift's references to God are always formal: "It is apparent from Scripture, and most agreeable to reason, that the safety and welfare of nations are under the most peculiar care of God's providence," Swift writes in his sermon on doing good (*PW,* 9:238). This is a perfectly orthodox statement in every respect. It is not personal but collective experience that is invoked: Swift's religion is a matter of what is said in the sacred book and what is acceptable to the human faculty of reason; what is ascribed to God is a vast and indeed lifeless abstraction, the safety and welfare of nations. Missing, notably, is the sense of a fully engaged writer, the vivid particularity and feeling of Swift's satire.

Over all, Swift's references to God suggest a conventional, institutionally correct concept in keeping with what we know of Swift's life within the Church of England. He felt that this church was the best religious institution to maintain society in its most desirable form and its God accordingly stands for the state of things as they ought to be. In his sermon on the duty of mutual subjection Swift wrote that "the subject must obey his Prince, because God commands it, human laws require it, and the safety of the public maketh it necessary" (*PW,* 9:144). Sacred and secular law and public safety are all in harmony in mandating the basic political hierarchy.

Swift's God thus provides transcendental authority for Swift's deeply held political, social, and moral tenets. He is not a God created in Swift's image but rather a God who responds to Swift's particular needs for order. Lacking a source of power in the world, Swift spent his energies, both in his life and in his writings, trying to impose order with the means available to him. It pleased him to envision God as the source and rationale for this order, not endowed with the specific attributes that a real father would appear to a child to possess but simply the ultimate authority. "All government is from God, who is the God of order," his sermon on doing good asserts, "and therefore whoever attempts to breed confusion or disturbance among a people, doth his utmost to take the government of the world out of God's hands, and to put it into the hands of the Devil, who is the author of confusion" (*PW,* 9:238). This is a succinct statement of Swift's fundamental stance, the espousal of order in every category of life and the rejection of confusion: the stark polarities of God and the devil.

The value of duly constituted authority and public order is so important to Swift that he is even willing to countenance hypocrisy in order to achieve it. In *A Project for the Advancement of Religion and the Reformation of Manners* he proposes to make religion a necessary step to preferment although this would increase hypocrisy: "But if one in twenty should be brought over to true piety by this and the other nineteen be only hypocrites, the advantages would still be great. Besides, hypocrisy is much more eligible than open infidelity and vice; it wears the livery of religion; it acknowledges her authority" (*PW*, 2:57).

For Freud, religion is another form of transference, and like all transference phenomena, it is only a replay of childhood. In *Totem and Taboo* (1914) he locates the origin of religion, like that of the neuroses,[21] in the Oedipal triangle, beginning in the history of the primal horde of sons who kill the father because he has forbidden sexual relations with the women of the clan. The murder is repressed but returns as a guilt that can be assuaged through reconciliation with the dead father. Historically, this impulse is first projected on to a totem animal and later onto a heavenly father.

In *The Future of an Illusion* (1927) religion appeases not only the primal Oedipal guilt but cosmic anxieties as well: [The gods] "must exorcise the terrors of nature, they must reconcile men to the cruelty of Fate, particularly as it is shown in death, and they must compensate them for the sufferings and privations which a civilized life in common had imposed on them."[22] Such beliefs are illusions, that is, they are the product of wishes. Freud sees these illusions as extension of infantile gratification into adulthood, a persistence of immaturity in which "the benevolent rule of a divine Providence allays our fear of the dangers of life; the establishment of a moral world-order ensures the fulfillment of the demands of justice, which have so often remained unfulfilled in human civilization; and the prolongation of earthily existence in a future life provides the local and temporal framework in which these wish-fulfillments shall take place."[23] Unbelievers are the true adults because they forgo the comforts of childhood illusions in order to embrace reality: "Men cannot remain children forever; they must in the end go out into hostile life."[24]

Swift, although he accepts God and religion as Freud does not, avoids the attitude that Freud attributes to believers and instead seems to embrace a view almost as bleak as Freud's. On his birthday Swift always read the third chapter of Job, one of the most despairing in the Bible. It begins: "After this opened Job his mouth, and cursed his day. And Job spoke, and said, Let the day perish wherein I was born, and the night in which it was said, there is a man child conceived" (King James Version, Job 3:1–3). The chapter continues in a bitter invocation of nonbeing, a desire not to end being but never to have been.

Religion does not mask the harsh reality of human existence for Swift so much as provide an explanation for this reality. As he asserted in his sermon on the poor man's contentment, and reiterated elsewhere in similar language, "God never intended this World for such a Place of Rest as we would make it; for the Scripture assureth us, that it was only designed as a Place of Trial" (*PW*, 9:196). Religion for Swift is a means of escaping infantile illusions of all sorts and accepting life as it is.

Freud would comment that any Christian belief system is immature in its refusal to accept the finality of death. Swift believes in the afterlife, yet he eschews the possibility of a heaven that would give him his heart's desire. He writes to Pope in 1727, "I have often wish'd that God almighty would be so easy to the weakness of mankind, as to let old friends be acquainted in another state; and if I were to write an Utopia for heaven, that would be one of my Schemes" (*Corres.*, 3:131). But, he continues, "This wildness you must allow for, because I am giddy and deaf." In numerous letters Swift chronicles an obsession with death that indicates neither the thoughtful memento mori nor the triumph represented by the afterlife, both orthodox Christian responses to death. In 1729 he writes to John Browne, "I was 47 Years old when I began to think of death; and the reflections upon it now begin when I wake in the Morning, and end when I am going to Sleep" (*Corres.*, 3:261). To Pope in 1733, when he was sixty-six, he writes: "As to Mortality, it hath never been out of my head eighteen minutes these eighteen years" (*Corres.*, 3:615). And again to Bolingbroke, "Death . . . is never out of my mind" (*Corres.*, 3:294). These somber yet matter-of-factly stated remarks are often coupled with his assertions that he values life very little or thinks that it is not of much value.

Landa's conclusion that "there is nothing about Swift's pessimism as a churchman that is strange or pathological or wilful or self-indulgent or even uniquely personal and temperamental"[25] is accurate but incomplete. That Swift had reason to be pessimistic about the condition of the Church in his time is correct. His words to Ford in 1736, "I have long given up all hopes of Church or Christianity" (*Corres.*, 4:316), must be taken as a despairing recognition that his religious institution would continue to lose ground to competing congregations. Since Swift saw this church as the foundation of all forms of order in the body politic, he was deeply affected.

But Swift's pessimism moves from the proper Christian depreciation of worldly life to an all-encompassing, un-Christian despair. This is, after all, a man who on the anniversary of the day of his birth habitually read a lament that goes beyond a call for death as an end of suffering to condemn birth and life itself. James once again provides a useful description: "There are people for whom evil means only a mal-adjustment with things, a wrong correspondence of one's life with the environment. Such evil as this is curable, in principle at least, upon the natural plane, for merely by modifying either the self or the things, or both at once, the two terms may be made to fit, and all go merry as a marriage bell again. But there are others for whom evil is no mere relation of the subject to particular outer things, but something more radical and general, a wrongness or vice in his essential nature, which no alteration of the environment, or any superficial rearrangement of the inner self, can cure and which requires a supernatural remedy."[26] This is similar to Swift's own division of the world into "two Sects, those that hope the best, and those that fear the worst" (*Corres.*, 1:226). As he himself admitted, Swift belongs to this second category: his satire is often directed against human nature itself rather than against remediable evils. But arguably his early parental deprivation left a self too needy to be fully consoled by the supernatural remedy James alludes to. Intellectually Swift could make the commitment that he describes in the *Sentiments of a Church-of-England Man:* "Whoever professes himself a Member of, the Church of England ought to believe in God, and his Providence, together with Revealed Religion, and the Divinity of Christ" (*PW* 2:4). Emotionally, even in times of great stress, Swift was never able to renounce his own ego, to be consoled by his religion. This egotism is the most striking aspect of the passage on Stella's approaching death in a letter of 1726 to James Stopford: "I think there is not a greater Folly than that of ent'ring into too strict and particular a Friendship, with the loss of which a man must be absolutely miserable, but especially at an Age when it is too late to engage in a new Friendship. Besides this was a Person of my own rearing and instructing . . ." (*Corres.*, 2:660). This is surely a statement revealing strong emotion, but it is the form that the affect takes that is striking. The image of the real person mourned is overwhelmed by the paradigm situation in which she cannot be replaced, not because she is unique, and in her uniqueness valuable, but for a practical reason (that is, he is too old to find another such friend, too old to undertake again the forming of character that he alludes to).[27]

Surprisingly, the scientific skeptic and the orthodox churchman share some common ground on religion. In *The Future of an Illusion*, Freud writes, "If [religion] succeeded in making the majority of mankind happy, in comforting them, in reconciling them to life and in making them into vehicles of civilization, no one would dream of attempting to alter the existing conditions."[28] Freud saw religion as losing its ability to realize these objectives which are also Swift's, particularly the last, that of enabling the advancement of civilization. The majority of Swift's pronouncements about religion and God have that concern, as when he writes in his sermon on doing good that "all wilful injuries done to the public are very great and aggravated sins in the sight of God" (*PW*, 9:234). In *A Letter to a Young Gentleman, Lately Entered into Holy Orders* he observes that "men always grow vicious before they become Unbelievers" (*PW*, 9:78). In Swift's view the hope of future reward and the threat of future punishment that only religion provides gives it power in the present to control the forces of disorder. Swift, in an earlier age than Freud's, was still able to see religion as the means of achieving their common goals.

NOTES

This essay originally appeared in *Eighteenth-Century Ireland* 4 (1989): 31–40. Reprinted by permission of the editor.

1. *The Prose Works of Jonathan Swift*, ed. Herbert Davis, 14 vols. (Oxford: Clarendon Press, 1937–68), 9:97. Further references will be given parenthetically in the text following citations and using the abbreviation *PW*.

2. See Jonathan Swift, *Journal to Stella*, ed. Harold Williams, 2 vols. (Oxford: Clarendon Press, 1948), 1:358–59: "Did I tell you of the archbishop of Dublin's last letter? He had been Saying in several of his former, that he would shortly write to me something about myself, and it looked to me as if he intended something for me: at last out it comes, and consists of two parts. First, he advises me to strike in for some preferment now I have friends; and secondly, he advises me, since I have parts, and learning, and a happy pen, to think of some new subject in Divinity not handled by others, which I should imagine better than any body. A rare spark this, with a pox! but I shall answer him as rarely. Methinks he should have invited me over, and given me some hopes or promises. But hang him!"

3. "Jonathan Swift: 'Not the Gravest of Divines,'" *Jonathan Swift 1667–1967: A Dublin Tercentenary Tribute*, ed. Roger McHugh and Philip Edwards (Dublin: Dufour Editions, 1968), 39.

4. Landa, 39.

5. *La Pensée religieuse de Swift et ses antiomies* (Lille: Facultes Catholiques, 1935), quoted in Milton Voigt, *Swift and the Twentieth Century* (Detroit: Wayne State University Press, 1964), 135.

6. James, *The Varieties of Religious Experience* (Cambridge, MA: Harvard University Press, 1985), 34.

7. Ibid., 115.

8. Ibid.

9. *Psychoanalysis and Religious Experience* (New Haven, CT: Yale University Press, 1984), 18.

10. James W. Jones, "Transference and Transcendence: Towards a New Psychoanalysis of Religion," 26–27. I am grateful to Professor Jones for making his work in progress available to me.

11. Ana-Maria Rizzuto, *The Birth of the Living God* (Chicago: University of Chicago Press, 1979), 51. A valuable summary and assessment of psychoanalytic criticism of Swift can be found in Hermann J. Real and Heinz J. Vienken, "Psychoanalytic Criticism and Swift: The History of a Failure," *Eighteenth-Century Ireland*, 1 (1986): 127–41.

12. "Some Reflections on Schoolboy Psychology," *The Standard Edition of the Complete Psychological Works of Sigmund Freud*, ed. and trans. James Strachey, 23 vols. (London: Hogarth Press, 1953), 13:243. Further references will be abbreviated as *Standard Edition*.

13. Ibid., 243.

14. *The Correspondence of Jonathan Swift D.D.*, ed. David Woolley, 4 vols. (Frankfurt: Peter Lang, 1999–), 3:230. Further references will follow citations in the text and use the abbreviation *Corres.*

15. Because his nurse separated him from his mother for three years during infancy, Swift lacked both parents during the crucial early period of his life (*PW*, 5:192). While this undoubtedly intensified his overall sense of loss, my discussion is limited to the effect of paternal lack of relationship on the image of God the father.

16. "To his Grace the Arch-Bishop of DUBLIN, A Poem" (1724), *The Poems of Jonathan Swift*, ed. Harold Williams, 2d ed., 3 vols. (Oxford: Clarendon Press, 1958), 1:339, 11.7–8.

17. Dedication to "Horace, Book IV, Ode IX," *Poems*, 243, 1. 7.

18. *Swift: The Man, His Works, and the Age*, 3 vols. (Cambridge, MA: Harvard University Press, 1962–83), 3:533.

19. *"God's Grandeur," Poems of Gerard Manley Hopkins*, ed. W. H. Gardner (Oxford: Oxford University Press, 1948), 70.

20. George Herbert, "The Collar," *The Works of George Herbert*, ed. F. E. Hutchinson (Oxford: Clarendon Press, 1941), 153.

21. This conjunction remained constant in Freud from its early formulation in "Obsession Actions and Religious Practices" (1907), *Standard Edition*, 9:126–27: "In view of these similarities and analogies one might venture to regard obsessional neurosis as a pathological counterpart of the formation of religion, and to describe that neurosis as an individual religiosity and religion as a universal neurosis."

22. *Standard Edition*, 22:17–18.

23. Ibid., 21:30.

24. Ibid., 21:49.

25. Landa, "Jonathan Swift: 'Not the Gravest of Divines,'" 42.

26. James, 114.

27. A similar example occurs in a letter Swift wrote to Pope after the death of their mutual friend John Gay. Noting the recent deaths of "two persons of great merit whom I loved very well . . . in the prime of their years, but a little above thirty," Swift remarks: "I would endeavour to comfort my self upon the loss of friends, as I do upon the loss of mony; by turning to my account-book, and seeing whether I have enough left for my support?" (*Corres.*, III, 580).

28. *Standard Edition*, 21:37.

"in the mean time": Jonathan Swift, Francis Bacon, and Georgic Struggle

John Shanahan

I

DURING HIS STAY IN LAPUTA, THE FLYING ISLAND POWERED BY MAGNETISM and home to frenzied experimenters, Gulliver meets a "great Lord" who has no skill in mathematics and therefore is "reckoned the most ignorant and stupid Person among them" (*PW*, 11:173).[1] This unnamed lord supplies Gulliver with a letter of introduction to a like-minded friend on the mainland of Balnibarbi. This friend, Lord Munodi, invites Gulliver to his country house outside the metropolis, and they pass from an urban landscape of poverty and ill-constructed homes to contiguous surroundings of suburban agricultural blight. In the fields around the city there is no "Expectation either of Corn or Grass, although the Soil appeared to be excellent" (*PW*, 11:75). Gulliver is increasingly puzzled by this dearth since many people are visible in the fields, busy with unrecognizable tools (*PW*, 11:174–75). The apocalyptic landscape changes, however, as the carriage nears Munodi's lands farther from the city. His estates, quite separate from the barrenness surrounding them, affords a prospect of a "beautiful Country" where small, enclosed, farms produce a variety of crops. Munodi's great house is "built according to the best Rules of ancient Architecture" and the surrounding environs are "disposed with exact Judgment and taste" (*PW*, 11:176). The startling contrast between Munodi's seat and the greater realm of Balnibarbi is the result of the former's resistance to a great social experiment undertaken by the state. In a thinly veiled swipe at the Royal Society, Munodi relates to Gulliver the origins of the crisis: "[A]bout Forty Years ago [i.e., the 1660s], certain Persons went up to Laputa, either upon business or Diversion; and after five Months Contrivance, came back with a very little Smattering of Mathematicks, but full of Volatile Spirits acquired in that Airy Region. . . . [T]hese Persons upon their Return, begun to dislike the Management of every Thing below; and fell into Schemes of putting all Arts, Sciences, Languages, and Mechanics upon a new Foot" (*PW*, 11:176). A royal patent was granted for the establishment of an "Academy of PROJECTORS" and the popular scheme spread among the populace of Balnibarbi. The satire of specific experiments of the Royal Society here and in later chapters when Gulliver visits the Lagadan Academy is well documented and will not concern us here, for more important than the content of any particular experiments is the very form of the Laputan quest and its remarkable failures.[2] I would like to suggest that this brief episode in book 3 presents to the reader in an emblematic manner the worldview that informs Swift's thought as a whole. In his focus on form, Swift makes his most compelling statement about the relationship of the sciences to the arts and to the world at large.

Munodi explains to Gulliver the effects produced when Lagadan promises are applied to the recalcitrant, earthly, Balnibarbian world. In their "College" the Lagadan Projectors

> contrive new Rules and Methods of Agriculture and Building, and new Instruments and Tools for all Trades and Manufactures, whereby, as they undertake, one Man shall do the Work of Ten; a Palace may be built in a Week, . . . [a]ll the Fruits of the Earth shall come to Maturity at whatever Season we think fit to chuse, and increase an Hundred Fold more than they do at present; with innumerable other happy Proposals. The only Inconvenience is, that none of these Projects are yet brought to Perfection; and *in the mean time* the whole Country lies miserably waste, the Houses in Ruins, and the People without Food or Cloaths. By all which, instead of being discouraged, they are Fifty Times more violently bent upon prosecuting their Schemes, driven equally on by Hope and Despair. (*PW*, 11:177, emphasis added)

Culminating as it does in particularly devastating humor, this description of Lagadan plans and Balnibarbian reality portrays more economically than perhaps any other passage in Swift the gap so notable between present and future, reality and illusion. We have been taught in several excellent recent studies how the "burden of the future" weighed on Swift.[3] That burden takes concrete shape in the description of Lagadan plans quoted above. Swift rivets the reader's attention first on the promises, only to shock him or her with the disarmingly savage portrait of "the mean time," where real individuals must survive day to day while systematic planning and larger forces—in this case scientific, but often economic as well—play havoc from above with the means of subsistence. The simultaneous existence in Balnibarbi of work in the fields and people in rags and tatters exposes the cruelty of such unaccountable systems; it was a landscape familiar to Swift from a lifetime spent almost wholly in Ireland. The misery of the country peasantry and the Dublin under-class, exacerbated by absentee landlords and vicious economic poli-cies, made a mockery of the fact that Ireland was, Swift noted in a sermon, "capable of producing all Things necessary, and most Things convenient for Life, sufficient for the support of four Times the number of its Inhabitants" (*PW,* 9:199).

That "mean time" Gulliver notices is Swift's time as an activist and moralist. It typifies the temporality of his pastoral mission. The pres-ent, that passing flow of such mean times, the here-and-now, is the time of real life and praxis with limited means. Swift's "mean time" can be considered a middle temporality bridging the gap between open-ended goals and limited time and resources, where work can-not be removed and work always remains; it designates the gap be-tween mental models and real mechanisms. In this essay I will argue first that Swift expressed such a precise concern for "the mean time" because of a sensibility centered on the injunction to labor commanded in georgic and biblical accounts of mankind's place in the creation. What I'll call the georgic impulse that characterizes Swift's voice at the same time made him an attentive reader of the works of Francis Bacon, spokesperson of the new science and also a profoundly georgic thinker. In the second half of this essay I'll exam-ine how and why Swift placed himself ambivalently in the wake of the project of iconoclasm Bacon pioneered.

II

As an Anglican priest in Ireland, Swift literally embodied the con-flicts of a vocation in the "mean time" of early eighteenth-century Ireland—both mediator and shepherd in a double dispensation, theological and epistemological. His liturgy was a via media poised unsteadily between Catholic priestcraft and dissenting enthusiasm. But Swift soon found that breaking the icons of popery and zealotry could easily endanger one's own intimately held truths and images, at least in the public's eyes, as the furiously divided reception of his youthful "&c.," the *Tale of a Tub,* proved. Simultaneously, his tenure as priest constituted only one small temporal point in an eternal sweep, after the Fall, the revelation, and the age of miracles, but be-fore final justice and felicity; another extended present where the single mind could lose itself in eternal truths incomprehensible to finite human reason. Swift's early and late works evince this com-

mon stance focused on "the mean time" and immersed in its pain
and ambiguity. The *Tale*, we recall, functions as a kind of stopgap
straddling the grimy reality of publishing for the new Grub Street
market and the shallow ease of patronage rhetoric. A parody of
Christian providentialism and pastoral oversight, the *Tale* is the
hack's self-described "*Interim*" contribution to human care "till the
perfecting of the Great Work," an academy of Wits at public expense (*PW*, 1:25). The hack assures his dedicatee Prince Posterity
that the document is "literally true this Minute I am writing," because for this all-too-modern author the present has been com-
pressed to a mere punctum of validity and authenticity (*PW*, 1:22).
In his later work Swift continued to focus on the "mean time" of
mundane experience, for example in his portrayal of the time
Strephon takes wandering Celia's empty chamber after the latter's
own extended ("Five Hours") period of self-making. After the de-
parture of "the goddess," Strephon takes his own extended time in
the garret, "[r]esolved to go through *thick* and *thin*," in order to
experience fully her "pomatums, paints, and slops" (ll.1, 3, 80, 35
[*PW*, 448–450]). Consistent with Swift's wide-angle aesthetic, aware
of what lies beyond the frame and what has been repressed and excluded, the poem limns both ends of the process from the middle;
it notes the idealized product ("gaudy tulips") and the sordid materials from whence it came ("dung"), but ultimately to concentrate
the reader on the process in the middle—the sweat and struggle that
takes time and where, in fact, all of human life is actually, physically,
lived. Carole Fabricant has shown a similar structure present in the
clash of country house ideal and country reality in Swift's work.[4]
Others have pointed out the way this stubborn realism tied to gritty
struggle in this world manifests itself in his religious sensibility. Michael DePorte, for instance, has noted how little any real intimations
of the next world play in Swift's works; instead, "[w]hat comes across
most strongly in Swift's references to God is his sense of His remoteness and unknowability."[5] But the consequence of such inaccessibil-
ity was not to be the cynical passivity of the Swiftian freethinker who
because of a variant reading of the Trinity in an "antient Manuscript" felt authorized to "safely whore and drink on, and defy the
Parson" (*PW*, 2:38). It required instead a transfer of energy from
speculative or "theological" to practical care. In other words, given
the obscurity of eternal verities such as the Trinity, the practical
"mean time" solution was to do within the Church what Lord Munodi has done on his estates, namely to "go on in the old forms"
and mitigate, as best one could, man's constitutional and institutional infirmities. Swift's focus on the present, his ability to occupy

and then concentrate others' attention upon moments of grimy actuality, constitutes his characteristically unstable voice of altruism mixed with brutality. It was a voice and temperment ultimately georgic in its orientation.

Virgil's *Georgics* became especially important in England after the restoration of the monarchy and Anglican Church. Already a central part of the humanist curriculum, the *Georgics* took on additional resonance for many Englishmen after 1660 because it was a poem explicitly about the reestablishment of productive agriculture after a period of destructive neglect due to fraternal bloodshed. In the early 30s BCE, in the aftermath of the civil wars that brought the republic to an end, Virgil expressed a hope for peace and virtue in the constancies of agricultural labor under an enlightened elite. After the marches of armies, the vicissitudes of martial fortune and political ambition, the fields as ever continued to demand attention. The two great wishes of the *Georgics* are peace and useful work. In a powerful passage at the end of book 1, Virgil hopes for a future era when the battles of the recent past become a hazy conjecture and future plowmen who inadvertently unearth the relics of war will only imperfectly recognize the lost purposes of the objects:

> after length of Time, the lab'ring Swains,
> Who turn the Turfs of those unhappy Plains,
> Shall rusty Piles from the plough'd Furrows take,
> And over empty Helmets pass the Rake.
>
> (1:493–96; 1:662–65)[6]

The landscape of previous carnage of brother against brother (*sanguine nostro* / "Roman blood" 1:491; 1:661) yields in Virgil's long-term vision to a focus on objects that with luck might be taken from the furrows to be beaten back into farm tools. The future yeomen envisioned here occupy themselves with appropriate labor, in stark contrast to their roles in warfare when, in an inversion of Isaiah 2, "crooked Scythes are streightned into Swords" (1:508; 1:684). Though the strange agricultural tools that Gulliver sees in the fields of Balnibarbi are never particularly specified, they might be thought to resemble those unfortunately reshaped instruments described by both Virgil and Isaiah.

But the hope of redirecting labor from warfare to agriculture, so important for situating Virgil's occasion, is secondary to the ultimate concern of the poem: ceaseless but ultimately redeeming work. Virgil described the necessity of productive labor in a famous metaphor of rowing against the current (1:199–203): "Thus all things are fated to rush toward the worst, and are borne backward to glide away; they are no different from one who can bravely row his small boat upstream; if for a moment he rests his arms, the boat sweeps him away headlong down the swift current."[7] Human effort gets special attention in the poem, but the *Georgics* also notes the cobwebs of spiders and the warrens of small field creatures, the nests of birds and, most famously, the hives of bees in a climactic passage in the fourth book. Virgil casts mankind as just one part of a teeming landscape, tugged like other creatures by sexual desire, sweating like other creatures for sustenance and survival. The Swift who enjoyed reading and himself wrote Aesopian fables in verse, and who queried human nature most radically by analyzing it not for any potential mirroring of the divine image but by holding it vis-à-vis equestrian form, found suggestive precedents in the *Georgics*. In a rich essay on the place of Virgil's poem in *Gulliver's Travels,* Margaret Anne Doody has described the fecundity of the former for Swift in this way: the "whole poem is populated by animals, birds, insects—secondary characters in relation to man who yet live their own independent lives with a homely beauty. . . . The constant presence of other lives than ours gives to man's rural existence its truth to varied reality, a deep consciousness of life that makes for sanity."[8] Swift's georgic vision resembles what we might term an ecological sensibility that anchors man into a stable landscape of shared responsibilities and duties. All living things must work in order to preserve themselves. But the *Georgics* and the injunction to labor is present not only allusively in the *Travels,* as Doody has persuasively shown. It serves more, I'd argue, like a fundamental personal orientation animating all of Swift's works. In his "Thoughts on Various Subjects," for example, he cited directly a well-known passage from book 1 of the *Georgics* so that it might stand as both a philosophy of life and a justification of Providence:

> One Argument used to the Disadvantage of Providence, I take to be a very strong one in its Defense. It is objected, that Storms and Tempests, unfruitful Seasons, Serpents, Spiders, Flies, and other noxious or troublesome Animals . . . discover an Imperfection of Nature; . . . But the Design of Providence may clearly be perceived in this Proceeding. The Motions of the Sun and Moon; in short, the whole System of the Universe, as far as Philosophers have been able to discover and observe, are in the utmost Degree of Regularity and Perfection: But wherever God hath left to Man the Power of interposing a Remedy by Thought or Labor, there he hath placed Things in a State of Imperfection, on purpose to stir up human Industry; without which Life would stagnate, or indeed rather could not subsist at all: *Curis acuens mortalia corda* [*Georgics* 1:123] (*PW,* 4:245).

The closing allusion is to Virgil's account of the loss of the Golden Age, the subsequent requirement of labor and, ultimately, the story of human accomplishment, for after that loss *tum variae venere artes. labor omnia vicit / improbus* ("art followed hard on art. Toil triumphed over every obstacle" [1:145–146, (Fairclough's trans.)]). Dryden rendered the same passage in couplets:

> The Sire of Gods and Men, with hard Decrees,
> Forbids our Plenty to be bought with Ease:
> And wills that Mortal men, inur'd to toil,
> Should Exercise, with pains, the grudging Soil.
> Himself invented first the shining Share,
> And whetted Humane Industry by Care.
>
> (1:121–24; 1:183–88)

Virgil's lament at the loss of the Golden Age was by a long exegetical tradition brought into accord with the second and third chapters of Genesis, where God placed Adam in the garden "to till it and keep it" (2:15) and later cursed and exiled him after the fall (3:17). Sweat "in the mean time" due to inevitable imperfection is, as we've seen above, an abiding theme in the Dean's works as a whole. Attention to spoiled objects and to gritty effort for temporary illusion are central parts of the conflictual mixture of fascination and abjection that propels the dressing room, birthday, and country house poems Swift penned over decades. Attention to ongoing labor in the mean time typifies his understanding of all human existence, including his own. In his sermon "On Mutual Subjection," he told his listeners that God "hath pleased to put us into an imperfect State, where we have perpetual occasion of each others' Assistance" (*PW,* 9:143); in the sermon on the "Poor Man's Contentment" he reminded the congregation that "Scripture assureth us, that [the World] was only designed as a Place of Trial" (*PW,* 9:196). The dean who struggled to keep the blasted Naboth's vineyard against regular flooding, and its "cursed wall" of stone from bad masons and gravity, was the same Swift who could style himself a simple daily workman in his letters and laud (through Gulliver) the King of Brobingnag, that "georgic hero" who sought "whoever could make two Ears of Corn, or two Blades of Grass to grow upon a Spot of Ground where only one grew before." Such a man, the prudent King continues, would "do more essential Service to his Country, than the whole Race of Politicians put together."[9]

The injunction to labor, derived doubly from Scripture and from Virgil, also provides the key for understanding Swift's criticism of the "new science" as inferior to the arts in the battle of ancients and moderns. The effort required of the arts constituted their superiority, and it was this ineradicable sweat that was threatened by the apparent ease of the sciences. As I noted above about the time spent in Laputa, Swift's is less a content-based criticism of particular experiments (though it is also that) than it is an assault on scientific form itself: *scientia* is suspect because it is frictionless—it costs the projecting mind virtually nothing to practice—but rather displaces its cost onto others, and in almost every case the most vulnerable in society. While touring the Academy at Lagado, Gulliver notes that in addition to Munodi on the mainland, an entire segment of the population of the flying island has refused the efforts of the projectors. He reports that "Women in Conjunction with the Vulgar and Illiterate" continue to resist the works of the Academy, "[s]uch constant irreconcileable Enemies to Science are the common People" (*PW*, 11:185).[10] Like those stubborn souls, Swift does not reject the new sciences according to specific ideas or experiments so much as he divides arts and sciences according to a different criterion based on sweat and social *usefulness.*

III

Swift's evaluations of the natural philosophy of his day has been a perennially contested issue in the scholarship. The antiscientific Swift, confirmed "ancient" standing against the tide of the new physics, chemistry and anatomy, has roots in the first biographies and continues in some modern criticism. John Boyle, Earl of Orrery, opined in 1754 that the voyage to Laputa was written "against chymists, mathematicians, mechanics, and projectors of all kinds."[11] Swift did, of course, write against excessive systematicity and abstraction in learning, from his early complaints against studying logic to his late, perhaps disingenuous, quip that "I understand not mathematics."[12] In a well-known letter to John Winder in January 1698/9, he threatened to burn a returned copy of Joseph Glanvill's *Scepsis Scientifica* as a "fustian piece of abominable curious Virtuoso stuff" (*C,* 1:30). Cited with some readings of *Gulliver* part 3 and the *Tale,* such comments make it easy to place Swift in the orbit of his former employer Sir William Temple and similarly out of his intellectual depth, stubbornly attacking misunderstood targets, unable to concede to a superior opponent.[13] But a defense of Swift as one who understood and to some degree even appreciated the natural sciences took shape in the wake of Nicolson and Mohler's pioneering essay on Laputa and R. F. Jones's broad study *Ancients and Moderns.*[14] These reassessments inaugurated decades of important investigation of Swift's engaged intimacy with the science of his day and especially how he read the *Philosophical Transactions* and other reports of the virtuosi.[15] Defenses of Swift's adequate knowledge of his targets has been augmented by readings of him as, in fact, rather accomplished in science and mathematics, choosing only to criticize abuses of science rather than the enterprise as a whole. The roots of this view are also as old as the eighteenth century, where Deane Swift's *Life* explains that "Dr Swift has laughed egregiously . . . not against the whole tribe of chymists, projectors, and mathematicians in general; but *against those, and only those, who despise the useful branches of science,* and waste their lives in the pursuit of aerial vanities and extravagances."[16] Colin Kiernan, for example, has argued that Swift was a fine mathematician able to use Kepler's third planetary law in order to determine the value of the time of revolution of one of Mars' satellites in *Gulliver's Travels* (*PW*, 11:170–71).[17] But such defenses of Swift are as flawed as the readings they challenge, both sides marred by conceptual anachronism.

The most important intervention into this interpretive dichotomy in the history of studies of "Swift and science" has come from recent work by Douglas Lane Patey on the definitional logic subtending early modern understandings of the differences between the "arts" and the "sciences" and the "ancients" and the "moderns."[18] Paying close attention to word usage in seventeenth- and eighteenth-century encyclopedias, dictionaries, and trade manuals, Patey has brought much needed clarity to the topic of the *querelle,* making possible subtle and historically attuned analysis of the terminology of the antagonists. Such work has helped critics avoid polarized and ultimately, misconstrued, indictments and defenses of Swift's supposed "attitude" to science based on late modern assumptions about the boundaries and epistemology of the "two cultures." Both critical camps have paid insufficient attention to the categories of knowledge in use at the time Swift was writing. According to Patey: "Swift does not . . . use these terms [arts and sciences] as they were redefined by the Moderns; rather, he uses them to mark a division of knowledge familiar since Aristotle (a figure the *Travels* more than once defends): Swift's science is still what centuries of thinkers would have recognized as the realm of certainty, whose instrument is logical demonstration; his arts are not the fine arts or humanities, but the older arts of prudence—those fields in which, because of the limitations of the human mind, demonstrative certainty is not to be had."[19] Of the first mode of thought, scientia, Swift had a dim view.

Often scientia/science is used interchangeably with "system," where both words describe mental acts of abstraction and reduction (for example, attempts to bring the welter of phenomena under a single principle: Descartes' vortices, Epicurus' atoms, the Aeolists' winds). Paradoxically, scientia is most unstable because it is based on reason, that quality that might be, but so often is not, the glory of human creatures. Reason that might "strike . . . with immediate Conviction" if uncorrupted, instead is made perverse, "discolored by Passion and Interest," in the flawed species Swift ultimately would define as *rationis capax,* not *animal rationale* (*PW,* 11:267; *C,* 3:103). Rather than the simplicity of unadorned natural processes and observed teleologies on the Aristotelian model, virtuoso scientia turns the mind toward ungoverned speculations. The Houyhnhnms, for example, as Gulliver notes, use the traditional humanist formulation of scientia and its boundaries: "Reason taught [them] to affirm or deny only where [they] are certain; and beyond [their] knowledge [they] cannot do either" (*PW,* 11:267).

As pure intellection, scientia is the branch of human knowledge most susceptible to the corruptions of pride and triviality. It is also the mental endeavor most closely associated with the production of idols. For the unfortunate thinker caught up in scientific theorizing, logical schemata and numerical mediators are given the reverence due ultimately only to God. Swift might have remembered Augustine's damning description of the hermetic magicians and pagan mathematicians who fashioned wondrous new mechanisms so compelling that they seemed to require worship: "as if there could be anything more wretched than for a man to be in thrall to what he himself has made."[20] The air pumps, logarithms, and chemicals associated with the Royal Society, not to mention the worldwide abuses of gunpowder—a special preoccupation of the *Travels*—exemplified this modern temptation to fall down before one's own technological goods. In a similar way, the political arithmetic of the "Modest Proposer" epitomizes the cruel results when numerical values replace unique human dignity. For the projecting mind, the ease with which simple algebraic problems and geometrical proofs are solved is carried over to the messiness of life and objects where they have no proper business. Here science is a manifestation of hubris; it is premature satisfaction with the model of the moment, a refusal to acknowledge the long-term truth that systems by their nature have periods of fashion and (as the ghost of Aristotle counsels Gulliver in Glubdrubdrib) "would vary in every age . . . even those [formed upon] mathematical principles" (*PW,* 11:198). When mathematics is applauded by Swift, it serves as a practical help, for example in Brobdingnag, where calculation is "wholly applied to what may be useful in life; to the Improvement of Agriculture and all mechanical Arts" (*PW,* 11:136). In themselves, unaccompanied by practical use, numbers are little better than the scribbles of magic formulae; at the level of narrative text, as it were, Newton could appear a useless conjurer as readily as William Partridge.[21] What we could call mathematical number magic unsurprisingly dominates the mind of the hack-author of the *Tale,* as it does his ideal readers and intellectual models ("Philosophers and Great Clerks") who would look forward to future works like "A Panegyrical Essay Upon the Number THREE" and analysis of the four winds in the Aeolist sects (*PW,* 1:34, 1, 34, 96–97).

The appeal of the arts to Swift, by contrast, was their useful, practical, and prudential nature. From cooking to history, and from poetry and agriculture to politics, the "arts" were human endeavors both time bound and subjectively inflected, by their very nature incapable of being mathematized. In the arts, one worked by emulation and imitation, not by demonstration and logic. Since logical proofs were not possible, in the arts the history of technique and opinion was the sole guide. Artistic practice meant taking a place in a vast formal struggle, never to be accomplished, toward what Horace described as *miscuit utile dulci,* profit blended with delight.[22] The arts, therefore, are georgic in their very essence, products of the sweat commanded as a consequence of the fall in Eden; they were skills of "cultivation" requiring immersion in processes larger than the human ego and because of that ultimately, partially, redemptive. In the story of their unfolding through human history the arts tell of processes, now more and now less glorious, of work with nature and with others collectively. To study the arts was to study the historical aggregation of wisdom and folly in order to acquire prudence and ultimately, in Patey's words, to "isolate . . . what writers from Pico della Mirandola to Alexander Pope [called] the 'proper dignity' of man."[23] With the "book-frame" that mechanically produces text in Lagado serving as a perfect antithesis, the arts required long-term care and the judicious exercise of taste, as Aesop reminds the moderns in the *Battle of the Books:* " We ['Antients'] *are content with the* Bee, *to pretend to nothing of our own, beyond our* Wings *and our* Voice: . . . *whatever we have got, has been by infinite Labor, and search, and ranging thro' every Corner of Nature"* (*PW,* 1:151). By contrast, the hack-author of the *Tale* hopes to see soon "an universal System in a small portable Volume, of all Things that are to be Known, or Believed, or Imagined, or Practiced in Life" (*PW,* 1:78). Swift celebrated the arts for their prudence and kept an iconoclast's hammer poised for scientia.

IV

In this, perhaps surprisingly, Swift's stance has much in common with the thought of Francis Bacon, one of the most influential early modern theorists of intellectual idolatry and reform. But Bacon was a contradictory intellectual and textual legacy for Swift. By the second half of the seventeenth century, no educated Englishman could ignore the influence of the former lord chancellor. To a handful of vocal critics like the Hobbesian physician Henry Stubbe, Bacon was a "Dictator" and his experiment-minded progeny a slavish *"Bacon-face"* generation.[24] But for the overwhelming majority of Englishmen, Bacon was a touchstone and prophet for the gathering enlightenment of the globe.[25] Swift was by no means uniformly hostile to this herald of the new philosophy. He owned several editions of Bacon's works, including the multivolume *Opera Omnia* of 1730, and his engagement with the lord chancellor's ideas was lifelong. Swift annotated his copy of Bacon's *History of Henry VII* and often cited and alluded to the *Essays, or Counsels.*[26] Brean Hammond is correct that Swift had a "grudging admiration" for Bacon (and for Hobbes) that provoked him to some of his most daring prose.[27] Brian Vickers has excavated a number of possible allusions to Bacon in the most complete study of the subject so far.[28] In his formative years Swift was surrounded by admirers of Bacon—his tutor, St. George Ashe and provost, Narcissus Marsh were professed virtuosi; even Sir William Temple, no friend of the new science, admired Bacon.[29] It is widely held that Swift drew his spider and bee imagery in the *Battle of the Books* from Bacon.[30] Though Bacon is probably the "Troglodyte Philosopher" mockingly glanced at in section 10 of the *Tale,* it should also be noted that the Aristotle who dismisses Gassendi and Descartes in *Gulliver,* when aiming to kill Bacon in the *Battle of the Books* misses him, only to impale Descartes instead (*PW,* 1:116; 11:197; 1:156).[31] Given the slaughter of Bentley, Wotton, and many others self-professed "moderns," the survival of Bacon, great herald of modernity, is significant. Swift's anxiety over how to characterize the latter's legacy can be seen writ large in the fact that the outcome of the battle is left uncertain as the manuscript breaks off.

Bacon was like Swift a profoundly georgic thinker; his works stress ongoing engagement and effort with recalcitrant matter and stubborn thoughts. His meditations on method, "these Georgics of the mind," as he termed them in the *Advancement of Learning,* coupled a painstaking compilation of facts with a readiness to acknowledge error and failure (*Works,* 3:419).[32] In a Swiftian phrase that would not be out of place in the *Tale,* Bacon lamented how "the mind loves to leap to generalities, so that it can rest; it only takes it a little while to get tired of experience" (*NO,* 36). Similarly, Bacon blasted zeal in religion and philosophy in ways congenial to Swift's temperment and ridiculed the enthusiasm of (al)chemists and natural philosophers who "out of a few experiments of the furnace have built up a fantastic philosophy" (*Works,* 4:59). Such virtuosi practiced what Bacon called *Ad quod vult Scientas,* or "*As-you-like-it* Sciences. For man would rather believe what he wishes to be true" (*OFB,* 11:87). By contrast, the *New Organon* (1620), Bacon's replacement method, recommended long-term and labor-intensive work to learn truths not as individual men wished them to be but as in fact they really were. The *New Organon*'s catalogs of phenomena are called "harvests" and "vintages," reinforcing in its very metaphorical system the georgic sensibility that underwrites it. In his many comments on method Bacon contrasted the dialectic of the schoolmen that too quickly sprung to universals and logical categories with his own inductive process that built slowly its results: "[W]e must not allow the understanding to leap and fly from particulars to remote and highly general axioms (such as the so-called *principles* of arts and things), . . . since the mind's natural bent is prone to do this, and is even trained to it and made familiar with it by the example of syllogistic demonstration. . . . Therefore we do not need to give men's understanding wings, but rather lead and weights, to check every leap and flight" (*NO,* 83). Repeated in many other forms throughout his oeuvre, this passage summarizes the kind of mediation lying at the root of the georgic sensibility Bacon shares with Swift. For Bacon, the grounded intellect works simultaneously from sense experience to axioms and from axioms to further sense experiences, sometimes "vexing" nature with tools and sometimes simply watching additional phenomena. Significantly, these processes are figured by Bacon as roads winding uphill and downhill. In experimental work, "the road is not flat, but goes up and down" (*NO,* 83). Like the "mean time" so important to Swift, the uneven road of empirical knowledge is the byway of common humanity and its long-term cultural accomplishments, not the smooth path of fancy where the road might rise to meet the walker. The inductive road is one of labor and friction—precisely more accurate for its painful resistance; true knowledge, for Bacon as later for Swift, is what hurts. According to Bacon, "[t]he lowest axioms are not far from bare experience. And the highest axioms (as now conceived) are conceptual and abstract and have no solidity. It is the intermediate axioms which are true, sound, living axioms on which human affairs and human fortunes rest" (*NO*, 83). Even the deductive sciences are to be practiced much more like arts, cultivated by long-term effort and the recirculation of data for use in immediately practical ends. In Bacon's *Sylva Sylvarum* (1627), an immensely popular collection in the seventeenth century, and from which Swift may have borrowed hints for the *Tale*,[33] a collection of piecemeal experiences serves as a groundwork of simples and observations with which to begin learning about phenomena. For the notoriously nonmathematical Bacon, the focus was almost exclusively on the middle-sized world of visible qualities and quantities and all those physical and historical principles that spur on human endeavor. For this reason, Bacon held that work in correct natural philosophy paralleled the prudence of the statecraft recommended in his *Essays, or Counsels,* another book Swift knew well.[34] The effective royal state must busy itself with empirical work that coincides with the "mean time" of its inhabitants. On Bacon's utopian island of Bensalem, unlike Laputa, the work of the natural philosophers helps the inhabitants in their present (*Works*, 3:156–66).

Though it has rarely been a sustained subject of Swift scholarship, Bacon's account of the "idols" that plague mankind was surely an important source for Swift in that it deployed the ethical force of theological iconoclasm while directing it at broadly secular and psychological targets. In his *Institutes,* Calvin maintained that the mind was "a perpetual forge of idols."[35] Bacon and Swift would surely agree, but both transformed Calvin's strictly religious diagnosis by grafting it to the humanist-derived commonplace that one could measure the validity of a philosopher's doctrine by analyzing his manner of living. Effective diagnosis of mental idols was one part of such an evaluation, and the psychology of the knowing (and writing) subject is a principle focus throughout Swift's work. "There are four kinds of *Idols* which beset human minds," according to the *New Organon* (*OFB*, 11:79). Each kind of mental distortion is given a figurative appellation; to each Bacon then devotes a diagnosis and partial remedy. Three idols are innate to the fallen human subject, constituting, as Swift's "Troglodyte Philosopher" in the *Tale of a Tub* would have it, the "Grains of Folly . . . annexed, as Part of the Composition of Human Nature" (*PW*, 1:116). Idols of the Tribe arise from sensory distortion, and are ineradicable since the mind is an "uneven mirror" that must to some degree shape and distort its perceptions (*OFB*, 11:79–81). Idols of the Cave are individual prejudices and misconceptions—the hobbyhorses that, combined with the idols of the tribe, make all humans more and less troglodytes passing time in a Platonic cave of shadows. Individual prejudices can arise in a man from "his education and association with others, or the books he reads and the several authorities of those whom he cultivates and admires," especially when such influences are not checked by humility and history (*OFB*, 11:81). The third flaw born with man as a kind of secular original sin is the Idol of the Market-place, and this describes the distortions of language by the traffic of human community and trade. Inevitably languages change with time and expansion; pidgins and slang words develop in commercial areas; high concepts are appropriated to the "capacity of ordinary people" (*OFB*, 11:81), and all of these lead to mental distortion and instability of reference. To these three, Bacon adds a fourth—the Idol of the Theatre—different in kind because it is not innate, but the conscious production of men through flawed models of knowledge. This last kind of idol is so called because the various natural philosophical theories are, Bacon writes, "so many stories made up and acted out, stories which have created sham worlds worthy of our stage" (*OFB*, 11:81–83). Every philosopher has a system to save the phenomena; from Pythagoras and Plato to Copernicus and Paracelsus entire schools have flourished since antiquity to promote mutually exclusive models of reality. Given Swift's disdain of systematic philosophy, Bacon's critique of the Idols of the Theatre must have seemed particularly congenial: "[J]ust as many *Theories* of the heavens can be fabricated from the *Phenomena* of the ether, so much more can different dogmas be erected and established on the *Phenomena* of Philosophy. And such *stage-plays* share this with the plays of the dramatists, that tales got up for the stage are more harmonious and attractive, and to one's taste, than true stories from the historical record" (*OFB*, 11:97). As each dramatist is a minor divinity, peopling and moving a microcosm on the boards, so every philosopher fashions a full metaphysics in order to reflect back to himself vanity and consistency. Swift's critique of this propensity to fashion intellectual systems whole cloth—to "reduce the Notions of all Mankind, exactly to the same Length, and Breadth, and Heighth of his own"—spans his career, from the ironic attack on the hack of the *Tale* who wishes to launch his own, to the savaging of all metaphysical absolutes in *Gulliver's Travels* over two decades later (*PW*, 1:105). For Bacon as for Swift, the core criticism remains that having *a* system invariably prizes vanity over humility; to have *the* singular model prohibits openness to new data and alternate views. Aristotle, himself a dogmatist and therefore perhaps less trustworthy, informs Gulliver that "new Systems of Nature were but new Fashions, which would vary in every Age" (*PW*, 11:189). But Isaac Bickerstaff, a persona closer to Swift, makes much the same point in the Partridge papers in 1709, namely that "Philosophers have differed in all Ages" (*PW*, 2:159).

According to Bacon, the four idols are innate and acquired propensities so deeply embedded in the human intellect that one cannot finally abolish them. The mind is simply by nature a compromised receptacle, an "uneven mirror" or "enchanted glass, full of superstition and imposture" (*Works*, 4:431). The only solution to this form of secular idolatry is vigilance: "All that can be done is to use a kind of thoughtful prudence to guard against them [idols]" (*Works*, 4:432). Diagnosis and correction for the idols is one part, the destructive or negative half, as it were, of Bacon's project. This diagnostic iconoclasm was, as I've suggested, quite useful to Swift as a georgic model of intellectual critique stressing humility, labor, and vigilance. But Bacon's reconstructive, or positive, philosophy, and particularly its rhetorical presentation, is much harder to reconcile with Swift's commitments. It is with regard to this latter, "positive" philosophy that Swift parts company with Bacon's views and finds grounds for rejecting the "Troglodyte Philosopher." Swift will stay resolutely georgic and iconoclastic, ultimately turning Bacon's tools of critique against Bacon himself, staying vigilant against idols at all cost.

For all that Swift may have adopted from the former lord chancellor, he would not become a Baconian like so many of his contemporaries because Bacon's was in the end an *incomplete* georgic. That is to say, Bacon the valiant diagnostician of the idols, the useful iconoclast who exposed the "stage-play" systems of all previous philosophies, in the end produced his own system despite his many strictures against them. Swift would ultimately make no such compromise; the power of his work lies precisely in its stark ability to leave the reader in the destructive moment, dwelling upon broken idols and pierced illusions without suggesting that a future move might dissolve the problematic. Ronald Paulson has usefully described these risky and fraught tactics this way: Swift "breaks and empties the idol and then climbs (or suspects that he climbs) inside the shell himself, becoming what he has broken now that it is clearly broken and no longer idolizable."[36] By contrast, Bacon presented his constructive philosophy, the "great instauration" of induction and accumulation, as a series of open-ended promises, agenda, catalogs, and wishes—placeholders for "the mean time," if one likes—for a future synthesis of royal power-knowledge. Though underdeveloped textually, (Bacon left gaps and drafts and empty tables in his published works that resemble those in Swift's early satires), the promises of the coming instauration were grandiose. The charge of the fathers of Solomon's House in *New Atlantis*, that utopia of state-supported technology, for example, is "the knowledge of Causes, and secret motions of things; and the enlarging of the bounds of Human Empire, to the effecting of all things possible" (*Works*, 3:156). Bacon's dedication of the *New Organon* to James I, who he calls the "new Solomon," makes it seem that with Bacon's work, the critique of all hitherto philosophical systems might finally be at an end and "at last, after so many ages of the world, philosophy and the sciences may no longer float in the air [as in Laputa!], but rest upon the solid foundations of every kind of experience properly considered. I have supplied the instrument [*organum*], but the material must be sought in things themselves" (*NO*, 5). Hence the Janus-faced nature of Bacon's work. At one moment a humble laborer and helpful diagnostician, at another a breathless projector seeking extended patronage in the currency of promises of wonderful things. To Swift, Bacon's textual legacy must have appeared maddeningly twofold: both Balnibarbian "mean time" and Lagadan frenzy, both georgic struggle and "Schemes of putting all Arts, Sciences, Languages, and Mechanics upon a new Foot" (*PW*, 11:176). Swift dwelt in the former dynamic of each pairing; unlike Bacon, he knew that a diagnosis was not the same thing as a cure. Despite his own cautions, Bacon espoused a new philosophy that tends in its proleptic cadences to divorce itself from the very ravages of time. For Swift, by contrast, georgic in his very bones and, as Kenneth Craven has elegantly noted, wedded to the melancholy mythology of Kronos/Time, "Evil vanquished is no part of the Kronos-Saturn myth."[37] While Bacon would routinely set aside his georgic and iconoclastic voices for one more positive about human remedy, Swift pursued the biblical injunctions to labor for bread and smash popular idols to their literary and social limits.

V

This made Bacon's work a troubling inheritance. But Swift's ruthless iconoclasm made all of his sources and targets, even his own texts, occasions of anxiety as well. The vocation of iconoclast, religious or secular, is hardly a stable one, as Swift portrays, for example, in his story of the brothers' hermeneutic and sumptuary innovations in the *Tale*. Swift's iconoclasm was directed both outward and in-

ward, and produced a wildly multivalent satiric principle—a troubling "iconoclash," to use a term recently coined by sociologist
Bruno Latour to describe the haunting sense that in smashing idols
one may simultaneously break one's hammer, damage the idol's "innocent" pedestal, and/or replace the old idol with another candidate no less impure. Latour's description of the manner by which
an iconoclast's hammer can appear to "strike sideways, destroying
something else that seems, after the fact, to matter immensely," fits
Swift's melancholy case quite well.[38] Directed externally at absentee
landlords and predatory projectors, Swift's "savage indignation"
could produce remarkable exercises in satiric attack, from the play-
ful indirection of the *Tale* and *Modest Proposal* to the overt personal
venom of his sermon on the "Causes of the Wretched Condition
of Ireland" and his letters to the stingy Robert Percival.[39] Directed
internally, Swift was hardly less ruthless. The "Apology" added to
the 1710 edition of the *Tale* notes that the young author sought "to
strip *himself* of as many real prejudices as he could" in the process of
making public others' corruptions of religion and learning (*PW*, 1:1,
emphasis added). His self-representation as a priest was overwhelm-
ingly that of a bedraggled paternalist, committed to a divine but
often losing cause; he was a troubled shepherd among a populace
with a propensity for backsliding and irreligion. There is, for example, the alienated, adversarial, sense of vocation in his "Thoughts on
Religion": "I look upon myself, in the capacity of a clergyman, to be
one appointed by providence for defending a post assigned me, and
for gaining over as many enemies as I can" (*Works*, 9:262).

Ultimately, I am tempted to join together Swift's self-presentation
as "monarch in the *Liberties,* and King of the Mob" of Dublin with
his biblical understanding of monarchy wherein "kings were reckoned good or ill, as they suffered or hindered Image-Worship and
Idolatry" as the best way to capture the georgic contours of his double role as priest and satirist, scourge and buffoon.[40] If he was to be
a good king, even of the rabble of Dublin, idol breaking must be his
cause, and Ireland badly needed such vigilance. Of Wood's attempt
to introduce brass coins, Swift in his sermon on "Doing Good"
pointed out that "the poor ignorant people . . . did not discover the
serpent in the brass, but were ready, like the Israelites, to offer in-
cense to it . . . until some, of good intentions, made the cheat so
plain to their sight" (*PW*, 9:238). Such careful pastoral attention
might not even be rewarded, as the Drapier later learned; instead,
"when a Person writes with no other intention then to *do you good,*
you will not be at the Pains to read his Advices . . . neither do you know
or enquire, or care who are your friends, or who are your enemies.

. . . I cannot but warn you once more of the manifest Destruction before your Eyes, if you do not behave yourselves as you ought" (*PW,* 10:3–4). Preacher and jester, priest and satirist, each identity forged by serious attention to injunctions to labor, in the end Swift's conscious humbling to make himself useful to the vulnerable was perhaps modeled most directly on the example of Christ, who "was pleased to chuse his Lot among Men of the lower Condition" in a paradoxical *mean time* both brief and eternal (*PW,* 9:198). Equal parts lamenting Jeremiah and disgusted social worker, Swift's focus on the mean time of vulnerable lives kept him engaged in worldly struggle no matter how lost he felt particular causes.[41]

NOTES

1. Citations from Swift's works will be from the following editions and parenthetical in the text: *The Prose Works of Jonathan Swift,* ed. Herbert Davis et al., 14 vols. (Oxford: Basil Blackwell, 1939–68) [*PW*]; *The Correspondence of Jonathan Swift, D.D.,* ed. David Woolley, 4 vols. (Frankfurt am Main: Peter Lang, 1999 [*C*]; *The Complete Poems of Jonathan Swift,* ed. Pat Rogers (New York: Penguin, 1983) [*P*]).

2. On the experiments in part 3, see Marjorie Nicolson, "The Scientific Background of Swift's *Voyage to Laputa* (with Nora Mohler)," rpt. in *Science and Imagination,* (Ithaca: Great Seal Books, 1956), 110–54; Dennis Todd, "Laputa, the Whore of Babylon, and the Idols of Science," *Studies in Philology* 75 (1978): 93–120; John R. R. Christie, "Laputa Revisted," *Nature Transfigured: Science and Literature 1700–1900,* (Manchester: Manchester University Press, 1989), 45–60.

3. Cf. Alan D. Chalmers, *Jonathan Swift and the Burden of the Future,* (Newark: University of Delaware Press, 1995); Kenneth Craven, *Jonathan Swift and the Millenium of Madness; The Information Age in Swift's* Tale of a Tub (Leiden: E. J. Brill), 1992.

4. Carole Fabricant, *Swift's Landscape* (Baltimore, MD: Johns Hopkins University Press, 1982), 116.

5. "Swift, God, and Power." *Walking Naboth's Vineyard: New Studies of Swift,* ed. Christopher Fox and Brenda Tooley (Notre Dame: Notre Dame University Press, 1995), 73–97, at 89.

6. Unless otherwise specified, I will use Dryden's translation because it was the most influential in Swift's lifetime. Citations in the body of the text will be the original Latin book and line numbers followed by Dryden's book and line numbers. The editions I've used are Virgil: *Eclogues, Georgics, Aeneid I–VI.* English translation by H. Rushton Fairclough, rev. ed. G. P. Goold, (Cambridge, MA: Harvard University Press, 1999), and *The Poems of John Dryden.* ed. James Kinsley, 4 vols., (Oxford: Clarendon Press, 1958), vol. 2 [1687–97].

7. Here I've preferred the translation of Anthony Low in his *The Georgic Revolution* (Ithaca, NY: Cornell University Press, 1985), 46.

8. "Insects, Vermin, and Horses: *Gulliver's Travels* and Virgil's *Georgics*." *Augustan Studies: Essays in Honor of Irvin Ehrenpreis,* ed. Douglas Lane Patey and Timothy Keegan (Newark: University of Delaware Press, 1985), 145–174, 150. As Doody and John Chalker (*The English Georgic: A Study in the Development of a Form* [Baltimore: Johns Hopkins University Press, 1969], 20–30) have pointed out, due to its own generic instability the *Georgics* could also serve as a kind of ready-made mock-heroic

poem. Virgil's treatise is certainly a serious paean to peace and nature and a practical (if stylized) handbook for the gentleman-farmer, but the potential for comic
effects is always present due to its striking mixture of high verse form and rustic
content. Joseph Addison's description of Virgil's accomplishment in his prefatory
essay to Dryden's translation would surely have given Swift pause: "He delivers the
meanest of his precepts with a kind of grandeur; he breaks the clods and tosses the
dung about with an air of gracefulness." On changing ways of reading the *Georgics*
through the eighteenth century, see Rachel Crawford, "English Georgic and British
Nationhood," *ELH,* 65:1 (1998), 123–58, and Frans de Bruyn, "Reading Virgil's
Georgics as a Scientific Text: The Eighteenth-Century Debate between Jethro Tull
and Stephen Switzer," *ELH,* 71:3 (2004), 661–89.

    9. The "cursed wall": *C,* 3:60; Swift as workman: *C,* 4:91; the phrase "georgic
hero" is from Douglas Lane Patey, "Swift's Satire on 'Science' and the Structure of
Gulliver's Travels," *ELH,* 58 (1991): 809–39, at 832; the King of Brobdingnag's
words: *PW,* 11:135–36.

    10. Cf. the "little old Treatise" of "Morality and Devotion" in "little Esteem [in
Brobdingnag] except among Women and the Vulgar" (*PW,* 11:137).

    11. *Remarks on the Life and Writings of Dr. Jonathan Swift* (London, 1754), 147,
quoted in Patey (op cit. note 9), 810.

    12. According to Orrery, Swift "held logic and metaphysics in the utmost con-
tempt and . . . scarce considered mathematics and natural philosophy unless to turn
it into ridicule. The studies which he followed were history and poetry," quoted in
Joseph M. Levine, *The Battle of the Books: Literature and History in the Augustan Age*
(Ithaca, NY: Cornell University Press, 1991), 110; *C,* 3:240.

    13. For representative examples of this view, see Levine (op cit. note 12), esp.
110–20; Florence Moog, "Gulliver Was a Bad Biologist," *Scientific American* 179
(1948): 52–55; Ernest Tuveson, "Swift and the World-Makers," *Journal of the History
of Ideas* (1950): 54–74; Richard G. Olson, "Tory High-Church Opposition to Science and Scientism in the Eighteenth Century: The Works of John Arbuthnot, Jonathan Swift, and Samuel Johnson," in *The Uses of Science in the Age of Newton,* ed. John
G. Burke (Berkeley: University of California Press, 1983).

    14. Nicolson and Mohler (op cit. note 2); Richard Foster Jones, *Ancients and Mod-
erns: A Study of the Rise of the Scientific Movement in Seventeenth-Century England,* 2nd
ed. (St. Louis, MO: Washington University Press, 1961).

    15. For important studies of Swift as a reader of the works of the virtuosi, see
Todd (op cit. note 2); T. Christopher Bond, "Keeping up with the Latest Transactions: The Literary Critique of Scientific Writing in the Hans Sloane Years," *Eighteenth-Century Life* 22, no. 2 (1998): 1–17; Frank T. Boyle, *Swift as Nemesis: Modernity
and its Satirist* (Stanford, CA: Stanford University Press, 2000), esp. chapters 4–6.
Larry Stewart claims that Swift "cannot be seen as an unregenerate opponent of
science"; rather, he was an opponent of "projecting" generally, whether in politics,
science, or literature (*The Rise of Public Science: Rhetoric, Technology, and Natural Philosophy in Newtonian Britain, 1660–1750,* [Cambridge: Cambridge University Press,
1992], 208). Although it is impossible to fix definitively Swift's role in its composition, relevant also is the *Memoirs of the Extraordinary Life, Works, and Discoveries of Martinus Scriblerus* [1741], ed. Charles Kirby-Miller (New York: Oxford University Press,
1988).

    16. Quoted in Patey (op cit. note 9), 810, my emphasis.

    17. "Swift and Science," *The Historical Journal* 14:4 (1971): 709–22, at 711–12.

    18. Patey, (op cit. note 9); idem, "'Ancients' and 'Moderns,'" *Cambridge History
of Literary Criticism, vol. 4: The Eighteenth Century,* ed. H. B. Nisbett and Claude Raw-

son (Cambridge: Cambridge University Press, 1997), 32–71. Patey draws in part on the rich treatment of eighteenth-century dictionaries in David Spadafora's excellent *The Idea of Progress in Eighteenth Century England* (New Haven, CT: Yale University Press, 1990), especially chapter 2.

19. Patey (op cit. note 9), 812.

20. *The City of God Against the Pagans.* Trans. R. W. Dyson (Cambridge: Cambridge University Press, 1998), 347 [book 8, chapter 23].

21. Cf. Simon Wagstaffe, in his introduction to *Polite Conversations,* who notes the gossip about "one Isaac Newton, an Instrument-Maker, . . . knighted for making Sun-Dyals better than others of his Trade, and was thought to be a Conjurer, because he knew how to draw Lines and Circles upon a Slate, which no Body could understand" (*PW,* 4:122–23).

22. *Ars Poetica,* l. 343, quoted in *Classical Literary Criticism,* trans. T. S. Dorsch (New York: Penguin, 1965), 22.

23. Patey (op cit. note 9), 826.

24. Quoted in Jones, (op cit. note 14), 236, 258.

25. For comprehensive studies of Bacon's influence, see Jones (op cit. note 14), and Charles Webster, *The Great Instauration, Science, Medicine and Reform 1626–1660* (London: Duckworth, 1975). For Bacon's influence into the eighteenth century, see Stewart (op cit. note 15), chapter 1.

26. *The Library and Reading of Jonathan Swift: A Bio-Bibliographical Handbook,* ed. Dirk F. Passmann and Heinz J. Vienken. 4 vols. (Frankfurt-am-Main: Peter Lang, 2003), 1:127.

27. "Swift's Reading," *The Cambridge Companion to Jonathan Swift,* ed. Christopher Fox (Cambridge: Cambridge University Press, 2003), 73–86, at 80.

28. Brian Vickers, "Swift and the Baconian Idol," in *The World of Jonathan Swift: Essays for the Tercentenary,* ed. Brian Vickers (Cambridge, MA: Harvard University Press, 1968), 87–128. Cf. Chalmers (op cit. note 3), 21–23. I differ from Vickers's claim that Swift rejected Bacon for the latter's "destructive" philosophy that tore down idols of the past. In fact, it is precisely the opposite: Bacon's positive, reconstructive, work was unacceptable to Swift. Irvin Ehrenpreis has rightly noted that Swift's allusions and borrowings from Bacon are often less abusive than Vickers maintains: see "The Doctrine of *A Tale of a Tub,*" *Proceedings of the First Münster Symposium on Jonathan Swift,* ed. Hermann J. Real and Heinz J. Vienken (München: Wilhelm Fink Verlag, 1985), 59–71, at 62.

29. Irvin Ehrenpreis, *Swift: The Man, His Works, and the Age,* 3 vols. (Cambridge, MA: Harvard University Press, 1962–83), 1:48–88, 232–35.

30. E.g., Ehrenpreis, (op cit. note 27), 1:232–233.

31. Following Vickers (op cit. note 25), I assume that "Troglodyte" probably refers to Bacon due to the his doctrine of the "idol of the cave" and fondness for metaphors of digging, mining, foundations, and depths.

32. Citations from Bacon's works are from the following editions, cited parenthetically in the text: *The Oxford Francis Bacon,* gen. ed. Graham Rees and Lisa Jardine (Oxford: Clarendon Press, 2000), vol. 4, *The Advancement of Learning,* ed. Michael Kiernan, and *vol. 11: The Instauratio Magna Part II: 'Novum Organum' and Associated Texts,* ed. Graham Rees with Maria Wakely [*OFB*]; Francis Bacon, *The New Organon,* ed. Lisa Jardine and Michael Silverthorne (Cambridge: Cambridge University Press, 2000) [*NO*]; *The Works of Francis Bacon,* ed. James Spedding, Robert Leslie Ellis, and Douglas Denon Heath, 14 vols. (London, 1864–74) [*Works*].

33. Bacon's "History of Winds" (*Works* 5:137–201) may be a source for section 8 of the *Tale.* Section 1 of the *Tale* seems to me indebted to the *Sylva's* century 3 on

sounds, where Bacon notes, for example, that sounds "move strongest in a right line" and queries: "It may be doubted, that sounds do move better downwards than upwards. Pulpits are placed high above the people . . . This may be imputed to the stops and obstacles which the voice meeteth with, when one speaketh upon the level" (*Works*, 2:414, 415); cf. century 10, on the "transmission of spirits and imagination" as relevant to sections 8 and 9 of the *Tale* (*Works*, 2:640–43).

34. Vickers (op cit. note 25) has noted many direct references to the *Essays* in Swift's works, 199n28. For examples of Bacon's fusion of statecraft and natural philosophy, see especially *New Organon* book one, aphorism 127, and the dedication to King James (*NO*, 4–5, 96), as well as Julian Martin's *Francis Bacon, the State, and the Reform of Natural Philosophy* (Cambridge: Cambridge University Press, 1992).

35. *Institutes of the Christian Religion*, book 1, chap. 11, 8, quoted in Christopher Hill, *The English Bible and the Seventeenth-Century Revolution* (New York: Penguin, 1993), 253.

36. *Breaking and Remaking: Aesthetic Practice in England 1700–1820*, (New Brunswick: Rutgers University Press, 1989), 38.

37. Craven (op cit. note 3), 195.

38. "What is Iconoclash?" *Iconoclash: Beyond the Image Wars in Science, Religion, and Art*, ed. Latour and Peter Weibel (Cambridge: MIT Press, 2002), 14–37, at 15. Cf. idem., "How to be Iconophilic in Art, Science, and Religion?" *Picturing Science, Producing Art*, ed. Caroline A. Jones and Peter Galison (New York: Routledge, 1998), 418–40.

39. Swift to Robert Percival: "This odd way of dealing among you folks of great estates in Land and money, although I have been used to, I cannot well reconcile my self with, especially when you never give me above a quarter value of your tythes, on which account alone you should not brangle with me. It is strange that Clergymen have more trouble with one or two squires and meet with more injustice with them than with fifty farmers. If your Tenants payd your Rents as you pay your Tyths, you would have cause to complain terribly," *C*, 3:274, [December 11, 1729].

40. *Memoirs of Laetitia Pilkington*, ed. A. C. Elias, 2 vols. (Athens: University of Georgia Press, 1997), 1:35; *PW*, 2:89.

41. But not without some venom: e.g., *An Answer to a Paper, Called 'A Memorial'*: "methinks I could have a malicious Pleasure, after all the Warning I have in vain given the Publick, at my own Peril, for several years past; to see the Consequences and Events answering in every Particular" (*PW*, 12:22), or the late *Proposal for Giving Badges to Beggars* (1737). On Swift's ambivalent views of charity, see David Nokes, *Jonathan Swift: A Hypocrite Reversed* (Oxford: Oxford University Press, 1985), 273–77.

Concise Bibliography

Chalmers, Alan D. *Jonathan Swift and the Burden of the Future.* Newark: University of Delaware Press, 1995.

Connery, Brian A. *Representations of Swift.* Newark: University of Delaware Press, 2002.

Connolly, S. J. *Religion, Law, and Power: The Making of Protestant Ireland 1660–1760.* Oxford: Clarendon Press, 1992.

Craven, Kenneth. *Jonathan Swift and the Millenium of Madness; The Information Age in Swift's* Tale of a Tub. Leiden: E. J. Brill, 1992.

DePorte, Michael. "Avenging Naboth: Swift and Monarchy." *Philological Quarterly* 69 (1990).

Downie, J. A. *Jonathan Swift: Political Writer.* London: Routledge, 1984.

Ehrenpreis, Irvin. *Swift: The Man, His Works, and the Age.* 3 vols. Cambridge, MA: Harvard University Press, 1962–83.

Elias, A. C. Jr. "Swifts Corrected Copy of *Contests and Discussions,* with Other Pamphlets from his Library *Philological Quarterly* 75 (1996): 167–95; 169.

Fabricant, Carole. *Swift's Landscape.* Baltimore: Johns Hopkins University Press, 1982.

Fauske, Christopher. *Jonathan Swift and the Church of Ireland: 1710–1724.* Dublin: Irish Academic Press, 2002.

Fox, Christopher, and Brenda Tooley. *Walking Naboth's Vineyard: New Studies of Swift.* Notre Dame: University of Notre Dame Press, 1995.

———, ed. *The Cambridge Companion to Jonathan Swift.* Cambridge: Cambridge University Press, 2003.

Franklin, Ben. *Poor Richard's Almanac.* London, 1743.

Freud, Sigmund. *The Standard Edition of the Complete Psychological Works of Sigmund Freud.* Ed. and trans. James Strachey. 23 vols. London: Hogarth Press, 1953.

Frye, Roland Mushat. "Swift's Yahoo and the Christian Symbols for Sin." *Journal of the History of Ideas* 15 (1954).

Harth, Phillip. *Swift and Anglican Rationalism: The Reigious Background of A Tale of A Tub.* Chicago: University of Chicago Press, 1961.

Hawes, Clement C. *Mania and Literary Style: The Rhetoric of Enthusiasm From the Ranters to Christopher Smart.* Cambridge: Cambridge University Press, 1996.

Higgins, Ian. *Swift's Politics: A Study in Disaffection.* Cambridge: Cambridge University Press, 1994.

James, William. *The Varieties of Religious Experience.* Cambridge, MA: Harvard University Press, 1985.

Kelly, Ann Cline. *Jonathan Swift and Popular Culture: Myth, Media, and the Man.* New York: Palgrave, 2002.

Kristeva, Julia. "Approaching Abjection." In *Powers of Horror*. New York: Columbia University Press, 1982.

Landa, Louis. Introduction to *The Prose Works of Jonathan Swift*. Vol. 9, *Irish Tracts and Sermons 1720–1723*, ed. Herbert Davis and Louis Landa. Oxford: Basil Blackwell, 1968.

———. "Jonathan Swift: Not the Gravest of Divines." Reprinted in *Essays in Eighteenth-Century English Literature*. Princeton, NJ: Princeton University Press, 1980.

———. *Swift and the Church of Ireland*. Oxford: Clarendon Press, 1954.

———. "Swift, the Mysteries, and Deism," Reprinted in *Essays in Eighteenth-Century English Literature*. Princeton: Princeton University Press, 1980.

Levine, Joseph M. *The Battle of the Books: Literature and History in the Augustan Age*. Ithaca, NY: Cornell University Press, 1991.

Low, Anthony. *The Georgic Revolution*. Ithaca, NY: Cornell University Press, 1985.

Lund, Roger, ed. *The Margins of Orthodoxy: Heterodox Writing and Cultural Response 1660–1750*. Cambridge: Cambridge University Press, 1995.

Mahony, Robert. *Jonathan Swift: The Irish Identity*. New Haven, CT: Yale University Press, 1995.

Mell, Donald C., ed. *Pope, Swift, and Women Writers*. Newark: University of Delaware Press, 1996.

Milton Anthony. *Catholic and Reformed: The Roman and Protestant Churches in English Protestant Thought 1600–1640*. Cambridge: Cambridge University Press, 1995.

Monk, Samuel Holt. "The Pride of Lemuel Gulliver." *The Sewanee Review* 63 (1955).

Morgan, Peter E. "Lost Week I Saw a Woman *flay'd*": Swift's Meta-Social Discourse and the Implication of the Reader." *Swift Studies* 1 (1999): 59.

Nicolson, Marjorie. "The Scientific Background of Swift's *Voyage to Laputa* (with Nora Mohler)," rpt. in *Science and Imagination*, (Ithaca, NY: Great Seal Books, 1956)

Nokes, David. *Jonathan Swift: A Hypocrite Reversed*. Oxford: Oxford University Press, 1985.

———. "Swift and the Beggars." *Essays in Criticism* 26 (1976): 219.

Olson, Richard G. "Tory High-Church Opposition to Science and Scientism in the Eighteenth Century: The Works of John Arbuthnot, Jonathan Swift, and Samuel Johnson." In *The Uses of Science in the Age of Newton*. Edited by John G. Burke. Berkeley: University of California Press, 1983.

Otto, Rudolph. *The Idea of the Holy*. Oxford: Oxford University Press, 1958.

Parker, Todd C. *Sexing the Text: The Rhetoric of Sexual Difference in British Literature, 1700–1750*. Albany: State University of New York Press, 2000.

Passman, Dirk F., and Heinz J. Vienken, eds. *The Library and Reading of Jonathan Swift: A Bio-Bibliographical Handbook*. 4 vols. (Frankfurt-am-Main: Peter Lang, 2003).

Patey, Douglas Lane, and Timothy Keegan, eds. *Augustan Studies: Essays in Honor of Irvin Ehrenpreis*. Newark: University of Delaware Press, 1985.

Phiddian, Robert. *Swift's Parody*. Cambridge: Cambridge University Press, 1995.

Pilkington, Laetitia. *Memoirs of Laetitia Pilkington*. Edited by. A. C. Elias, 2 vols. Athens: University of Georgia Press, 1997.

Rawson, Claude J. *The Character of Swift's Satires: A Revised Focus*. Newark: University of Delaware Press, 1983.

———. *God, Gulliver, and Genocide: Barbarism and the European Imagination, 1492–1945.* Oxford: Oxford University Press, 2001.

———. "Mandeville and Swift." In *Eighteenth-Century Contexts: Historical Inquiries in Honor of Phillip Harth.* Edited by Howard D. Weinbrot, Peter J. Schakel, and Stephen E. Karian. Madison: University of Wisconsin Press, 2001.

Real, Hermann J., and Heinz J. Vienken, eds. *Proceedings of the First Münster Symposium on Jonathan Swift.* München: Wilhelm Fink Verlag, 1985.

———. "Psychoanalytic Criticism and Swift: The History of a Failure." *Eighteenth-Century Ireland* 1 (1986).

Said, Edward. "Swift's Tory Anarchy." *Eighteenth–Century Studies* 3 (1969).

Spadafora, David. *The Idea of Progress in Eighteenth Century England* (New Haven, CT: Yale University Press, 1990.

Spurr, John. *The Restoration Church of England, 1646–1689.* New Haven, CT: Yale University Press, 1991.

Swedenberg, H. T., Jr. *England in the Restoration and the Eighteenth Century: Essays on Culture and Society.* Berkeley, Los Angeles: Univeristy of Berkeley Press, 1972.

Swift, Jonathan. *The Correspondence of Jonathan Swift.* Edited by Harold Williams. 5 vols. Oxford: Clarendon Press, 1963–65.

———. *The Correspondence of Jonathan Swift D.D.* Edited by David Wolley. 4 vols. New York: Peter Lang Publishing, 1999–2007.

———. *Jonathan Swift: The Complete Poems.* Edited by Pat Rogers. New Haven, CT: Yale University Press, 1983.

———. *Journal to Stella.* Edited by Harold Williams. 2 vols. Oxford: Clarendon Press, 1948.

———. *The Prose Works of Jonathan Swift.* Edited by Harold Williams et al. 14 vols. Oxford: Basil Blackwell, 1939–68.

———. *A Tale of a Tub and Other Works.* Edited by A. C. Guthkelch and D. Nichol Smith. 2nd ed. Oxford: Clarendon Press, 1958.

Todd, Dennis. "Laputa, the Whore of Babylon, and the Idols of Science." *Studies in Philology* 75 (1978).

Vickers, Brian, ed. *The World of Jonathan Swift: Essays for the Tercentenary.* Cambridge, MA: Harvard University Press, 1968.

Virgil. *Eclogues, De Senectute, De Amicitia, De Divinatione.* Loeb Classical Library, 1923.

Williams, Kathleen. "Gulliver's Voyage to the Houyhnhnms." *ELH* 18 (1951).

Young, B.W. *Religion and Enlightenment in Eighteenth-Century England: Theology and Debate from Locke to Burke.* Oxford: Clarendon, 1998.

Contributors

LOUISE K. BARNETT is Professor of English at Rutgers University. She is the author of numerous books and articles, including *Swift's Poetic Worlds* (University of Delaware Press, 1981), *Authority and Speech: Language, Society, and Self in the American Novel* (1993), and *Ungentlemanly Acts: The Army's Notorious Incest Trial* (2000). Her latest work, *Jonathan Swift in the Company of Women* appeared in the fall of 2006.

BRIAN A. CONNERY is the editor of *Representations of Swift* (University of Delaware Press, 2002). He has published work on Swift, satire, and the public sphere in early eighteenth-century England, and university fiction. He is Professor of English at Oakland University, Rochester, Michigan.

CHRISTOPHER FOX is Professor of English at the University of Notre Dame and Director of the Keough-Naughton Institute for Irish Studies. Fox is the author of *Locke and the Scriblerians: Identity and Consciousness in Early Eighteenth-Century Britain* (1988) and the editor or coeditor of several books, including *The Cambridge Companion to Jonathan Swift, Walking Naboth's Vineyard: New Studies of Swift* (with Brenda Tooley), *Gulliver's Travels: An Authoritative Text with Case Studies in Contemporary Criticism, Inventing Human Science: Eighteenth-Century Domains* (with Robert Wokler and the late Roy Porter), *Teaching Eighteenth-Century Poetry,* and *Psychology and Literature in the Eighteenth Century.* Fox is currently working on a study of the eighteenth-century response to the English Civil Wars.

ANNE BARBEAU GARDINER is Professor Emerita in the Department of English at John Jay College, City University of New York. She has published two books on John Dryden: *The Intellectual Design of John Dryden's Heroic Plays* (1970) and *Ancient Faith and Modern Freedom in John Dryden's The Hind and the Panther* (1998). She has also published numerous essays on Milton, Dryden, Pope, Swift, and Catholic authors of the late seventeenth century.

DANIEL LUPTON is a PhD candidate at the University of North Carolina at Chapel Hill. He is currently working on a dissertation examining mid-eighteenth-century men's clubs in Britain and America and the influence these clubs had on political and social philosophy. He is also working on an edition of William Blake's annotations of Sir Joshua Reynolds's *Discourses on Painting*.

ROBERT MAHONY is Professor of English at The Catholic University of America in Washington, D.C., where he served as the first director of the Center for Irish Studies from 1983–97. The focus of his research has shifted over his career from the eighteenth century in England, specializing in the poet Christopher Smart, to the seventeenth and eighteenth centuries in Ireland, specializing in Swift, and his most important work to date is *Jonathan Swift: The Irish Identity* (1995). Since 2002 he has organized the annual Dublin Symposium on Jonathan Swift, an international scholarly gathering that meets in the deanery of St. Patrick's Cathedral.

Until recently, TODD C. PARKER was Associate Professor of English at DePaul University in Chicago. A former winner of the Rodino Prize for Swift Criticism, he also won the 2004 SCSECS Presidential Essay Prize. He is the author of *Sexing the Text: The Rhetoric of Sexual Identity in British Literature 1700–1750* (2000), in addition to articles on Swift, Smart, and Händel. His 2006 graduate seminar on Jonathan Swift was the subject of an ongoing series of articles by the *Chicago Tribune*'s Pulitzer Prize-winning cultural critic, Julia Keller. After eleven years at DePaul, Parker left to join the Society of St. Francis, an order of Franciscans in the Episcopal Church.

JOHN SHANAHAN is Assistant Professor of English at DePaul University where he specializes in Restoration and eighteenth-century literature. His work has appeared in *Genre* and *Shakespeare Bulletin,* and he is completing a book entitled *Elaborate Works: Untangling Drama and Science in Early Modern England.*

JAMES WARD is Lecturer in Early Modern English at the University of Ulster, Northern Ireland. He has published articles on *A Modest Proposal* and on the writing of history in early eighteenth-century Ireland. He is working on a monograph on Swift.

Index